Impacts of the
Mild Winters and
Hot Summers
in the United Kingdom in
1988–1990

Edited by M.G.R. Cannell and C.E.R. Pitcairn

Institute of Terrestrial Ecology
Bush Estate, Penicuik
Midlothian, Scotland EH26 0QB

London: HMSO

ISBN 0 11 752642 8

Contents

List of Figures   vii
Introduction   xiii
Contributors   xv
Acknowledgements   xvi

SECTION A   **Impacts of the mild winters of 1988/89 and 1989/90**

Chapter A1   **The Climate**   3
                       A1.1   Temperatures and Windiness   3
                               P.D. Jones and M. Hulme
                               1.1.1   Introduction   3
                               1.1.2   Central England temperatures, November–April   3
                               1.1.3   Temperatures over the United Kingdom, November–April   5
                               1.1.4   Weather types during November 1988–April 1989   5
                               1.1.5   Windiness over the United Kingdom and the north sea
                                       region in 1989/90 compared to previous years   8
                               1.1.6   Conclusions   10
                       A1.2   Hydrology   11
                               N.W. Arnell, N.S. Reynard, T.J. Marsh, S.J. Bryant and R.P.C. Brown
                               1.2.1   Introduction   11
                               1.2.2   November 1988–April 1989   11
                               1.2.3   November 1989–April 1990   18
                               1.2.4   Conclusions   23
                       Appendix   23

Chapter A2   **Impacts on the Terrestrial Environment**   25
                       A2.1   Impacts on Plants   25
                               2.1.1   Introduction   25
                               2.1.2   Observations of First Flowering at ITE Stations   25
                                       J.M. Sykes
                               2.1.3   Phenology of Flowering Plants at Longniddry, East Lothian   29
                                       F.T. Last
                               2.1.4   Herbaceous Flora in Central England   30
                                       J.G. Hodgson and J.P. Grime
                               2.1.5   Impacts on Forestry   33
                                       J.N. Gibbs and M.G.R. Cannell
                               2.1.6   Conclusions   34
                       A2.2   Impacts on Animals   35
                               2.2.1   Introduction   35
                               2.2.2   Invertebrates   35
                                       L.K. Ward
                               2.2.3   Amphibia and Reptiles   40
                                       L.K. Ward
                               2.2.4   Birds   41
                                       M. Marquiss
                               2.2.5   Mammals   43
                                       L.K. Ward and M.G.R. Cannell
                               2.2.6   Conclusions   45
                       Appendix   46

Chapter A3   **Impacts on Freshwater Systems**   47
                       D.G. George
                       A3.1   Introduction   47
                       A3.2   Physical Aspects   47
                               3.2.1   River temperatures   47

		3.2.2	Lake ice cover	48
		3.2.3	Lake water temperature	48
	A3.3	Chemical Aspects		49
		3.3.1	The influence of road salt on water chemistry	49
		3.3.2	The winter concentration of nitrate in rivers and lakes	49
	A3.4	Biological Aspects		50
		3.4.1	Lake phytoplankton	50
		3.4.2	Aquatic invertebrates	51
		3.4.3	Freshwater fish	52
		3.4.4	River birds	53
	A3.5	Conclusions		53

Chapter A4   **Impacts on Agriculture and Horticulture**   54

M.H. Unsworth, R.K. Scott, J.S. Cox and K. Bardell

	A4.1	Introduction		54
	A4.2	Pests		54
		4.2.1	Birds	54
		4.2.2	Rodents	54
		4.2.3	Slugs	54
		4.2.4	Aphids	54
	A4.3	Weeds		55
	A4.4	Effects on Agricultural Crops		55
		4.4.1	Cereals	55
		4.4.2	Oilseed rape	57
		4.4.3	Sugarbeet	57
		4.4.4	Legumes	57
		4.4.5	Potatoes	57
	A4.5	Effects on Horticultural Crops		58
		4.5.1	Brassicas	58
		4.5.2	Carrots	58
		4.5.3	Leeks and onions	58
		4.5.4	Flowers	59
	A4.6	Frost Damage		59
	A4.7	Grass Growth and Associated Animal Production		59
		4.7.1	Grass Production	59
		4.7.2	Livestock	60
	A4.8	Conclusions		61
	Appendix			62

SECTION B   **Impacts of the hot summers 1989 and 1990**

Chapter B1   **The Climate**   65

| | B1.1 | Temperature and sunshine duration | | 65 |

P.D. Jones and M. Hulme

		1.1.1	Introduction	65
		1.1.2	Central England temperatures, May–October 1989 and 1990	65
		1.1.3	Temperature over the United Kingdom, May–October 1989 and 1990	66
		1.1.4	Sunshine hours. May–October 1989 and 1990	70
		1.1.5	The heatwave of early August 1990	72
		1.1.6	Conclusions	74
	B1.2	Hydrology		74

N.W. Arnell, N.S. Reynard, T.J. Marsh, S.J. Bryant and R.P.C. Brown

		1.2.1	Introduction	74
		1.2.2	Rainfall	74
		1.2.3	Evaporation and soil moisture	80
		1.2.4	Groundwater	81
		1.2.5	River flows	82
		1.2.6	Water management responses during summer 1989 and 1990	86

| | | 1.2.7 | Discussion | 87 |
| | | 1.2.8 | Conclusions | 88 |

Chapter B2   **Impacts on the Terrestrial Environment**   90

	B2.1	Impacts on Plants		90
		2.1.1	Introduction	90
		2.1.2	Herbaceous Flora	90
			T.C.E. Wells, P. Carey and R. Rose	
		2.1.3	Phenology of Flowering Plants at Longniddry, East Lothian	95
			F.T. Last	
		2.1.4	Forest and Amenity Trees	96
			J.N. Gibbs	
		2.1.5	"Countryside Survey 1990" Observations	98
			C. Barr	
		2.1.6	Conclusions	98
	B2.2	Impacts on Animals		100
		2.2.1	Introduction	100
		2.2.2	Invertebrates	100
			L.K. Ward	
		2.2.3	Birds	110
			M. Marquiss	
		2.2.4	Fires and the Hot Dry Summers 1989 and 1990	113
			L.K. Ward	
		2.2.5	Conclusions	114
	Appendix 1			115
	Appendix 2			117

Chapter B3   **Impacts on Freshwater Ecosystems**   119

	B3.1	Introduction		119
	B3.2	Physical aspects		119
			D.G. George	
		3.2.1	Stream and river temperature	119
		3.2.2	Lake temperatures	119
	B3.3	Chemical aspects		120
		3.3.1	Concentrations of nitrate in a lowland river	120
			D.G. George	
		3.3.2	The effects on streamwater chemistry flowing from an upland wetland in mid-Wales	120
			B.A. Emmett and N. Reynolds	
	B3.4	Biological aspects		122
			D.G. George	
		3.4.1	Lake phytoplankton	122
		3.4.2	Algal blooms	122
		3.4.3	Freshwater fish	124
	B3.5	Conclusions		125

Chapter B4   **Impacts on Agriculture and Horticulture**   127

M.H. Unsworth, R.K. Scott, J.S. Cox and K. Bardell

	B4.1	Introduction		127
	B4.2	Soil conditions		127
	B4.3	Pests and diseases		127
	B4.4	Effects on agricultural crops		128
		4.4.1	Cereals	128
		4.4.2	Sugarbeet	129
		4.4.3	Oilseed rape	129
		4.4.4	Sunflowers	130
		4.4.5	Linseed	131
		4.4.6	Potatoes	131
		4.4.7	Legumes	131
	B4.5	Effects on horticultural crops		132

		4.5.1	Vegetables	132
		4.5.2	Fruit and Flowers	133
	B4.6	Grass growth and associated animal production		134
		4.6.1	Grass growth and silage production	134
		4.6.2	Dairy cattle and milk production	135
		4.6.3	Beef cattle and sheep	136
	B4.7	Conclusions		138
	Appendix			139

| **SECTION C** | **Conclusions** | 143 |
| | **References** | 150 |

List of Figures

SECTION A

Chapter A1

1 Average Central England Temperatures for the (a) conventional and (b) extended winters, 1959/60 to 1989/90. The smooth lines are 30-year Gaussian filters fitted through both series. The dotted lines show the two standard deviation limits calculated over the entire period. 4

2 Mean maximum (a), mean minimum (b) and mean temperature (c) anomalies with respect to the 1961–80 average for conventional winters, 1988/89 (left) and 1989/90 (right). Contours drawn by objective interpolation using UNIRAS graphics. (Taken from Hulme and Jones 1992, with permission of the Royal Meteorological Society). 6

3 Mean maximum (a), mean minimum (b) and mean temperature (c) anomalies with respect to the 1961–80 average for extended winters, 1988/89 (left) and 1989/90 (right). Contours drawn by objective interpolation using UNIRAS graphics. (Taken from Hulme and Jones 1992, with permission of the Royal Meteorological Society). 7

4 Anomalous number of air frosts (minimum temperature below 0°C) (a) and days with mean temperature below 5°C (b) with respect to the 1961–80 average for the conventional winters, 1988/89 (left) and 1989/90 (right). Contours drawn by objective interpolation using UNIRAS graphics. (Taken from Hulme and Jones 1992, with permission of the Royal Meteorological Society). 8

5 Number of gales over the UK region for the conventional (a) and extended (b) winters, 1880/81 to 1989/90 (see Appendix for the definition of a gale). The dotted lines are the two standardised deviation lines calculated over the entire period. The smooth lines are 15-year Gaussian filters fitted through both series. 9

6 Mean sea-level pressure anomalies (mbar) with respect to the 1961–80 average for conventional winters, 1988/89 (a) and 1989/90 (b). The analysis is based on grid-point data on a 5° latitude by 10° longitude grid. Twenty grid points (the 16 in Figure A1 in the Appendix plus the 4 corner points) were used. Contours drawn by objective interpolation using UNIRAS graphics. (Taken from Hulme and Jones 1992, by permission of the Royal Meteorological Society). 10

7 Winter precipitation over England and Wales and winter Central England Temperatures from 1766/67 to 1989/90. (Winter is defined as December, January and February). The long-term homogenised monthly rainfall data for England and Wales were derived by the Climatic Research Unit, who also supplied the Central England Temperature data. 12

8 Winter rainfall (December to February) in (a) 1988/89 and (b) 1989/90, expressed as a percentage of the 1961–1980 average: MORECS data. 13

9 Soil moisture deficit (SMD), actual evapotranspiration (AE) and potential evapotranspiration (PE) for five MORECS boxes, 1985–1990. 15

10 Location of the MORECS boxes shown in Figure 9. 16

11 Groundwater levels in three wells in the chalk aquifer in 1988, 1989 and 1990. 17

12 Monthly river runoff in six catchments from October 1988 to December 1990, expressed as a percentage departure from the long-term monthly mean. 21

13 Location of sites shown in Figures 11 and 12. 22

Appendix

A1 Location of grid points over the UK used in the construction of the gale index. Grid-point numbers are those used in the equations (from Hulme and Jones, 1991, with the permission of the Royal Meteorological Society). 23

1   Dates of first flowering or leafing of (a) 17 native species in 1989 and (b) 16 native species in 1990, recorded at 6 ITE stations, compared with long-term mean dates recorded as part of the Phenological Records of the Royal Meteorological Society 1891–1947.   26

2   Records made at 6 ITE stations in 1990 compared with 1989 of (a) first flowering of 17 species and (b) first leafing of 5 tree species.   27

3   Dates of first flowering in (a) 1989 and (b) 1990 compared with the mean dates for 1978–88 inclusive, for a range of plant species in a garden in East Lothian. First flowering in 1989 and 1990 was either the same (●) or significantly different (○) from the mean for 1978–88.   28

4   Numbers of garden plant species/hybrids in flower at Longniddry, East Lothian in 1989 and 1990 compared with the average for 1978–88. Stars indicate that 1989 and 1990 values differed from the 1978–88 average by more than two standard deviations.   29

5   (a) The relationship between DNA amount and the time of shoot expansion (date to nearest quarter month at which 50% of maximum shoot biomass was obtained) in 24 plant species commonly found in the Sheffield region (redrawn from Grime and Mowforth, 1982). Temperature at Sheffield is expressed as the long-term average for each month of daily minima (□) and maxima (▮) in air temperature 1.5 m above the ground.
    (b) The relationship between DNA amount and the mean rate of leaf extension over the period 25 March–5 April in 14 grassland species coexisting in the same turf (redrawn from Grime, Shacklock and Band, 1985). 95% confidence limits are indicated by vertical lines.   31

6   The relationship between (a) leaf size at the end of March 1989 as a percentage of leaf size in April/May 1989, and (b) nuclear DNA amount. Data collected from around Hathersage, North Derbyshire.

Ae, *Arrhenatherum elatius*; Am, *Arum maculatum*; As, *Anthriscus sylvestris*; At, *Arabidopsis thaliana*; Au, *Allium ursinum*; Bp, *Bellis perennis*; Br, *Bromus ramosus*; Ca, *Cardamine amara*; Cc, *Carex caryophyllea*; Cf, *Cardamine flexuosa*; Cha, *Chamaenerion angustifolium*; Cm, *Conopodium majus*; Cn, *Centaurea nigra*; Cp, *Caltha palustris*; Cs, *Calystegia sepium*; Eh, *Epilobium hirsutum*; Eo, *E. obscurum*; Er, *Elymus repens*; Fg, *Festuca gigantea*; Ga, *Galium aparine*; Gp, *G. palustre*; Hn, *Hyacinthoides non-scripta*; Hs, *Heracleum sphondylium*; La, *Lamium album*; Ln, *Lysimachia nemorum*; Lv, *Leucanthemum vulgare*; Ma, *Mentha aquatica*; Mo, *Myrrhis odorata*; Mp, *Mercurialis perennis*; Ms, *Myosotis scorpioides*; Nm, *Nasturtium microphyllum*; Pa, *Phalaris arundinacea*; Ph, *Petasites hybridus*; Pm, *Plantago major*; Pp, *Poa pratensis*; Rb, *Ranunculus bulbosus*; Rfi, *R. ficaria*; Rfl, *R. flammula*; Rj, *Reynoutria japonica*; Ro, *Rumex obtusifolius*; Rr, *Ranunculus repens*; Sa, *Stellaria alsine*; Sd, *Silene dioica*; Se, *Sparganium erectum*; Sh, *Stellaria holostea*; So, *Stachys officinalis*; Sp, *Succisa pratensis*; To, *Taraxacum officinale*; Ud, *Urtica dioica*; Vb, *Veronica beccabunga*.

Most species are denoted by a closed circle (●). However, species whose phenology was markedly abnormal are indicated as the following symbols:

□   Shoots abnormally large by end of March.
○   Above-ground shoots not normally produced until late April – early May.
△   Foliage overwintering in species whose shoots normally die back in late autumn – early winter.
▲   Early flowering observed in the period January to March; onset at least one month earlier than normal.

Some species (*e.g. Lamium album*) are identified by two symbols.   32

7   (a) Correlation of mean January-April temperatures with the first record of the peach-potato aphid (*Myzus persicae*) in the suction trap at Rothamsted, and
    (b) correlation of mean December–June temperatures with numbers of aphids in the suction trap by 1 July (from Harrington, 1990, unpublished report).   36

8   Total catch of the moth, Hebrew character, *Orthosia gothica* (L.) (Lep. Noctuidae) in light traps in 1989 compared to the mean for all the previous years of trapping. Data from the Rothamsted Insect Survey.   38

9   First appearances of moths in the light trap at Furzebrook in Dorset in 1989: (a) first appearance contrasted to average date of the first appearance for all records from 1972–76, (b) first appearance contrasted to all records from 1972–76.   39

10 Phenological records of first date of spawning of the common frog in 1984, 1985 and 1989 (Morrison, 1989).   40

11 Duration of the breeding periods (vertical lines) of the common toad in Dorset 1980–89. (Reading, pers. comm.). ● – first spawn laid.   41

12 Percentage of marked oystercatchers which returned to Banchory, Kincardineshire during February and March in 1987 (●, n=42), 1988 (■, n=60) and 1989 (▲, n=67) (from Picozzi, pers. comm.).   42

13 Numbers of rat infestations recorded by Ealing District Council 1967–89. (a) Total numbers per year; (b) mean monthly total; (c) numbers recorded in November (——) and December (. . . .) in each year.   43

14 Mean catch of bank voles and wood mice trapped in winter (November/December) and summer (May/June) at 10 standard woodland sites recorded by the Mammal Society, National Small Mammal Survey (Flowerdew, 1989; 1990 and pers. comm.).   44

Chapter A3

1 Plots of 5-day mean water temperatures against 5-day mean air temperatures for (a) Black Brows Beck in Cumbria and (b) Mattergill Sike in the Pennines. (From Crisp and Howson, 1982).   47

2 Twenty year records of winter water temperatures in (a) the River Tees, (b) the River Tyne, (c) Black Brows Beck, and (d) the River Frome. The plotted temperatures are the average of daily readings in January, February and March.   48

3 The number of days each winter when there was some ice cover on: (a) Windermere, Cumbria; and (b) Loch Leven, Fife.   48

4 The long-term trend in (a) air, and (b) surface temperatures at Windermere in 1989 and 1990 compared with the range recorded between 1943 and 1987. All values were smoothed with a three point, centre weighted running average.   49

5 (a) Means of weekly nitrate concentrations in the River Frome plotted against time of year for the period 1965–1975. From Casey and Clarke, 1979.
   (b) The twenty year trend in winter nitrate levels and water temperatures in Windermere.   50

6 (a) Typical limits of "light" and "dark" water in four lakes of different depths in April, showing the morphometric/mixing factor.
   (b) The spring increase in chlorophyll in a relatively shallow lake (Blelham Tarn), and a deep lake (the North Basin of Windermere).
   (c) Growth simulations of the diatom *Asterionella* in Windermere. The lower curve shows the predicted growth in an "average" year, the higher curve the predicted growth in 1989 (Figures (a) and (b) are taken from Talling, 1971).   51

7 The influence of the mild winter on the reproductive rate of *Daphnia*. The lower curve shows the standardised birth rate in an "average" year (see George *et al.*, 1990). The upper curve shows the predicted birth rate in Windermere during the first six months of 1989.   52

8 Survival of juvenile sea trout in a Lake District stream between 1966 and 1990. The curve shows the strong "density dependent" relationship between the number of survivors and parent stock (number of eggs), apparently unaffected by the mild temperatures in 1989 and 1990.   53

Chapter A4

1 Dates when T-SUM 200 was reached at Nottingham University School of Agriculture, Sutton Bonington, Notts. (Data courtesy of N. Sweet). T-SUM is the accumulated day degrees above the base temperature for grass growth.   59

2 A perennial ryegrass sward, var. Cropper was allowed to grow after cutting in November the previous year. Grass was cut again from March onwards at 4 weekly intervals in a staggered sequence. The yields from these clearing cuts are given. (Data courtesy of R.H. Lavender, R. Sheldrick and R. Martyn, IGER North Wyke).   60

SECTION B

Chapter B1

1 Comparisons of May to October temperatures for 1990, 1989, 1976 and for the 1961–80 reference period.   66

2   Mean maximum (a), mean minimum (b), and mean temperatures (c), with respect to the 1961–80 period for the June to August 1989 and the May to October 1989 seasons.   67

3   Mean maximum (a), mean minimum (b), and mean temperatures (c) with respect to the 1961–80 period for the June to August 1990 and the May to October 1990 seasons (contour intervals 0.2°C).   68

4   Numbers of days with (a) the mean temperature above 20°C and (b) the maximum temperature above 25°C with respect to the 1961–80 period for the June to August 1989 and the May to October 1989 seasons.   69

5   Number of days with, (a) mean temperature above 20°C (contour intervals 2 days) and, (b)maximum temperature above 25°C (contour interval 3 days) with respect to the 1961–80 period for the June to August 1990 and May to October 1990 seasons.   70

6   Number of sunshine hours per day and seasonal totals for the June to August (a) and May to October (b) periods. The dotted lines are one hour per day deviations from the 1909–1990 average. The smooth lines are ten year Gaussian filters fitted through both series.   71

7   Number of anomalous sunshine hours with respect to the 1961–80 period for the June to August 1989 and the May to October 1989 seasons.   72

8   Number of anomalous sunshine hours over the United Kingdom with respect to the 1961–80 period for the June to August 1990 (left) and the May to October 1990 (right) seasons (contour intervals 0.4 hours/day).   72

9   Absolute maximum temperature occurring during the hot spell of August 2–4 1990. The dots show the locations of the 171 stations used. (a) Contoured at 2°C intervals to show finer detail. (b) Contoured at 5°C intervals for comparison with Brugge (1991).   73

10   Comparison of temperature and rainfall in England and Wales in summer (June to August). The data extend back to 1766.   76

11   Rainfall between February and November in 1990, 1989 and 1976, expressed as a percentage of the 1961–80 average.   77

12   Ratio of winter (October – March) rainfall to summer (April – September) rainfall for England and Wales, 1766–1990.   78

13   Potential (PE) and actual evapotranspiration (AE) in summer (June, July and August) 1976, 1989 and 1990 as a percentage of the 1961–80 average. MORECS data.   79

14   Number of months ending with a soil moisture deficit greater than 100 mm in 1990.   81

15   Ground water levels in three wells in the chalk aquifer in 1988, 1989 and 1990.   81

16   Location of sites shown in Figures 15 and 17.   82

17   Monthly river runoff in six catchments from October 1988 to December 1990, expressed as a percentage departure from the long-term monthly mean.   83

18   Reservoir contents for Stithians Reservoir, South West Water, in 1976, 1989 and 1990.   84

19   Monthly runoff from February to November expressed as a percentage departure from the long-term monthly mean, for 1990, 1989 and 1976.   85

20   Area with hosepipe bans as of August 21 1990. (Redrawn from Water Bulletin, August 24).   87

Chapter B2

1   The musk orchid (*Herminium monorchis*) – number of plants flowering in a 444 m^{-2} area at Totternhoe, Bedfordshire, 1966–90.   93

2   (a) Numbers of flowers per plant of marsh gentian (*Gentiana pneumonanthe*) (——) shown in relation to mean summer temperature (– – – –). Data are means for sites in east Dorset and the New Forest.
     (b) Relationship between mean summer temperature in the previous year and the numbers of flowers per plant on marsh gentian (*Gentiana pneumonanthe*). Letters refer to flowering years, A=1977, B=1978 . . ., N=1990.   94

3 (a) Total numbers of butterflies of all species counted each year at Kingley Vale NNR in the ITE Butterfly Monitoring Scheme (Williamson, pers. comm.).

(b) Total numbers of holly blue (*Celastrina argiolus*) butterflies counted each year at Kingley Vale NNR in the ITE Butterfly Monitoring Scheme (Williamson, pers. comm.).   101

4 Mean UK trend in the abundance of the speckled wood (*Pararge aegeria*) butterfly since 1976, taken from the ITE Butterfly Monitoring Scheme. Collated indexes are shown numerically with numbers plotted on a logarithmic scale (the 1976 index was arbitrarily set at 100 and subsequent years are related to this (Pollard and Yates, 1989)).   102

5 Distribution of the hedgebrown (or gatekeeper) butterfly (*Pyronia tithonus*) in the UK and Ireland. The hatched areas mark the northward expansion of the species range since 1970 as determined by the ITE Biological Records Centre. The closed circles mark the distribution of the species since 1940. The open circles mark sighting of the species north of its present range before 1940.   102

6 The flight period of the meadow brown (*Maniola jurtina*) 1976–1990, showing the mean flight date for each year.   104

7 Long term records (1934–1989) for honey yields from the Bee Farmers Association (Ellis, pers. comm.) (a) mean yield in lbs/colony of bees, (b) 7 and 10 year running mean yield in lbs/colony of bees.   106

8 Range expansion in 1990 of the long-winged cone head bush cricket (*Conocephalus discolor*) (from Haes, 1990 and Biological Records Centre, Monks Wood).   107

9 Influence of weather on slug activity in 1988, 1989 and 1990 (Young and Port, pers. comm.).   109

10 Number of outdoor secondary fires in grassland (includes heathland), crops, woods *etc.* (Fire Statistics UK, 1987, 1988; Home Office Statistical Bulletin, 38/90).
(a) In the UK 1968–90.
(b) In the Dorset Fire Brigade area 1978–90.   112

11 The monthly occurrence of fires throughout the year. (——) total outdoor fires in Dorset in each month in 1990 (Greet, pers. comm.); (– – – –) total numbers of fires on National Nature Reserves in each month since 1968 (using all available records from the NCC).   113

Appendix 1
A1 Generalised phenology of five species of orchids growing in Bedfordshire and Cambridgeshire.   116

Chapter B3

1 Sixteen year records of the average summer (June, July, August) water temperature in (a) the River Tyne (Northumberland), (b) Black Brows Beck (Cumbria) and (c) the River Frome (Dorset).   119

2 Sixteen year records of the summer surface temperatures in (a) Windermere (Cumbria), (b) Esthwaite Water (Cumbria) and (c) Loch Leven (Fife). The plotted temperatures are the average of weekly readings in June, July and August.   119

3 The seasonal variation of surface water temperatures in (a) Loch Leven (Fife) and (b) Windermere (Cumbria). The temperatures recorded during 1990 (thick line) are compared with the maxima and minima recorded between 1979 and 1989 (thin line).   120

4 Observed (●) and predicted (—) concentrations of nitrate in the River Frome in (a) 1976 and (b) 1989. The 1989 curve has been adjusted to account for recent general increases in the concentration of nitrate (estimated as *ca.* 0.11 mg/year).   120

5 Concentrations of aluminium, iron, dissolved organic carbon and reduced nitrogen in water flowing into and out of a wetland area at Llanbrynmair Moor, mid-Wales in 1989/90.   122

6 The effect of sinking *Oscillatoria bowellyi* on the deoxygenation of deep water in the South Basin of Windermere. (a) 1976 a warm year with a poor growth of *Oscillatoria*. (b) 1989 a warm year with a strong growth of *Oscillatoria*. The *Oscillatoria* numbers are plotted as histograms and the points show the concentration of oxygen at a depth of 30 m.   123

7   The growth of the blue-green alga *Aphanizomen* in Esthwaite Water in 1985 and 1989. (a) 1985 on a cold windy summer. (b) 1989 a warm relatively calm summer. The *Aphanizomenon* numbers are plotted as histograms and the points show the average weekly wind speeds.   123

8   Factors influencing the growth of the blue-green alga *Oscillatoria agardhi* in the South Basin of Windermere between 1980 and 1990. (a) Winter concentrations of total phosphorus. (b) Year to year changes in the average summer crop of *O. agardhi*. (c) Year to year variations in the average winter (●) and summer (▮) temperatures.   124

9   The year to year variation in (a) the number of trout lost between the alevin stage and the parr stage in May/June (k1) and (b) the parr stages in August/September (k2). The loss rates have been calculated by key factor analysis.   124

10   The year to year variation in the production of trout under three years old in Black Brows Beck (Cumbria).   125

11   The year to year variation in the number of salmon moving up the River Frome in summer. The numbers are the numbers logged on a resistivity counter positioned in a gauging weir. The counter was not operating in 1983.   125

Chapter B4

1   Incidence of the pathogens *Altenaria (a) and Pyrenopeziza* (b) on leaves (April) and pods (July) of winter oilseed rape (cv. Bienvenu) for January-March and June respectively, 1985–1989. (Courtesy of C J Rawlinson *et al.*, Rothamsted Experimental Station).   130

2   Growth rate of Cropper Perennial Ryegrass at North Wyke, Devon, where 1985 represents an average year. Based on four-weekly cuts throughout the growing season. (Courtesy of R Sheldrick, IGER).   135

3   Monthly concentrate used in the UK (kg/cow), 1988–1990. Data courtesy of Milk Marketing Board, National Milkminder Results.   136

4   UK national milk production for the year 1990/91. (a) Weekly wholesale output and quota; (b) cumulative difference from quota (courtesy of the Milk Marketing Board).   137

Introduction

A remarkable climatological episode occurred in the UK from the autumn of 1988 to autumn 1990. Throughout that period, average temperatures were above normal in much of the UK, and rainfall was substantially below normal in the south-east. The period was remarkable in that there were two *successive* mild winters and hot summers (including record high temperatures) and *extended* drought conditions in much of eastern and central England. This episode was in many ways more significant ecologically than the hot, dry summer of 1976, because of the mild winters and the extended period of warmer/drier-than-usual conditions.

Following the summer of 1976, the Institute of British Geographers produced an atlas on the drought conditions and their impacts, as a record of that single unusual event (Doornkamp *et al.*, 1980). About the same time, the former Nature Conservancy Council commissioned a review of biological responses to climatic change (Ford, 1978). Following the mild winter of 1988/89, when spring came several months early, a similar decision was made by the Department of the Environment to collate as much information as possible on the impacts of that event on the natural environment in the UK. The motivation, in that case, was to gain information on the impacts in the UK of potential climatic warming, as well as to record what happened in 1988/89. At a time when researchers were planning experimental studies on the responses of ecosystems to warm temperatures, it seemed that a large natural experiment was going on outside from which a lot might be learned. Of course, the 1988/89 winter was then followed by a hot summer, another mild winter and an even hotter summer in 1990. The outcome was a set of three reports prepared for the Department of the Environment by NERC, in which a large number of observations were collated.

This book brings together all the information in the three DoE reports. For clarity, the information is divided into the mild winter events and hot summer events, although we realize that in some instances (concerning phenology, for instance) the events in the summers were dependent on what happened in the winters, and in all instances the consecutive nature of the warm/dry conditions was important. In addition, the information in this book has been updated in consultation with the individual authors, and all of the impact chapters have been independently refereed.

It is important to understand the type of information that is presented here and its purpose. In only a few instances was it possible to obtain data that had been systematically collected and rigorously analysed – notable exceptions were the climatological data, and some of the plant and animal phenological data. In order to cover the great breadth of events that occurred, we have included many anecdotal observations, many personal communications, and data from unreplicated sources at individual sites. Some of this information may be unconvincing, but it has been included to suggest the type of impacts that may have occurred and which might occur in the future. Remember that our intention was to gather observations made in 1988–1990 that might suggest the type of responses to climatic warming that may deserve attention. What should we worry about? What are the research priorities? Many records of what happened in the mild winters and hot summers, even casual ones, may be of value as indicators of what might happen in the future, although (as some referees pointed out) they would not satisfy a scientific editor. We thought, for instance, that when reporting outbreaks of insect pests or rat populations, we could get useful information from Rentokil, suppliers of insecticides, environmental health officers, and from farmers and the agricultural press, as well as from scientists. This sort of information gathering should be regarded as a precursor to more rigorous studies.

Several hundred people have contributed to this book. Some have generously shared data collected from experiments or surveys that happen to have been running at the time, while others have reported their personal observations. We are grateful to the authors, whose names appear on each chapter, to the many sources that are acknowledged below, and to the referees, who helped to point out some errors and deficiencies in the original reports.

We shall be rewarded if the observations reported here will help those making difficult decisions on research and policy priorities, and will serve as a useful record, however imperfect, of what happened in 1988–90.

Doornkamp, J.C., Gregory, K.J. and Burn, A.S. 1980. *Atlas of drought in Britain, 1975–76.* Institute of British Geographers, London.

Ford, M.J. 1978. *A study of the biological response to climatic change.* Nature Conservancy Council Report No. 218.

Melvin G R Cannell and Carole E R Pitcairn,
Institute of Terrestrial Ecology,
Edinburgh, February 1992.

Contributors

CLIMATE

– *Temperature*

P.D. Jones and M. Hulme (University of East Anglia)

– *Hydrology*

N.W. Arnell, N.S. Reynard, T.J. Marsh, S.J. Bryant and R.P.C. Brown (Institute of Hydrology)

IMPACTS ON TERRESTRIAL ENVIRONMENT

– *Plants*

F.T. Last (Longniddry), J.M. Sykes, M.G.R. Cannell, T.C.E. Wells, R. Rose, P. Carey and C.Barr (Institute of Terrestrial Ecology), J.N. Gibbs (Forestry Commission), J.G. Hodgson and J.P. Grime (University of Sheffield)

– *Animals*

L.K. Ward, M. Marquiss (Institute of Terrestrial Ecology)

IMPACTS ON FRESHWATER SYSTEMS

D.G. George (Institute of Freshwater Ecology), B.A. Emmett and B. Reynolds (Institute of Terrestrial Ecology)

IMPACTS ON AGRICULTURE AND HORTICULTURE

M.H. Unsworth, R.K. Scott, J.S. Cox and K. Bardell (University of Nottingham)

Acknowledgements

ADAS (Kendal, Pontypool, Leicester,
    Cambridge, Nottingham, Kirton, Bristol,
    Reading, Aberystwyth, Chichester,
    Harpenden Laboratory, Worcester,
    Leeds, Wolverhampton),
Agricultural Research Institute of Northern
    Ireland,
Ajax-Lewis A.,
Archer M.,
Arnold H.,
Arthur Rickwood Experimental Husbandry
    Farm (EHF),
Bagott B.,
Bee Farmers Association,
Benstead A.,
Boxworth Experimental Husbandry Farm
    (EHF),
Brigets Experimental Husbandry Farm
    (EHF),
British Herpetological Society,
Brooms Barn Experimental Station,
Central Veterinary Investigation Centre,
Chapman S.B.,
Chief Fire Officer (Dorset),
Churchfield S.,
Climatic Research Unit (East Anglia),
Cooke A.,
Coulson J.,
Cox R.,
Cummins C.,
DAFS (East Craigs),
Dagley J.,
Department of Agriculture for Northern
    Ireland,
Department of Agriculture and Fisheries for
    Scotland (DAFS),
East of Scotland Agricultural College,
Edinburgh School of Agriculture,
Efford Horticultural Station,
Elmes G.,
English Vineyards Association (Commander
    G. Bond),
Environmental Health Offices,
Evans D.,
Eversham B.,
Fielding J.,
Fire Research Station,
Flour Advisory Bureau,
Flowerdew J.,
Gleadthorpe Experimental Husbandry Farm
    (EHF),
Glue D.,
Goss-Custard J.,
Halstead A.,
Harrington R.,
Hayes C.,
Higgins J.,

High Mowthorpe Experimental Husbandry
    Farm (EHF),
Hill M.O.,
Hydrometric Authorities in England Wales
    and Scotland,
ICI Fertilisers,
Institute of Freshwater Ecology (NERC),
Institute of Horticultural Research (East
    Malling),
Institute of Horticultural Research
    (Wellesbourne),
Institute of Grassland and Environmental
    Research (North Wyke Research Station).
Institute of Horticultural Research
    (Department of Hop Research),
Institute of Arable Crops Research (Long
    Ashton Research Station),
Institute for Grassland and Animal
    Research,
Kelly D.,
Kenwood R.,
Kirton Experimental Horticulture Station,
Last F.T.,
Le Duc M.,
Leith I.D.,
Long Ashton Research Station,
Luddington Experimental Horticulture
    Station,
MAFF,
Majerus M.,
Mason W.L.,
Meteorological Office,
Milk Marketing Board,
Mills D.,
Morris P.,
Murray M.,
National Agricultural Centre (Stoneleigh),
National Institute of Agricultural Botany,
Nature Conservancy Council,
Newton I.,
Nottingham University School of
    Agriculture,
Owen D.F.,
Peak Park Planning Board,
Pearson B.,
Pickess B.,
Picozzi N.,
Pollard E.,
Processors and Growers Organisation,
Reading C.,
Rentokil plc,
Roewarne Experimental Horticulture
    Station,
Rosemaund Experimental Husbandry Farm
    (EHF),
Rothamsted Experimental Station,
Royal Meteorological Society
Royal Society for Nature Conservation,

Scottish Agricultural Colleges,
Scottish Crop Research Institute,
Shan Huen Chan,
Slatefield Fruit Farm (Forfar),
South A.,
South West Water plc,
Staines B.,
Stockbridge House Horticultural Station,
Stubbs A.,
Studland Heath NNR,
Surface Water and Groundwater Archives
  (Wallingford),
Swan M.,
Terrington Experimental Husbandry Farm
  (EHF),
Thomas J.,
University of Newcastle,

University of Wales (Catchment Research
  Group),
University of Nottingham,
Veterinary Investigation Regional Centres,
Veterinary Investigation Centre (Penrith),
Veterinary Investigation Centre (Sutton
  Bonington),
Watt A.D.,
Webb N.R.,
Welch D.,
Wellow Vineyards (Hants),
Welsh Office
Weston J.,
Wheeler A.,
Williamson D.,
Woiwodd I.,
Worplesdon Laboratory,
Wright M.,

Section A

Impacts of the Mild Winters 1988/89 and 1989/90

Chapter A1
The Climate

A1.1 TEMPERATURES AND WINDINESS

1.1.1 Introduction

This chapter compares temperatures and windiness over the United Kingdom during November to April in 1988/89 and 1989/90 with previous years. Data are presented for the conventional definition of winter, December to February, and the longer definition of winter, November to April.

The United Kingdom is endowed with the longest instrumental temperature record anywhere in the world. This 'Central England' record was constructed by Manley (1974) and extends back to 1659, although the years prior to 1721 are less reliable than the years since 1722. The record is regularly updated by the Meteorological Office (Jones, 1987) and is also available as a daily series since the late eighteenth century (Parker et al., 1991).

The 'Central England' temperature (Manley, 1974) is an average of the value at a site in the Lancashire plain and two sites located at the western and eastern extremities of the South Midlands. Since 1974 the series has comprised Rothamsted, Malvern and ½ (Squires Gate and Ringway). Descriptions of the series are given by Jones (1987) and Legg (1989), who assessed the influence of urbanization growth around the four sites. Potentially, the most seriously affected site is Malvern. Since about 1980, reductions of 0.1°C have been made to allow for urban influence in the series.

The Central England series provides mean monthly and daily temperatures which were used in comparisons. Regional variations in temperatures were also considered at 15 meteorological stations in the UK for which data were available for 1988/89, 1989/90 and the 1961–80 reference period.

1.1.2 Central England temperatures during November to April

MONTHLY TEMPERATURES IN THE CENTRAL ENGLAND SERIES

The mean monthly temperatures for the six month period, November to April in 1988/89 and 1989/90 are listed in Table 1, together with the 1961–80 average.

Although November 1988 and April 1989 were just over 1°C below average, the four months, December to March 1988/89 were all at least 2°C above the average and the December-March period for that winter was the mildest in the entire Central England record. In 1989/90, all months during both seasons were warmer than average except for November and the three months January, February and March were all at least 2.8°C warmer than the 1961–80 average. Taken together this three month period was the warmest three month start to a year in the Central England series. February 1990 was the third warmest such month in the entire series, which extends back to 1659. Only Februarys in 1779 (7.9°C) and 1869 (7.5°C) were warmer.

Using the normal definition of winter, December to February 1988/89 was 2.5°C above the 1961–80 average and December to February 1989/90 was 2.2°C above the 1961–80 average, making the two winters the second and sixth mildest, respectively, on record. The average for the two years clearly makes these two winters the mildest back-to-back winters in the entire record. The longer six-month definition of winter from November to April shows 1989/90 to be more extreme than 1988/89 (see Figure 1). The 1989/90 period was the fourth such mildest November to April period, exceeded by 1733/34 and 1821/22 by 0.1°C, and 1685/86 by 0.05°C.

Table 1: Monthly mean Central England temperatures (°C) November 1989 to April 1990

Month	1961–80 Average	1988/89 Mean Temperature	1988/89 Anomaly	1989/90 Mean Temperature	1989/90 Anomaly
November	6.4	5.2	−1.2	6.2	−0.2
December	4.4	7.5	+3.1	4.9	+0.5
January	3.6	6.1	+2.5	6.5	+2.7
February	3.9	5.9	+2.0	7.3	+3.4
March	5.5	7.5	+2.0	8.3	+2.8
April	7.9	6.6	−1.3	8.0	+0.1
Dec-Feb	4.0	6.5	+2.5	6.2	+2.2
Nov-Apr	5.3	6.5	+1.2	6.9	+1.6

a)

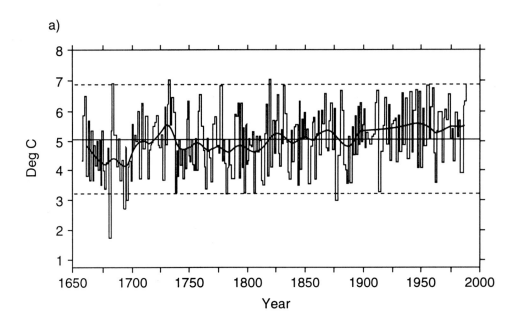

b)

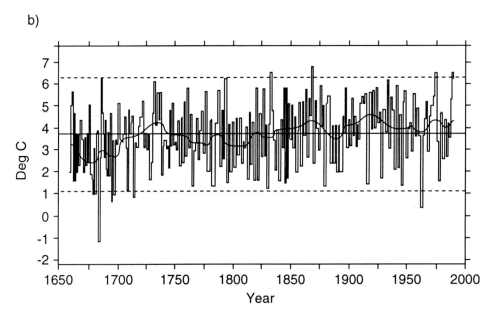

1   Average Central England Temperatures for the (a) conventional and (b) extended winters, 1959/60 to 1989/90. The smooth lines are 30-year Gaussian filters fitted through both series. The dotted lines show the two standard deviation limits calculated over the entire period.

Table 2:   Number of days with mean temperature below 0° and 5°C over Central England November to April 1988/89 and 1989/90.

Month	Days < 0°C			Days < 5°C		
	1961–80	1988/89	1989/90	1961–80	1988/89	1989/90
November	0.6	0	1	9.6	15	9
December	3.2	0	0	16.3	5	18
January	4.6	0	0	18.3	6	9
February	2.9	0	0	17.3	12	6
March	0.7	0	0	12.6	4	4
April	0.0	0	0	3.7	6	5
Dec-Feb	10.7	0	0	51.9	23	33
Nov-Apr	12.0	0	1	77.8	48	51

DAILY TEMPERATURES FROM THE CENTRAL
ENGLAND SERIES

The daily Central England temperature series was developed by Storey *et al.* (1986) and Parker *et al.* (1991), and extends back to the late eighteenth century. The series enables the number of days below or above specific thresholds to be counted and comparisons made with previous years. The number of days each month when the daily mean temperature was below two thresholds, (0° and 5°C) in 1988/89 and 1989/90 are compared with average values for 1961–80 in Table 2.

For the six-month period there were no days during 1988/89, and only one day during 1989/90, when the daily mean temperature dropped below 0°C (− 0.3°C was recorded on November 26, 1989). Since 1845, only four similar periods have recorded no days below zero, namely 1877/78, 1922/23, 1924/25 and 1974/75.

For the 5°C threshold over the same period, there were 29.8 and 26.8 fewer days below 5°C in 1988/89 and 1989/90, respectively, compared with the 1961–80 average. For the shorter winter period, there were again fewer days below 5°C in both winters compared to the 1961–80 average. During both the three and six-month winter season, there were slightly more days below 5°C in 1989/90 than in 1988/89. This result is somewhat surprising, particularly for the longer season, since the mean temperature for 1989/90 was 0.4°C warmer than 1988/89. This suggests that daily temperatures were more variable than in 1988/89, with more very mild winter days in 1989/90.

1.1.3 Temperatures over the United Kingdom during the November to April period

In the previous section, the two winter periods have been compared with the long historic record of Central England temperatures. In this section, the regional variations that occurred over the country are considered. Fifteen sites were chosen for which data were readily available for the 1988/89 and 1989/90 periods and for the 1961–80 reference period. The locations of the stations are listed in Table 3 and are shown as dots on the subsequent figures.

Table 3: Locations of the 15 meteorological stations over the United Kingdom

Station	Height (m)	Latitude (°N)	Longtitude (°W)
Aldergrove	68	54°39'	6°12'
Durham	102	54°46'	1°35'
Dyce	65	57°12'	2°12'
Elmdon	98	52°27'	1°45'
Eskdalemuir	242	55°19'	3°12'
Gatwick	59	51°09'	0°11'
Kirkwall	26	58°57'	2°54'
Long Ashton	51	51°26'	2°40'
Oxford	63	51°46'	1°16'
Plymouth	27	50°21'	4°07'
Ringway	75	53°21'	2°16'
Santon Downham	24	52°29'	0°41'E
Shawbury	72	52°48'	2°40'
Stornoway	15	58°13'	6°19'
Valley	10	53°15'	4°32'

MAXIMUM, MINIMUM AND MEAN TEMPERATURES

Figures 2 and 3 show the spatial patterns of mean maximum, mean minimum and mean daily temperature anomalies for conventional, three monthly (Figure 2) and extended, six-monthly (Figure 3) winter seasons for both 1988/89 and 1989/90 (Hulme and Jones 1991). In each case the anomalies are from the 1961–1980 period. Although anomalies were positive over the whole of the UK in both winters for maximum, minimum and mean temperatures, the spatial patterns of these anomalies in the two winters were quite different. Comparison of the 1988/89 and 1989/90 anomaly fields (Figures 2 and 3) shows that the 1988/89 anomalies were fairly uniform over the whole of the UK (e.g. about + 2.5°C in mean temperature for the conventional winter), whereas in 1989/90 there was a very marked south-east to north-west gradient for all three temperature variables. The largest anomalies in the 1989/90 conventional winter were + 3.0°C over south-eastern England, whereas anomalies over north-west Scotland were less than + 1.0°C. One result of this difference in spatial patterns is that over southern England the 1989/90 winter was milder than in 1988/89, whereas over northern England and Scotland the reverse was true.

DAYS BELOW TEMPERATURE THRESHOLDS

Another way of looking at the mildness of the winter is to examine the numbers of days with minimum temperatures below zero or the numbers of days with mean temperature below 5°C. These quantities were calculated for the 15 sites and compared with the average values for the 1961–80 period.

It was shown in the daily Central England Temperature record (Table 2) that similar reductions in the frequency of days with mean temperature below 0°C and those below 5°C occurred in both winters. However the spatial pattern of reductions in cold-day frequencies was not the same in both winters. Figure 4 shows the frequency anomalies over the UK for the two conventional winter seasons of days with minimum temperature below 0°C (air frosts) and days with mean temperature below 5°C (cold days) (Hulme and Jones 1991). These fields emphasise the distinction between the 1988/89 and 1989/90 winters identified above; the largest anomalies in 1988/89 (25–30 fewer air frosts and cold days than usual) occurred over north-eastern England and eastern Scotland, whereas in 1990 the largest reductions (25–30 fewer cold days) occurred over south-east England (Figure 4).

1.1.4 Weather types during the November 1988 to April 1989 period

Each day the daily weather pattern over the British Isles has been classified as being of a particular type (Lamb,

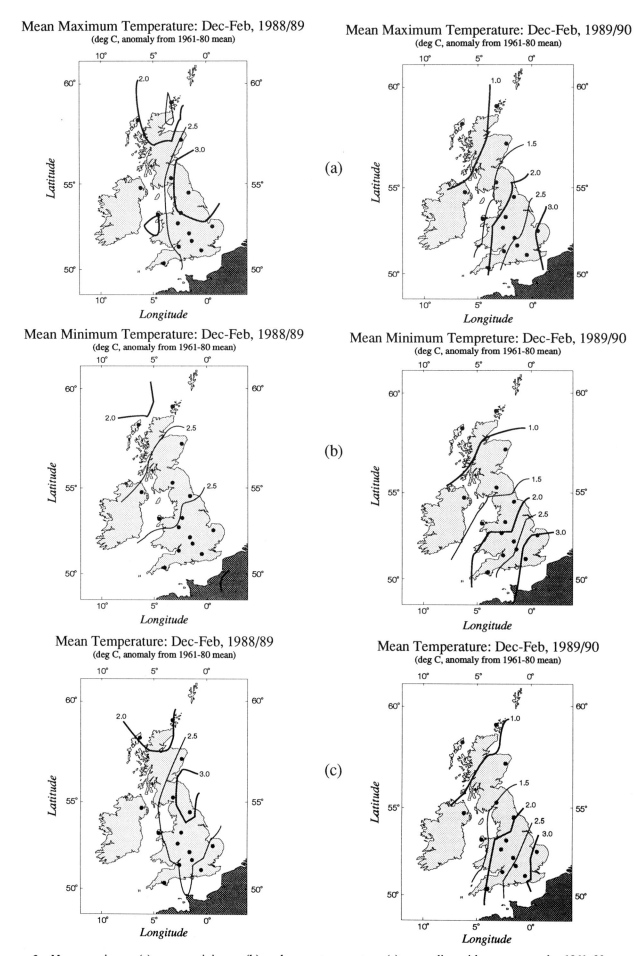

Mean Maximum Temperature: Dec-Feb, 1988/89
(deg C, anomaly from 1961-80 mean)

Mean Maximum Temperature: Dec-Feb, 1989/90
(deg C, anomaly from 1961-80 mean)

(a)

Mean Minimum Temperature: Dec-Feb, 1988/89
(deg C, anomaly from 1961-80 mean)

Mean Minimum Tempreture: Dec-Feb, 1989/90
(deg C, anomaly from 1961-80 mean)

(b)

Mean Temperature: Dec-Feb, 1988/89
(deg C, anomaly from 1961-80 mean)

Mean Temperature: Dec-Feb, 1989/90
(deg C, anomaly from 1961-80 mean)

(c)

2 Mean maximum (a), mean minimum (b) and mean temperature (c) anomalies with respect to the 1961–80 average for conventional winters, 1988/89 (left) and 1989/90 (right). Contours drawn by objective interpolation using UNIRAS graphics. (Taken from Hulme and Jones 1992, with permission of the Royal Meteorological Society).

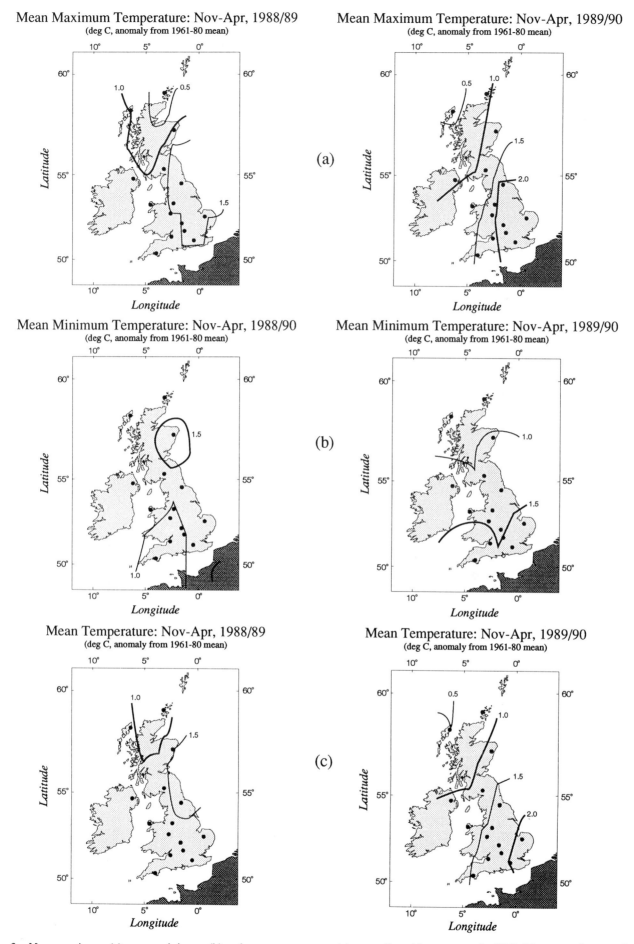

Mean Maximum Temperature: Nov-Apr, 1988/89
(deg C, anomaly from 1961-80 mean)

Mean Maximum Temperature: Nov-Apr, 1989/90
(deg C, anomaly from 1961–80 mean)

(a)

Mean Minimum Temperature: Nov-Apr, 1988/90
(deg C, anomaly from 1961-80 mean)

Mean Minimum Temperature: Nov-Apr, 1989/90
(deg C, anomaly from 1961-80 mean)

(b)

Mean Temperature: Nov-Apr, 1988/89
(deg C, anomaly from 1961-80 mean)

Mean Temperature: Nov-Apr, 1989/90
(deg C, anomaly from 1961-80 mean)

(c)

3   Mean maximum (a), mean minimum (b) and mean temperature (c) anomalies with respect to the 1961–80 average for extended winters, 1988/89 (left) and 1989/90 (right). Contours drawn by objective interpolation using UNIRAS graphics. (Taken from Hulme and Jones 1992, with permission of the Royal Meteorological Society).

Number of Air Frosts: Dec-Feb, 1988/89

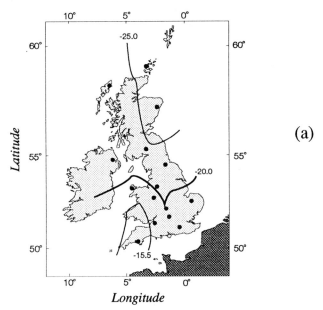

Number of Air Frosts: Dec-Feb, 1989/90

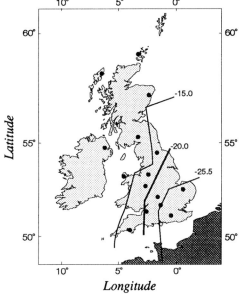

(a)

Number of Cold Days: Dec-Feb, 1989/90

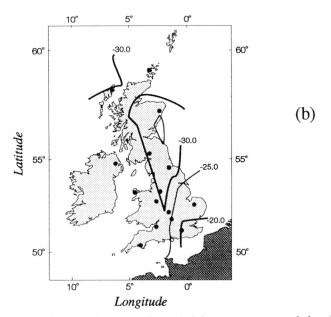

Number of Cold Days: Dec-Feb, 1989/90

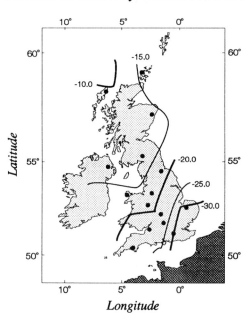

(b)

4   Anomalous number of air frosts (minimum temperature below 0°C) (a) and days with mean temperature below 5°C (b) with respect to the 1961–80 average for the conventional winters, 1988/89 (left) and 1989/90 (right). Contours drawn by objective interpolation using UNIRAS graphics. (Taken from Hulme and Jones 1992, with permission of the Royal Meteorological Society).

1972; Jones and Kelly, 1981; Briffa *et al.*, 1990). Twenty-seven different types are possible allowing for hybrids between the seven basic types: anticyclonic, cyclonic, northerly, easterly, southerly, westerly and northwesterly. Exceptionally cold winters (like 1862/63 and to a lesser extent 1978/79) tend to have a high number of days of easterly and northerly days. Wet and sometimes snowy winters have a high number of cyclonic days.

The anomalies of the seven basic types from 1961–80 reference period are listed in Table 4. The outstanding feature of the 1988/89 winter period was the dominance of westerly days. The last winter with the same levels of westerly days was 1974/75. Winters with high numbers

of westerly days were common during the 1920s and 1930s when, overall, the annual count of westerly days was at least one and a half times the average count during the 1980s. During some of the winters in the 1920s and 1930s snow was virtually absent and mild spells were common. Two of the winters with no days below 0°C in the Central England temperature series occurred during the 1920s. The number of westerly days during the 1988/89 season is similar to values reported during the 1920s.

1.1.5 Windiness over the United Kingdom and the North Sea region in 1989/90 compared to previous years

There are very few sites over the United Kingdom which have long records of daily wind strength. Both alterations

Table 4: Totals of the seven major Lamb daily weather types for the November 1988 – April 1989 period (days).

	Dec-Feb 1988-89	Dec-Feb 1861-80	Anomaly	Nov-Apr 1988-89	Nov-Apr 1961-80	Anomaly
Anticylonicity	22.3	19.6	2.7	45.2	40.6	4.6
Cyclonicity	7.8	15.1	−7.3	25.3	30.9	−5.6
Northerly	0.5	5.7	−5.2	10.7	14.7	−4.0
Easterly	2.0	9.1	−7.1	10.2	18.3	−8.1
Southerly	11.7	10.9	0.8	24.3	17.6	6.7
Westerly	43.2	20.1	23.1	56.9	38.8	18.1
Northwesterly	2.5	5.5	−3.0	2.5	11.6	−9.1
Unclassified days	0.0	4.0	−4.0	6.0	8.6	−2.6

a)

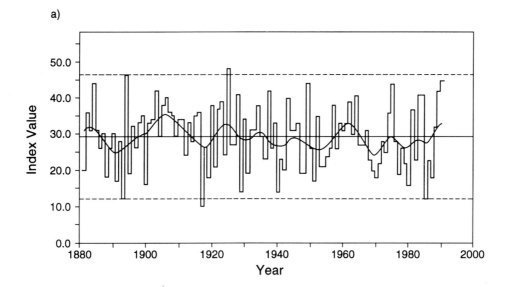

b)

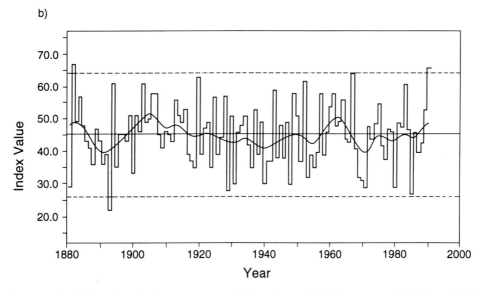

5   Number of gales over the UK region for the conventional (a) and extended (b) winters, 1880/81 to 1989/90 (see Appendix for the definition of a gale). The dotted lines are the two standard deviation lines calculated over the entire period. The smooth lines are 15-year Gaussian filters fitted through both series.

to sites and changes in instrumentation mean that the maximum length of homogeneous site records in the UK is about only 30 years. In order to derive a daily objective catalogue giving numerical values of wind flow and vorticity it is necessary to use the grid-point mean sea-level pressure data over the country. The guidelines of Jenkinson and Collison (1977) were used. They developed an objective definition of a gale day by calibration with

the monthly frequency of gales over the sea areas around the British Isles for a ten year period. Further details of their method of estimation of 'gale days' over the United Kingdom are given in the Appendix.

Figure 5 shows the number of gales over the UK region for the November to April and the December to February seasons. For the longer season in 1989/90, the number

(a)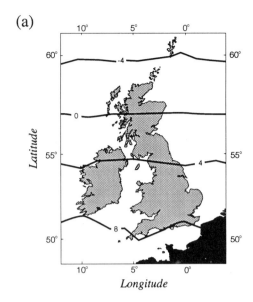

(b)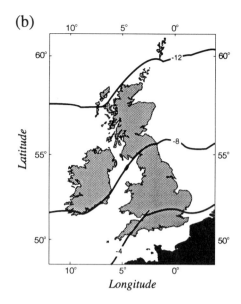

6 Mean sea-level pressure anomalies (mbar) with respect to the 1961–80 average for conventional winters, 1988/89 (a) and 1989/90 (b). The analysis is based on grid-point data on a 5° latitude by 10° longitude grid. Twenty grid points (the 16 in Figure A1 in the Appendix plus the 4 corner points) were used. Contours drawn by objective interpolation using UNIRAS graphics. (Taken from Hulme and Jones 1992, by permission of the Royal Meteorological Society).

of gales (66) was exceeded by only one other November to April period (1881/2), when 67 were recorded. For the shorter season, 45 gales were recorded, a value which has been exceeded twice before, in 1893/4 and 1924/25. The number of gales for the January to March period was the highest recorded since the series began in 1881. In this period, 54 gales were recorded, 19 in January, 21 in February and 14 in March. The February total easily exceeds the previous February maximum of 18. An analysis using the Smith (1982) index by Hammond (1990) also shows that February 1990 was the windiest February ever recorded. Although receiving less media attention than 1989/90, the 1988/89 conventional winter was the seventh windiest since 1881/82.

For the severe and very severe gale counts, the November to April period was not too unusual. There were, however, 16 severe gales in January and February which just exceeds the previous maximum of 15 in 1903 and 1962. The long time series shows that the most recent year only marks a return to the high gale level which prevailed earlier this century particularly during the 1900s and 1960s. The lowest number of gales occurred during the 1970s and the early 1980s. Coming after this period of low activity the January to March 1990 period seemed somewhat exceptional.

The grid-point mean sea-level pressure data have also been used to map the conventional winter pressure anomaly for the 1988/89 and 1989/90 winters (Figure 6). In both winters there was an enhanced westerly flow across the British Isles, from the west in 1988/89 and from the south-west in 1989/90. The greater windiness of 1989/90 is evident in below normal pressure over the entire region. In the earlier winter below normal pressure only occurred over northern Scotland.

1.1.6 Conclusions

1. Overall, the November to April 1988/89 period was among the twenty mildest such periods since the Central England temperature record began in 1659. That this period was not more exceptional is due to the relatively cool November and April. Taking the December to March period, 1988/89 was the warmest four month period in the Central England temperature series. If the more usual definition of winter is used the December to February 1988/89 period was the second mildest recorded – exceeded only by 1868/69.

2. The centre of the greatest temperature anomalies in 1988/89 was over northeastern England and eastern Scotland. The smallest anomalies occurred in south-east England where minimum temperatures in January and February were not much above normal.

3. The November to April 1989/90 period was the fourth mildest such period since 1659. The average temperature for this period was 1.6°C above the 1961–80 average. The January to March start to a calendar year was the warmest on record. The other three months of the extended winter, November, December and April experienced near normal conditions. The greater warmth of January to March was felt in both maximum and minimum temperatures.

4. The greatest anomalous warmth (>+ 3°C) was evident over southeastern England, with a strong west to east temperature gradient. In the extreme west of Britain the winter was only slightly warmer than normal.

5. Although the temperature anomalies of 1988/89 and 1989/90 were similar in many respects, the character

of the two years was completely different. This difference was most apparent in the windiness of the 1989/90 winter. The November to April 1989/90 period had the second greatest number of gale days according to an objective classification. Only 1881/2, with 67 gale days, exceeded the 1989/90 total, and this by just one day. Gale counts were anomalously high in January, February and March, with the February total of 21 gale days being the highest recorded February value on record.

6. The total number of severe gales was also a record during January and February 1990: the combined total for the two months of 16 severe gales exceeded the previous total of 15 which had occurred twice in the past.

A1.2 HYDROLOGY

1.2.1 Introduction

As it is difficult to separate hydrological characteristics of a year and their implications into summer and winter aspects, there will be some overlap in this section between Mild Winters and Hot Summers.

The winters of 1988/89 and 1989/90 were both substantially warmer than average but while the winter of 1988/89 was also remarkable for its low rainfall, 1989/90 was, in stark contrast, very wet in most regions. Because of the difference in rainfall between the two winters, it is necessary to consider each year separately.

Data used in this Chapter and in Chapter B1.2 come from a variety of sources. The river and groundwater data derive from the National Rivers Authority (before September 1989 the Water Authorities), and are taken from the Surface Water Archive and Groundwater Archive maintained by the Institute of Hydrology (IH) and the British Geological Survey (BGS), respectively. Some of the climatic data for the analyses are taken from MORECS (the Meteorological Office Rainfall and Evaporation Calculation System: Thompson et al. 1981), which produces weekly and monthly climatic statistics for 188 40 × 40 km boxes covering Britain. The long time series of homogenised England and Wales monthly rainfall data was derived and supplied by the Climatic Research Unit (CRU) of the University of East Anglia, who also provided the Central England Temperature series derived from data supplied by the Meteorological Office. The analyses and interpretations have been assisted by the monthly Hydrological Summaries for Great Britain prepared jointly by IH and BGS on behalf of the Department of the Environment.

1.2.2 November 1988 to April 1989

INTRODUCTION

The winter of 1988/89 was remarkable not just for its high temperatures but also for its low rainfall. The low rainfall in particular had significant implications for hydrological behaviour through the winter, and in some parts of Britain these implications were still being felt by the winter of 1989/90 (and beyond).

The dry winter followed a dry autumn, and by mid-February 1989 river flows and groundwater levels were well below average and causing real concern to water managers. High rainfall in March and April restored runoff and recharge (aquifer replenishment) rates to within the normal spring range in many parts of Britain, but in some areas the recovery was limited.

In this section, the dry winter is placed in its longer term context, and the spatial characteristics of its impact on precipitation, evaporation, soil moisture levels, river flows and groundwater levels are examined.

Rainfall and snowfall

SNOWFALL

Snow during the 1988/89 winter season was a rare commodity throughout Britain. Days with snow lying at 0900h are recorded at a network of observation stations, and for 22 such sites around Britain, Weather Magazine's "Weather Log" quotes monthly totals. Over the period from December to February, 12 of the 22 stations recorded no snow-days: most of these were in the east and south. The remaining 10 sites recorded only a little snow, all of which fell in February. The longer, November to April, definition of winter still produced 9 stations with no recorded snow-days, again around the east and south coasts.

The 14 snow days at Eskdalemuir in Scotland over the entire winter can be compared with a median over the period 1946/47 to 1987/88 of 32, and the one day recorded at Lyneham in Wiltshire compares with a long term median of 4 or 5 days. At both sites, fewer days with snow have been recorded on only two occasions: in 1975/76 (both sites) and in 1963/64 and 1966/67 at Eskdalemuir and Lyneham, respectively.

The mild winter of 1988/89 was therefore notable for its almost total lack of snowfall, particularly in southern and eastern areas between December and February.

RAINFALL

The period from November 1988 to mid-February 1989 was exceptionally dry, as is demonstrated within the context of the monthly homogenised time series of England and Wales rainfall. The period from December to February ranked as the 37th driest winter in the 223 years since the record began in 1766, and the 9th driest this century. Three December-February periods since 1960 have been drier – over England and Wales as a whole – namely, 1975/76 (18th driest since 1766), 1962/63 (15th and notably cold and anticyclonic), and 1963/64 (the driest

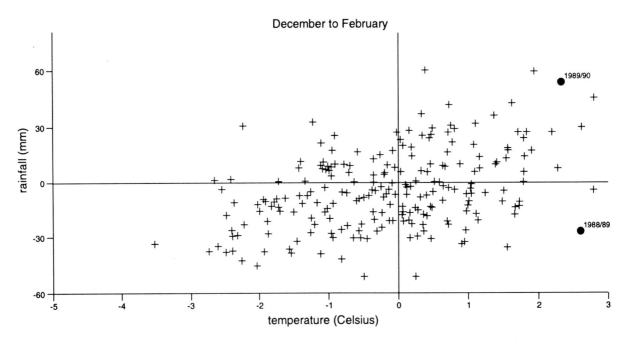

December to February

rainfall (mm)

temperature (Celsius)

1989/90

1988/89

Rainfall = difference from 1941-70 average
Temperature = difference from 1961-80 average

7   Winter precipitation over England and Wales and winter Central England Temperatures from 1766/67 to 1989/90. (Winter is defined as December, January and February). The long-term homogenised monthly rainfall data for England and Wales were derived by the Climatic Research Unit, who also supplied the Central England Temperature data.

on record). Rainfall in 1988/89 was only 70% of the average over the standard period 1941–1970. The period from November to January was more extreme still, and over England and Wales was the driest since 1879.

Heavy rainfall from late February through to April meant that the November to April total was less of a departure from the average (84% of the 1941–1970 mean), although the only drier November to April winter since 1960 was that of 1975/76.

Although the winter of 1988/89 was not unprecedently dry, it is notable for its combination of low rainfall with high temperatures. Warm winters in Britain tend to be wet, as shown by Figure 7 which plots the England and Wales rainfall data against the Central England Temperature series compiled by the Meteorological Office. The 1988/89 data point plots well away from the rest of the points, and the unusual combination of temperature and precipitation can be explained by recourse to the climatic conditions prevailing during the winter. In 1988/89, especially in December and January, the Azores High was located further north than usual, and anticyclonic conditions persisted over north west Europe, including southern Britain. This in turn meant that the Jet Stream took a more northerly course, feeding most of the frontal activity over Scotland rather than Britain as a whole. Warm winters in Britain are more usually characterised by frequent rain-bearing frontal activity across the whole country.

The spatial distribution of rainfall during the winter reflected these circulation controls, and the north and west of Britain experienced rainfall well above the long term average. Figure 8a shows the December to February rainfall in 1988/89 as a percentage of the 1961/62 to 1980/81 average for the 188 MORECS grid squares covering England, Scotland and Wales. Parts of Scotland recorded over 200% of average rainfall, whilst parts of eastern England experienced less than 50%. Table 5 shows the rainfall for each month within major water industry administrative divisions in England and Wales and Scotland, both in millimetres and as a percentage of the 1941–1970 average. The wet March and April stand out, and the particularly low winter rainfalls in southern and eastern England are clear. MORECS data show that the rain in March and April was least extreme in north-east Britain, and in March much of Scotland received below average rainfall. The table also gives total rainfall over both the short and long definitions of winter.

In summary, the winter of 1988/89 over Britain was not only mild, but also unusually dry. England and Wales as a whole had the 9th driest December to February this century, but this masks wide variations: the south and east were particularly dry, while parts of western England and Scotland recorded well above average rainfall. The shorter period from November to January was even more exceptionally dry. The low winter rainfall totals, together with the relatively high spring rainfalls in many areas, had important implications for river flows and groundwater

a: Winter 1988/89

b: Winter 1989/90

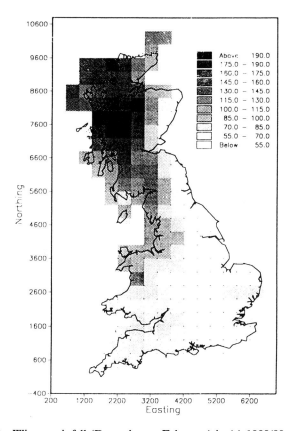
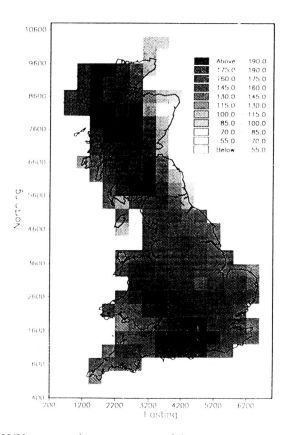

8   Winter rainfall (December to February) in (a) 1988/89 and (b) 1989/90, expressed as a percentage of the 1961–1980 average: MORECS data.

levels. In hydrological terms, the lack of rain was of greater importance than the high temperatures.

EVAPORATION AND SOIL MOISTURE

The mild temperatures meant that potential evapotranspiration was higher in the winter of 1988/89 than in most previous winters over virtually the entire country, with the greatest evapotranspiration in northern and western England and Scotland. MORECS data show, for example, that the potential evapotranspiration from grass over the period December to February 1988/89 exceeded 60mm in north west Scotland, in contrast to the average over the same months in the period 1961/62 to 1980/81 of between 20 and 35mm. In southern England, increases of 5 to 15mm on averages of 35 to 45mm were more typical. Potential evapotranspiration, however, has also been high in other winters in the 1980s. In large areas of southern England, for example, potential evapotranspiration was higher in December to February 1987/88 than in 1988/89 (the lower evapotranspiration in the latter, warmer, winter reflected lower windspeeds in the more stable anticyclonic conditions).

In the UK, soil moisture contents normally return to, or closely approach, field capacity (the maximum amount of water a soil can hold without further gravitational drainage) in early winter. The dry autumn and winter in 1988/89, together with the rather high evaporative losses, however, meant that the seasonal increase in soil moisture was very sluggish and by the end of January 1989 soils over large parts of lowland England and eastern Scotland had still not returned to field capacity. Deficits had been maintained for nearly a year in much of southern Britain. The rainfall of late February, March and April 1989 replenished stores in most areas, but soil moisture deficits (the amount of water needed to return soil moisture contents to field capacity) remained in those areas which experienced least rainfall, namely Lincolnshire, east Yorkshire and Kent. Figure 9 shows the potential evapotranspiration and soil moisture deficits under grass for five MORECS grid boxes since January 1985 (locations are shown in Figure 10). The lack of recovery of soil moisture in Lincolnshire (box 109) and Kent (box 174) is clearly evident, although the pattern in the west of Britain is less unusual.

Soil moisture deficits very probably imposed real constraints on evapotranspiration at some sites for short periods during the winter, but at the monthly scale, actual evapotranspiration was less than potential evapotranspiration only in a few areas, and even there the differences were small.

Table 5: Rainfall in 1988/89 in millimetres and as a percentage of the 1941–70 average. The return period estimates are based on tables provided by the meteorological office and assume a sensible stable climate.

		Oct	Nov	Dec	Jan	Feb	March	April	Dec-Feb Total	Nov-Apr Total
England & Wales										
North West	mm	120	69	117	75	142	144	87	334	634
	%	102	55	97	67	175	200	113	106	109
Northumbrian	mm	101	74	53	31	85	63	58	169	364
	%	135	79	71	39	129	121	105	76	86
Yorkshire	mm	90	55	47	27	70	78	78	144	355
	%	130	62	63	35	109	147	139	67	86
Severn Trent	mm	62	38	33	34	67	66	91	134	329
	%	95	48	47	49	126	127	175	70	88
Anglian	mm	52	35	22	30	36	49	75	88	247
	%	100	57	41	58	88	123	188	60	85
Thames	mm	66	28	16	34	61	66	79	111	284
	%	103	38	24	55	130	143	172	63	83
Southern	mm	84	32	19	30	69	76	81	118	307
	%	108	34	23	39	121	146	169	55	75
Wessex	mm	101	33	22	43	94	90	77	159	359
	%	123	34	24	51	159	155	143	69	81
South West	mm	144	55	59	66	146	126	87	271	539
	%	127	41	44	51	162	150	123	76	84
Welsh	mm	125	69	73	88	150	165	98	311	643
	%	97	48	50	65	156	190	114	94	93
TOTAL	mm	89	48	47	47	89	92	83	183	406
	%	107	49	52	55	137	156	143	76	89
Scotland										
Highland	mm	185	115	230	319	355	233	60	904	1312
	%	99	68	117	195	267	204	53	183	147
North-east	mm	138	66	51	52	113	83	54	216	419
	%	142	64	50	57	153	134	89	81	85
Tay	mm	197	89	89	156	197	173	45	442	749
	%	161	75	66	132	214	211	60	128	121
Forth	mm	130	77	81	133	158	151	44	372	644
	%	123	71	74	134	205	219	65	130	121
Clyde	mm	191	115	191	232	262	229	82	685	1111
	%	104	69	103	144	232	218	80	149	133
Tweed	mm	93	67	51	71	105	105	48	227	447
	%	106	64	57	76	152	181	79	90	94
Solway	mm	169	100	122	139	157	195	87	418	800
	%	117	69	81	99	169	214	99	109	113
TOTAL	mm	170	99	149	206	239	188	63	594	944
	%	114	70	95	150	230	204	70	151	132

GROUNDWATER

Groundwater aquifers form a major water resource over much of England and are the principal natural means of sustaining most river flows throughout the summer period. It is during the winter months, usually October to March or April, when rainfall exceeds potential evaporation, and when summer soil moisture deficits have been satisfied that replenishment (or recharge) to aquifers takes place. However, in the 1988/89 winter, soil moisture deficits had still not been satisfied in many areas in January and February – as indicated in the previous section – and no generally significant recharge to the major aquifer units had taken place up to that time. Consequently, borehole hydrographs in the carbonate aquifers were looking similar at the end of February to those of the winter of 1975/76, when commonly, the most depressed groundwater levels for the winter were registered.

Rainfall in late February, March and April 1989 was sufficient and in time (before accelerating evapotranspiration rates reduced the effectiveness of rainfall) to allow recharge in most areas. A rapid response was observed in the fissured Great Oolite and Lincolnshire Limestone aquifers and substantial recoveries occurred in much of the Chalk and Upper Greensand aquifers of central and much of southern England, in a period when groundwater levels are usually beginning to decline. In most areas, water table elevations recovered to, or above, the average level for the time of year (although the peak winter levels were generally well below normal peaks). The drought situation was thus considerably eased so that it was no longer comparable with the 1975/76 event which was most intense in the south east. By the end of April 1989 – when infiltration effectively ceased – the aquifers throughout much of lowland England had received between 50% and 80% of their mean annual recharge (Anon, 1990).

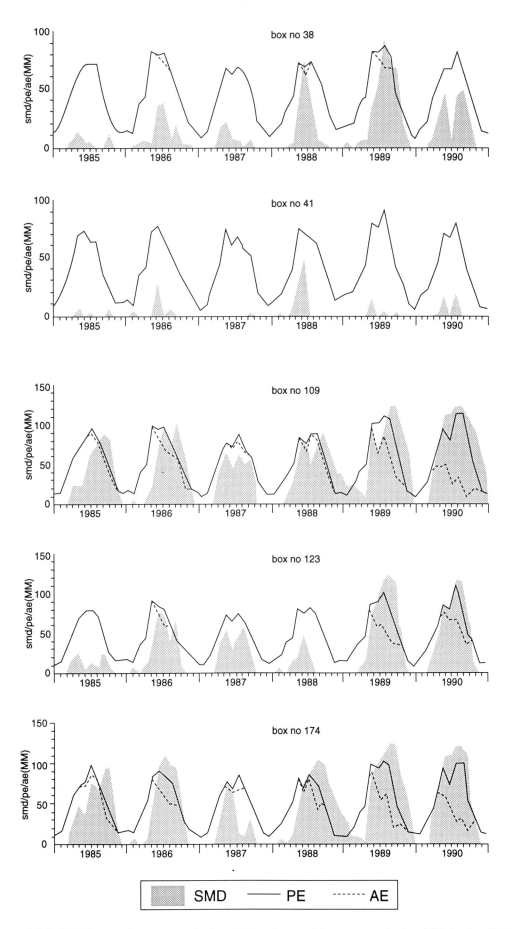

9 Soil moisture deficit (SMD), actual evapotranspiration (AE) and potential evapotranspiration (PE) for five MORECS boxes, 1985–1990.

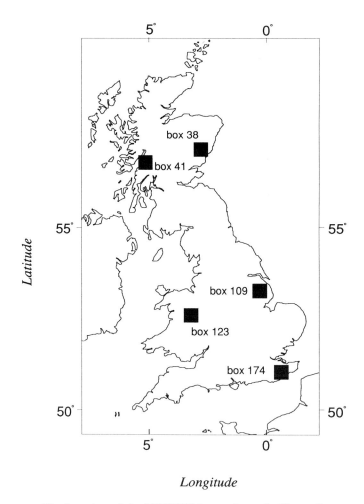

Longitude

10   Location of the MORECS boxes shown in Figure 9.

In east Lincolnshire, Humberside and east Yorkshire, where higher soil moisture deficits existed, little of the spring rainfall was effective as recharge. The groundwater hydrograph of the observation borehole at Dalton Holme, in the Yorkshire Chalk, showed an upward turn in April and May 1989 in response to the February rainfall (Figure 11). Up to that point the water level had been the lowest, for the spring, in a record reaching back 100 years. By the end of April the water table was still significantly below the corresponding 1975/76 level but that winter was not as dry in this area. It is estimated that the Yorkshire Chalk in general received no more than 10 to 15% of its mean annual recharge over the 1988/89 winter, with no further opportunity for recharge to occur before the next winter. The picture in the Permo-Triassic Sandstone aquifers of the north and north west was rather different as recharge had generally exceeded 100% of the mean annual total by the end of March, and no noticeable anomaly was evident.

RIVER FLOWS

River flows across Britain, with the notable exception of western Scotland, showed a very consistent evolution over the winter of 1988/89, although the intensity of the pattern showed strong variations. On the whole, flows remained depressed throughout November, December and January, picking up in February, and peaking in March or April.

In lowland England, winter flows normally result from a combination of high baseflow from recovering ground-water sources and response to rainfall on to surfaces with reducing soil moisture deficits. In 1989, a large area of the country, particularly in the east and south, still had significant soil moisture deficits at the end of January. The consequence was that rainfall up to that time was largely unavailable for the usual augmentation of winter flows from groundwater of saturated catchments. Starting at the end of February, substantial rainfall served to reduce the deficit in most parts of the country, thus allowing flows to recover (Lees et al. 1990). The highest monthly flow for most rivers usually occurs in January or February but, with the late winter rainfall the peak monthly flows observed in March and April 1989 introduced a lag into the annual hydrograph of two to three months.

The intensity of the winter drought displayed marked regional variation and in parts of Scotland runoff was abundant. The River Earn at Kinkell Bridge in the southern Grampians, for example, experienced its highest November to April flow in 29 years of record. Further north and east the River Dee at Park in the Cairngorms had its third lowest winter runoff in 17 years of record. In northern England flows were not significantly different from average but near the east coast winter flows on the River Lud at Louth would be expected to be lower only around once in ten years. In the West Midlands, also,

Site name: DALTON HOLME - East Yorkshire

National grid reference: SE 9651 4530   Well number SE94/5
Aquifer: CHALK AND UPPER GREENSAND   Measuring level: 33.50

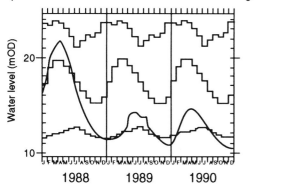

1988   1989   1990

Max, Min and Mean values calculated from years 1889 to 1987

Site name: WASHPIT FARM - Lincolnshire

National grid reference: TF 8138 1960   Well number TF81/2
Aquifer: CHALK AND UPPER GREENSAND   Measuring level: 80.20

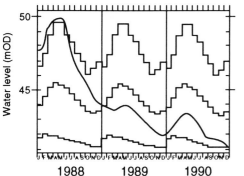

1988   1989   1990

Max, Min and Mean values calculated from years 1950 to 1987

Site name: COMPTON HOUSE - Sussex

National grid reference: SU 7755 1490   Well number SU71/23
Aquifer: CHALK AND UPPER GREENSAND   Measuring level: 81.37

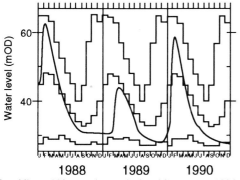

1988   1989   1990

Max, Min and Mean values calculated from years 1894 to 1987

A break in the data line indicates a recording interval

of greater than 8 weeks

11   Groundwater levels in three wells in the chalk aquifer in 1988, 1989 and 1990.

the River Roden at Rodington experienced low December to February flows with a return period of once in fifteen years, and November to April flows with a once in ten year frequency. Throughout the greater part of the English lowlands and in South Wales flows were slightly below normal, but no more than would be expected once in five years on average. Further south, however, along the south coast from Kent to Devon, November to April flows were particularly depressed with return periods in the order of once in ten years, and December to February flows, from Kent to Dorset, had return periods of around once in twenty five years. Indeed, on the Rivers Medway at Teston and Ouse at Gold Bridge, the lowest December to February flows in 30 and 28 years of record, respectively, were experienced.

The hydrological drought of the winter of 1988/89 was clearly more severe in the shorter December to February time period than in the longer November to April winter. In certain areas, notably the south coast, it gave rise to lower winter flows than the corresponding period in the winter of 1975/76. However, the rainfall at the end of February brought many March and April flows up to, or above, the average for that time of year, thereby alleviating the drought intensity in most areas. The associated general recovery of groundwater levels in most of the major aquifers contributed to this amelioration. However, the exceptionally dry May heralded a second phase of the drought, and by September 1989 flows had declined generally; in some areas exceptionally low runoff rates were recorded, and prospects for 1990 became a matter for concern.

SUMMARY: CONSEQUENCES OF THE 1988/89 MILD WINTER

The winter of 1988/89 was not only mild but was also dry, and as such was very unusual. Mild winters in Britain tend to be relatively wet, and in recent winters rainfall has been above average. The distribution of rainfall across Britain represented an accentuation in the normal north west/south east rainfall gradient. The north west – particularly Scotland – recorded more rain than on average whilst the east and south were very dry. The effect of the lack of rainfall was compounded by the relatively high evapotranspiration (although in southern England this was higher in the previous winter).

The low river flows and groundwater levels did not cause widespread water resources problems in the winter itself, and the greatest concern among water resources managers during the dry winter was that it would be followed by a dry spring and summer. In such circumstances, the lack of groundwater recharge and replenishment of surface reservoirs during winter would have had very significant implications for the ability to supply summer demand. The "Great Drought" of 1976, for example, followed a very dry winter when storages were not replenished. The heavy rainfall from late February 1989, however, eased the situation considerably, with much rainfall, particularly in the reservoir gathering grounds in the uplands of the west and north. By late April, virtually all reservoirs were at or near their normal levels. Although groundwater recharge was only a fraction of average recharge, levels in the chalk, limestone and permi-triassic sandstone aquifers in central and most of southern Britain recovered by the end of spring to levels close to seasonal averages, and in most cases well above those experienced at the same time in 1976. Exceptions to this included east Yorkshire, Lincolnshire and Kent, where groundwater levels recovered only slightly, with obviously important implications for summer supplies and the maintenance of summer river flows. Some water supply authorities along the south coast did apply drought restrictions in late winter in order to maintain stocks (by applying for Drought Orders allowing them to release less water from reservoirs), but in a few instances this was in part due to the deliberate lowering of reservoir levels early in the season for essential maintenance and a subsequent dry winter. The hot dry summer of 1989, however, triggered a second phase to the drought (Chapter B1.2), and the imposition of restrictions on water use: by October 1989 – the onset of the next winter – both surface and groundwater resources were at historically low levels.

Low river flows in winter can have very significant ecological implications, and although the influences of water temperature and quality are considered in Chapter A3, it is useful to refer briefly to three issues here which relate specifically to water quantity. First, the stream network in parts of southern and eastern England, particularly on the chalk, in the winter was more typical of that found in summer, and large stretches of some rivers and bournes were dry from autumn. In some instances the effect of the mild winter was exacerbated by groundwater pumping, but the lack of flow in early spring may have had implications for water and water-side flora and fauna: these do not appear to have been studied. As with water supply, the full ecological effects of the dry winter were not necessarily felt until during the following dry summer. The amenity loss due to the lack of water in some chalk bournes in winter also cannot be ignored, but is difficult to evaluate.

Secondly, the low river flows may have had an impact on freshwater and migratory fish. Salmon, for example, can pass obstacles in their passage upstream only during relatively high flows (although the link between flow and migration is currently poorly understood: Armitage, 1987), and these opportunities were limited along the east and south coasts in 1988/89. River flow conditions also influence spawning, for example, although many species appear relatively insensitive to flow variations, as long as flows remain within specified limits (Armitage, 1987). Thirdly, nitrates tend to be flushed from fields in winter. In 1988/89, the low flows in receiving channels may have increased the concentrations of nitrates in rivers draining catchments where sewage effluent is the primary nitrate source, although the warm temperatures and low rainfall

will have limited the flushing of nitrates from soil: more information is given in Chapter A3.

In summary, the most important hydrological characteristics of the winter of 1988/89 were a relatively low rainfall, a high evaporative demand and a preceding dry autumn, which, by mid-February, saw low river flows and groundwater levels over much of Britain. If the spring had not been unusually wet, these low flows and groundwater levels would have led to substantial resource and ecosystem problems in the 1989 summer. In many parts of England and Wales the consequences of the dry winter continued to be felt, but the wet spring eased fears for the summer. As it turned out, the summer of 1989 was very dry and the wet spring proved very beneficial: without it the water resources situation would have been very much more serious.

1.2.3 November 1989 to April 1990

SNOWFALL

The winter season 1989/90 produced very little snow. However, the relatively wet conditions of 1989/90 compared to 1988/89, did result in a little more snow than the previous year. Of the 22 network sites, 8 recorded no days with snow at 0900h throughout the entire winter (November to April) of 1989/90. For the shorter definition of winter (December to February) this figure rose to 9 sites. All of these sites lacking snow were south of a line joining Liverpool and Norwich.

The only noticeable falls were in Scotland, where Eskdalemuir recorded 21 days with snow lying at 0900h (during the 6 month winter). This compares to the 1988/89 value of 14 and the long term median (1946/47 to 1987/88) of 32 days. Fewer days than this have only been recorded on only 8 occasions. The falls were fairly evenly distributed throughout the December to April period. To the south, Lyneham in Wiltshire recorded no snow days compared to median value of 4–5 days and one day during 1988/89. The situation had arisen only once before, during the winter 1975/76.

RAINFALL

November was dry throughout Britain with the lowest rainfall figures, in terms of percentages of the long term average, occurring in Scotland. It remained dry during the first half of December, with some places recording 30 consecutive days with no rain. The rain that started in mid December saw the beginnings of what was to be the third wettest winter (December to February) in England and Wales since 1766 (1914 and 1876 were wetter). Plotting the difference from the long term average for both temperature and rainfall (Figure 7) the winter 1989/90 is seen to be at the very extreme end of the warm, wet sector, a dramatic change from the winter of 1988/89. The spatial distribution of rainfall was also very different from that of 1988/89. Figure 8b shows the

Table 6: Monthly rainfall for October 1989 to April 1990 in millimetres and as a percentage of the 1941–70 average

		1989			1990					
		Oct	Nov	Dec	Jan	Feb	Mar	Apr	Dec–Feb Total	Nov–Apr Total
England and Wales	mm	98	61	133	133	142	23	38	408	530
	%	118	63	149	154	218	39	65	170	116
NRA Regions										
North West	mm	145	84	100	197	193	45	57	490	676
	%	123	69	83	176	238	63	74	157	116
Northumbria	mm	71	35	75	111	135	32	25	321	413
	%	95	37	100	139	205	62	45	145	97
Severn Trent	mm	82	52	135	106	109	18	30	350	450
	%	126	66	193	152	206	35	57	181	120
Yorkshire	mm	77	45	98	118	112	24	24	328	421
	%	112	51	132	153	175	45	43	153	102
Anglia	mm	41	36	98	52	75	15	34	225	310
	%	79	58	185	100	179	38	85	153	108
Thames	mm	65	37	141	92	114	12	35	347	431
	%	102	51	214	148	243	26	76	198	127
Southern	mm	79	50	142	121	136	6	48	399	503
	%	101	53	175	159	239	12	100	186	124
Wessex	mm	101	58	165	124	158	14	35	447	554
	%	123	60	183	148	268	24	65	192	125
South West	mm	148	100	196	195	238	25	46	629	800
	%	131	75	145	151	264	30	65	178	125
Welsh	mm	180	109	199	240	215	37	48	654	848
	%	140	76	137	176	224	43	56	173	123
Scotland	mm	187	60	96	250	294	247	96	640	1043
	%	126	42	62	182	283	268	107	162	145
River Purification Boards										
Highland	mm	258	79	109	293	364	409	136	766	1390
	%	139	47	56	179	274	359	119	156	157
North East	mm	87	29	54	108	149	87	45	311	472
	%	90	28	53	119	201	140	74	116	96
Tay	mm	136	51	86	239	287	178	61	612	902
	%	111	43	64	203	312	217	81	178	145
Forth	mm	112	39	79	222	221	142	55	522	758
	%	106	36	72	224	287	206	81	184	143
Tweed	mm	68	30	78	166	178	53	31	422	536
	%	77	29	87	179	258	91	51	168	113
Solway	mm	145	59	119	254	285	94	72	658	883
	%	101	41	79	181	306	103	82	171	125
Clyde	mm	244	73	107	316	341	295	127	764	1259
	%	133	44	58	196	302	281	123	166	151

MORECS data for this period, where only 7 out the 188 boxes recorded below average rainfall, compared to Figure 8a for the same period during the 1988/89 winter which shows all areas but north west Scotland with below average rainfall. Vast areas of the country experienced rainfall in excess of 50% above the long term mean in 1989/90. Whilst something of a north west/south east gradient still existed, parts of Wales and southern England, as well as north west Scotland received over 200% of their average rainfall. In 1988/89, the areas with this sort of anomaly were restricted to the far north and west of Scotland. By referring to Table 6, February 1990 can be seen as the most outstanding month with 14 of the 17 water regions of Britain receiving over 200% of their average February rain. February was also the wettest month on record over Great Britain as a whole since at least 1869.

Whereas the mild winter of 1988/89 was brought about largely by the Jet Stream running in an abnormal position slightly to the north of Scotland, during the winter 1989/90 (mid-December to end of February), the Jet resumed its more usual position over the UK, so that the entire country received winter storms, and rainfall in the east was lower in the rain shadow areas. The very warm conditions in 1989 (see Chapter B1.1) had produced anomalously high sea surface temperatures, which may have accounted for the exceptionally high rainfall and run of very severe storms in January and February 1990 (a matter for debate).

EVAPORATION AND SOIL MOISTURE

Actual and potential evapotranspiration rates for the winter of 1989/90 were above the 1961 to 1980 average over the whole of the UK, with the highest rates in northwest Scotland and northeast England. The lowest values were found along the western seaboard, apart from the far north. The differences from the mean during winter were relatively small, only between

5 and 30 mm, and were very similar to the 1988/89 anomalies.

Soil moisture deficits (SMD) were also extraordinary for the year May 1989 to April 1990. Despite the relatively wet spring of 1989, field capacity was not reached in many eastern areas and appreciable SMDs were sustained throughout the winter. Time series of potential and actual evapotranspiration and SMD from 1985 to December 1990 are shown in Figure 9 (located on Figure 10).

Northwest Scotland (represented by MORECS box 41 (Figure 10)) shows SMD values that are not obviously different from any of the previous four years. It may be observed, however, that both potential and actual evapotranspiration rates were slightly higher, and this is seen to be true of every MORECS box selected.

The rapid decrease in the amount of rainfall from west to east Scotland between December 1989 and February 1990 produced very different SMD patterns. The east coast is represented by MORECS box 38. Unusually, deficits built up in January 1989, following the mild and dry winter. These deficits were removed during the more sustained rain in February 1989. With the very dry and warm conditions of the summer 1989, deficits reached 100mm in many boxes in eastern Scotland by July. This area saw the lowest rainfall of the winter 1989/90 in Scotland in terms of a percentage of the long term mean and this, coupled with very high potential evapotranspiration rates meant that, unusually, SMDs were maintained throughout the winter 1989/90 in eastern Scotland.

The pattern in eastern Scotland was repeated in most of eastern, southern and central England and many areas maintained deficits throughout the February 1988 to January 1990 period. In some districts of Northumbria, and in the extreme south east of England, SMDs were not fully replenished through the winter of 1989/90.

GROUNDWATER

Groundwater levels usually begin to rise again in the autumn as soil moisture deficits are replenished, but the dry November 1989 meant that there was very little widespread recharge until mid-December. Rainfall in October 1989 produced some local recovery in levels, but this proved short-lived. By the end of November, many wells were therefore close to or below their minimum recorded levels: at Dalton Holme in the Yorkshire chalk, levels in December 1989 were below the previous lowest in a 102-year record (Figure 11). Generally the groundwater resources at the beginning of the 1989/90 recharge season were in a worse position than at the beginning of the previous winter, particularly in the east.

Once the initial soil moisture deficits were replenished, however, the heavy rain in December led to rapid rises in groundwater levels, particularly in shallow or well-fissured aquifers. In western aquifers (such as the Permo-Triassic sandstones) levels in January 1990 were higher than average, although the recovery was slower further eastwards and was very limited in the extreme east. Groundwater levels rose further following the heavy rainfall in January and February. The well at Chilgrove in the Chalk in Sussex recorded a rise of 20m in seven days in February 1990, a rate well in excess of that terminating the 1976 drought and probably the fastest in a 154-year record (as far as can be ascertained from monthly data) (Marsh and Monkhouse 1990). A large rise was also recorded at nearby Compton House (Figure 11). For most British aquifers, groundwater recharge in the winter of 1989/90 was above – sometimes well above – average. Recharge was, however, below average in the chalk in parts of Yorkshire, East Anglia and Kent, and levels remained below the seasonal mean. The dry March and April meant that groundwater recharge finished considerably earlier than usual, and many well levels fell more rapidly than is usual: in some eastern wells this rapid decline was from an exceptionally low winter peak. By the end of May, 1990 groundwater levels across most of Britain were below average, but mostly within the normal range: however, in the east and parts of the south, water tables began the summer of 1990 at an exceptionally low level.

A comparison of groundwater behaviour in 1988/89 and 1989/90 shows the benefit of late, albeit limited, recharge. Rainfall was high during 1989/90 (except over the eastern Chalk), but the recharge season finished early and levels fell rapidly: levels in many wells were lower at the beginning of summer 1990 than at the same time in 1989 after the considerably drier winter of 1988/89. The experience of 1989/90 suggests that, when recharge is concentrated into a few weeks of intense rainfall, the improvement in resources in some aquifers (and hence ability to sustain summer levels) may not be as large as implied by the increase in levels. Even in well-fissured aquifers, a substantial amount of water may be held in intergranular storage rather than in the larger fissures. It is possible that short periods of intense rainfall may be insufficient to recharge this intergranular store, and water levels recede rapidly once recharge ceases. Such a rapid decline is apparent in the Compton House record (Figure 11). There is also some suggestion that, if rainfall is very intense, much of the excess of rainfall over evaporation runs off in floods rather than infiltrates as groundwater recharge. Both of these suggestions merit further research.

Figure 12 shows monthly flows from October 1988 to December 1990 for several representative catchments (shown on Figure 13), expressed as a percentage departure from the average flow for each month calculated over the entire period of record. Although there are some considerable differences between the magnitudes of the departures in each catchment, the data (together with data from catchments not plotted) show that flows were below average across virtually the whole of Britain until at least December 1989, although the rainfall in October 1989 produced higher than average flows in some western catchments.

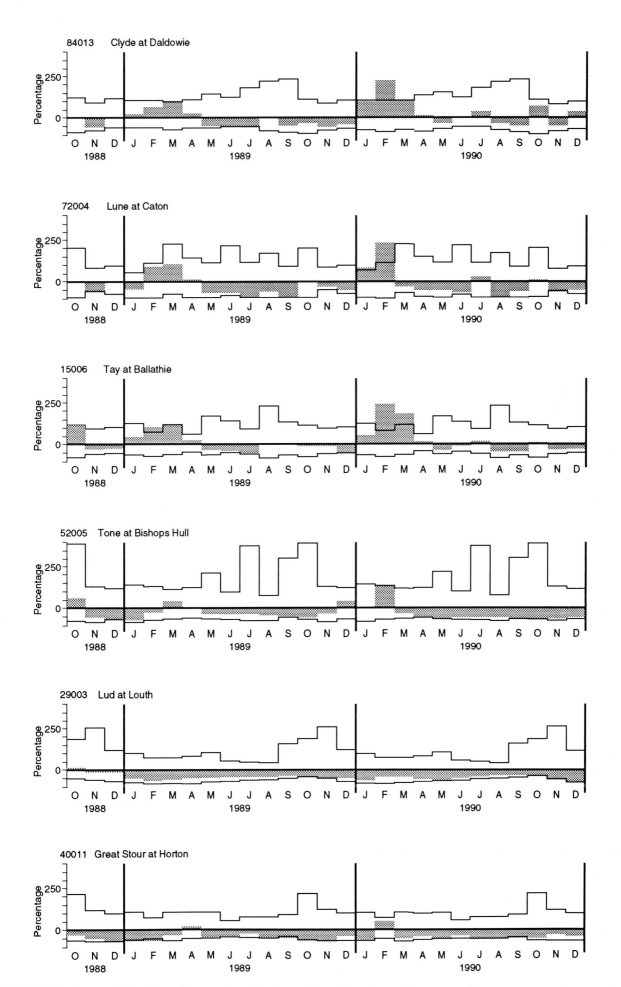

12　Monthly river runoff in six catchments from October 1988 to December 1990, expressed as a percentage departure from the long-term monthly mean.

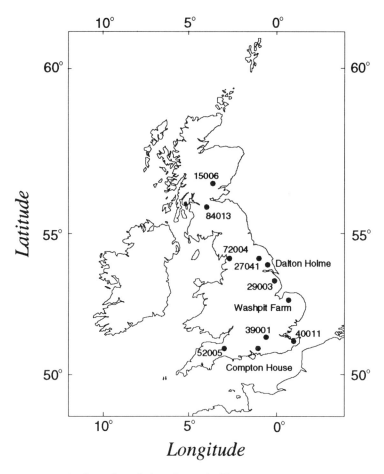

13   Location of sites shown in Figures 11 and 12.

Flows rose very rapidly in the middle of December. In many rivers, flows increased sharply from well below the seasonal mean to well above average in a matter of days. A number of lowland rivers recorded their lowest and highest flow rates for the year over the period of a fortnight in late December and early January, a rare event in the UK (Anon, 1990). Flooding occurred in December and, more widely, in February when runoff was exceptionally abundant in rivers draining the Scottish Highlands. The runoff volume for the Tay for February 1990 is the largest recorded on the Surface Water Archive for any month for any gauging station in the United Kingdom. Significant flooding also occurred on the Severn and the Thames where at Kingston (near the tidal limit) river flows remained above 300 m³s⁻¹ for 17 days, the longest period since 1947. February runoff totals exceeded previous maxima in many catchments, and the total runoff from England, Scotland and Wales in February 1990 was the largest recorded in any month over (at least) 30 years (Anon, 1991). Some catchments in eastern England and Scotland did not share in the high flows, however, and in several catchments flows remained below average through the winter (for example the Lud in Lincolnshire in Figure 12).

River flows fell rapidly during the dry March and April 1990, and by early summer were, in many catchments, again below the seasonal average. The variation in river flows over the winter from well below average, to record-breaking maxima and back to below average conditions is unprecedented (at least over the forty or so years with widespread, reliable hydrological records).

CONSEQUENCES OF THE MILD WET 1989/90 WINTER

Although rain during the winter of 1989/90 was late arriving, the winter was considerably wetter than 1988/89 and river flows were accordingly much higher (except in the east). Runoff totals over winter as a whole (December to February) were close to average in many catchments, but away from the Scottish Highlands this runoff was concentrated in a very few weeks. Reservoirs were generally filled by February, and in some cases could have been filled a second time. However, they began emptying sooner than usual (because of the dry spring and, in a few cases, because they were drawn down for flood alleviation purposes), so that by the beginning of the 1990 summer a number of reservoirs had lower stocks than at the corresponding time in the summer 1989. Surface water storages showed, therefore, a somewhat similar pattern to groundwater reserves: a little rain late in the winter season appears to be at least as beneficial for summer supplies as a larger amount of rain that ceases earlier in spring. Summer supply reliability depends not just on the amount of winter rainfall, but also on its timing.

1.2.4 Conclusions

1. The winter of 1988/89 was not only mild but was also very dry, and as such was unusual: mild winters in the UK tend to be relatively wet. The distribution of rainfall through the winter was also unusual. While the east and south were very dry, the northwest – and particularly in Scotland – recorded more rain than average. Over England and Wales as a whole the period from November to January was the driest since 1879, and followed a relatively dry autumn.

2. River flows and groundwater levels were very low from November to February, and in many parts of eastern England soil moisture contents failed to return to field capacity. By the middle of February, reservoirs were not filled and aquifers were not replenished to their usual extent. Some river networks in chalk areas were more typical of summer conditions.

3. Spring 1989 was very wet, and by the end of April river flows and groundwater levels in much of the UK were close to – but still below – average values.

4. The winter of 1989/90 was warm and wet (unlike the warm, dry winter of 1988/89). However, the winter rainfall in 1989/90 was notable in two respects: (i) the usual difference between the wet west of the UK and the drier east was exaggerated, so that parts of eastern Scotland and England received below average winter rainfall for the second year in succession, and (ii) rainfall was concentrated in a short period, from mid December to February, a feature more typical of Meriterranean climates.

5. The rise in groundwater levels and river flows in western UK was very rapid following the short, intense period of winter rainfall in 1989/90, and there was widespread flooding in February in the west.

6. The winter rain fell in too short a time to store all the surplus water in reservoirs, and, in the absence of normal rain in the spring 1990, some reservoirs were low at the start of the 1990 summer.

APPENDIX: ESTIMATION OF "GALE DAYS"

Jenkinson and Collison (1977) developed an objective definition of a gale day by calibration with the monthly frequency of gales over the sea areas around the British isles for a 10-year period using grid-point mean-sea-level pressure data. These data are available in daily form on a 5° latitude by 10° longitude grid extending back to the beginning of 1881. The grid-point pattern used for the

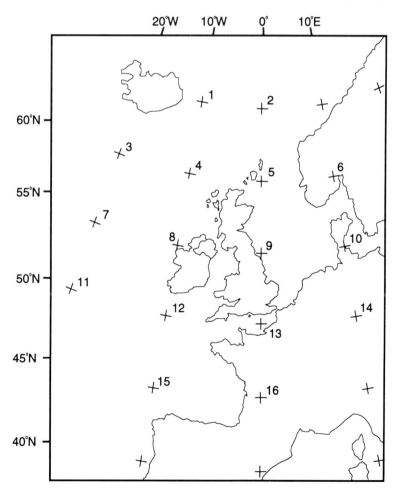

A1   Location of grid points over the UK used in the construction of the gale index. Grid-point numbers are those used in the equations (from Hulme and Jones, 1991, with the permission of the Royal Meteorological Society).

British Isles region is shown in Figure A1 and the wind-flow characteristics are computed as follows (grid-point numbers are as shown in Figure A1, the **emboldened** numbers are multipliers):

$$W = \tfrac{1}{2}(12 + 13) - \tfrac{1}{2}(4 + 5) \qquad \text{westerly flow}$$

$$S = 1.74\{\tfrac{1}{4}(5 + \mathbf{2} \times 9 + 13) - \tfrac{1}{4}(4 + \mathbf{2} \times 8 + 12)\} \qquad \text{southerly flow}$$

$$F = (S^2 + W^2)^{1/2} \qquad \text{resultant flow}$$

$$ZW = 1.07\{\tfrac{1}{2}(15 + 16) - \tfrac{1}{2}(8 + 9)\} - 0.95\,\{\tfrac{1}{2}(8 + 9) - \tfrac{1}{2}(1 + 2)\} \qquad \text{westerly shear vorticity}$$

$$ZS = 1.52[\tfrac{1}{4}(6 + \mathbf{2} \times 10 + 14) - \tfrac{1}{4}(5 + \mathbf{2} \times 9 + 13) - \{\tfrac{1}{4}(4 + \mathbf{2} \times 8 + 12) - \tfrac{1}{4}(3 + \mathbf{2} \times 7 + 11)\}] \qquad \text{southerly shear vorticity}$$

$$Z = ZW + ZS \qquad \text{total shear vorticity}$$

The gale index, G, is then defined as $G = \{F^2 + (0.5Z)^2\}^{1/2}$

Over the 10-year calibration period a gale is recorded for G greater than 30, a severe gale for G greater than 40 and a very severe gale for G greater than 50. The construction of the grid-point mean-sea-level pressure data over time, however, has not been consistent. Differences in the extraction of the grid-point data have led to some periods where the data are smoother (low and high pressure centres less intense) than other periods. Data for 1960–65 are particularly smooth. In order to allow for this, the threshold definitions of gale days have been adjusted accordingly (Table 1A).

Smith (1982) has also developed a monthly index of windiness over the United Kingdom using daily grid-point mean-sea-level pressure data. His index is based on the westerly and southerly flow components used here. Regression equations between measured anemometer wind speeds and these flow components are developed to reconstruct wind speeds prior to the commencement of modern anemometer measurements in the 1960s. The basic difference between the two approaches therefore is that the method used here includes a vorticity estimate.

Table 1A: Threshold values of the gale index, G, for diferent periods

Period	Threshold Value of G		
	Gale	Severe gale	Very severe gale
1880–1898	30	40	50
1899–1939	28	37	46
1940–1948	30	40	50
1949–1959	28	37	46
1960–1965	24	32	40
1966–1990	30	40	50

The definition of the index based on grid-point mean-sea-level pressure data has one potentially serious disadvantage. Gales which only affect a small region, such as the Great Storm of 16 October 1987, will not be classified as severe a gale as those which affect a much larger part of the country (e.g. 3 January 1976). Such a problem would presumably be greater with the Smith (1982) index which does not include the vorticity term. The problem would be lessened by a finer network of points at say 5° x 5° resolution.

Chapter A2
Impacts on the Terrestrial Environment

A2.1 IMPACTS ON PLANTS

2.1.1 Introduction

In this section, impacts of the mild winters of 1988/89 and 1989/90 on plants are described. The section is divided into four parts, covering observations of first flowering and leafing of native plant species, phenology of garden flowering plants, observations on herbaceous flora in central England and some impacts on forestry.

Some of the data come from sites throughout the UK while other data are more local.

2.1.2 Observations of first flowering and leafing at Institute of Terrestrial Ecology (ITE) Stations

Plants have evolved complex mechanisms to ensure that the date of flowering and leaf emergence in spring is optimized with respect to frosts, insect activity (as pollinators and herbivores), light interception and competition with other plants. Many temperate plants enter a state of dormancy in autumn which needs to be released by exposure to chill temperatures (ca 0–5°C). Long daylengths in spring can sometimes compensate for a lack of chilling. After dormancy release by chilling or long days, flowering or budburst will occur after a given thermal time (day degrees greater than a threshold temperature). Other plants have little or no dormancy, do not require much chilling, and grow and flower as soon as temperatures permit. Thus, plants can use chill temperatures, daylength and warm temperatures in complex ways as cues for spring emergence.

During 1989 and 1990, observations were made at the six ITE stations (Table 1) of first flowering of up to 17 of the species which had been included in the Phenological Reports of the Royal Meteorological Society between 1891 and 1947. In addition, the dates of budburst of up to five tree species were recorded in 1989 and 1990. The ITE observations were compared with each other and with the long-term Royal Meteorological Society observations made at sites within 20 miles of each ITE station, adjusted assuming one day's delay for every 20 miles north or 100 ft in altitude (Hopkins, 1938). Where there were few (<10) or no long-term records for a particular species close to an ITE station, 58 year means (1891–1948) of flowering times from the appropriate meteorological district, or 20 year means (1929–48) adjusted to 58 year means, (Jeffree, 1960) were used for comparisons. (Winter temperatures during the period 1891–1947 were fairly typical and similar to those of the period 1961–80 which was used in Chapter A1 for long term temperature

Table 1: Locations of ITE Stations

ITE Station	Grid Reference
Furzebrook, Dorset	SY 9383
Monks Wood, Cambridgeshire	TL 1980
Bangor, Gwynedd	SH 5771
Merlewood, Cumbria	SD 4079
Edinburgh, Midlothian	NT 2763
Banchory, Kincardineshire	NO 6995

comparisons with 1989 and 1990.) Regressions of local long-term flowering dates on the flowering dates for all species from the appropriate meteorological district provided a means of estimating local flowering dates for particular species when these were not available in the Phenological Reports.

In 1989, early flowering tended to be most pronounced in species which flowered before the end of April (Figure 1a). Of the 86 events recorded, 54 (63%) were earlier than the 58–year district means, 9 (10%) occurred on the same day and 23 (27%) were later. Blackthorn (*Pinus spinosa*) flowering, and leafing of horsechestnut (*Aesculus hippocastanum*), occurred earlier than average at all ITE stations.

The data for 1990 (Figure 1b) were similar although early flowering was found in species which normally flowered in April-June. Of the 89 recorded events for which long-term comparisons were available, 68 (76%) were earlier than the long-term district means, 4 (5%) occurred on the same day and 17 (19%) were later. Early flowering occurred in every recorded species at one or more of the stations with the exception of lesser knapweed (*Centaurea nigra*) which flowered later than average at all stations. Eight species - blackthorn, garlic mustard (*Alliaria petiolata*), hawthorn (*Crataegus monogyna*), horse-chestnut, lilac (*Syringa vulgaris*), elder (*Sambucus nigra*), dog-rose (*Rosa canina*), and hedge bindweed (*Calystegia sepium*) flowered earlier than average at all stations. Leafing in horse-chestnut was also earlier than average at all stations.

Figures 2a and 2b compare the first flowering and leafing dates of the same populations or individuals recorded at the ITE stations in 1989 and 1990. In general, species flowering in early spring and late summer tended to be later in 1990 than in 1989, while those flowering between April and June tended to be earlier. Five species, hawthorn, lilac, elder, dog-rose and hedge bindweed, flowered earlier in 1990 than in 1989 at each of the ITE stations. Sixty two (69%) of the possible comparisons between 1989 and 1990 showed earlier flowering in 1990, whilst 26 (29%) were later and two were the same in both

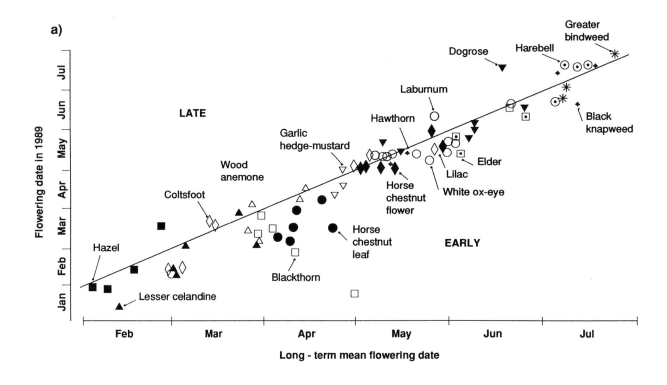

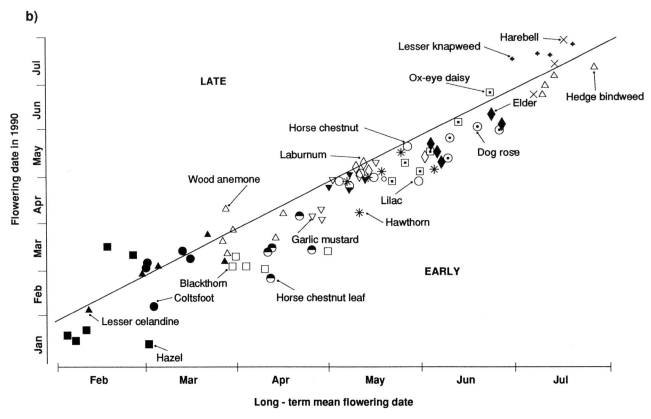

1   Dates of first flowering or leafing of (a) 17 native species in 1989 and (b) 16 native species in 1990, recorded at 6 ITE stations, compared with long-term mean dates recorded as part of the Phenological Records of the Royal Meteorological Society 1891–1947.

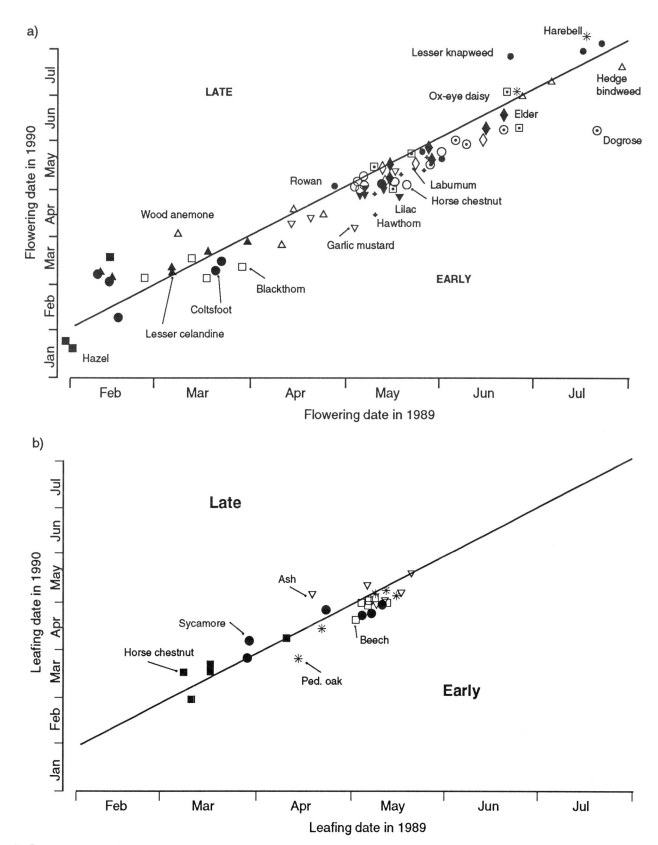

a)

LATE

Flowering date in 1990

Jul
Jun
May
Apr
Mar
Feb
Jan

Harebell

Lesser knapweed

Ox-eye daisy

Elder

Hedge
bindweed

Dogrose

Rowan

Laburnum

Horse chestnut

Wood anemone

Lilac

Hawthorn

Garlic mustard

EARLY

Blackthorn

Coltsfoot

Lesser celandine

Hazel

Feb   Mar   Apr   May   Jun   Jul

Flowering date in 1989

b)

Late

Leafing date in 1990

Jul
Jun
May
Apr
Mar
Feb
Jan

Ash

Sycamore

Beech

Horse chestnut

Ped. oak

Early

Feb   Mar   Apr   May   Jun   Jul

Leafing date in 1989

2   Records made at 6 ITE stations in 1990 compared with 1989 of (a) first flowering of 17 species and (b) first leafing of 5 tree species.

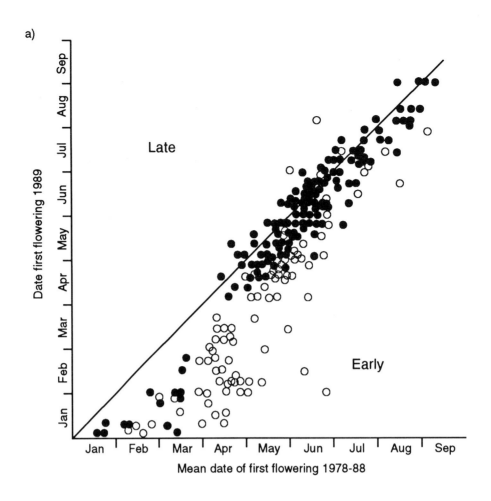

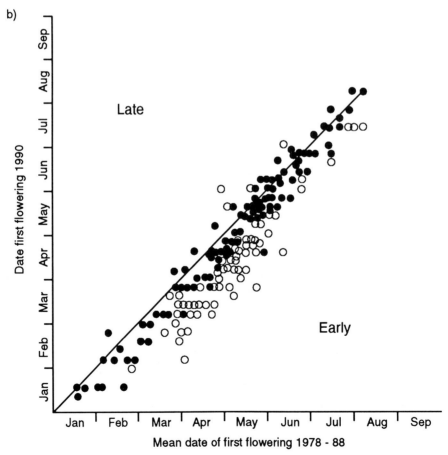

3   Dates of first flowering in (a) 1989 and (b) 1990 compared with the mean dates for 1978–88 inclusive, for a range of plant species in a garden in East Lothian. First flowering in 1989 and 1990 was either the same (●) or significantly different (○) from the mean for 1978–88.

years. Comparisons between leafing dates of five tree species in 1989 and 1990 showed trends similar to those of flowering, with 69% of the events being earlier in 1990, 28% later and 3% the same. Both pedunculate oak and beech were consistently earlier at all stations in 1990 than in 1989, on average by eight and six days, respectively.

The Appendix gives the values for each species at each station in 1989 and 1990, expressed as the number of days earlier (negative values) or later (positive values) than the long-term averages. On average, flowering or leafing occurred 10 days earlier in 1990 than in 1989.

In conclusion, both mild winters stimulated earlier flowering among species that normally flower between April and June. However, few records were broken. Not all species responded to early warming, probably because their phenology is controlled by daylength and/or winter chilling as well as spring warmth.

2.1.3 Phenology of flowering plants at Longniddry, East Lothian, Scotland

Professor F T Last has observed the presence or absence of flowers on over 200 species in his garden at Longniddry, East Lothian (55°58′N, 2°57′W) almost every week,

continuously for 12 years. Observations were made throughout the winter and spring of 1988/89 and 1989/90 and comparisons have been made with previous years. Figure 3 shows the dates of first flowering of a range of species in 1989 and 1990 compared with mean dates for the period 1978–1988. In 1989 and 1990, most species/hybrids that started to flower before July started earlier than the 1978–88 average. However, in 1990, few species were more than 8 weeks early, whereas in 1989 many species were 10 weeks or more early particularly those that started to flower before April.

The total number of species/hybrids in flower in each month in 1989 and 1990 are compared with the average for 1978–88 in Figure 4. In 1989, from early-January to mid-March approximately three times as many species were in flower compared with previous years; for example, in early-March 63 species were flowering compared with a mean of 20 in 1978–1988.

In 1990, the numbers of species/hybrids in flower during January were similar to the long-term average, but by March the numbers in flower in 1990 were larger than the 1978–88 average, although significantly fewer than in 1989. During April, there were similar numbers of species/hybrids in flower in 1989 and 1990.

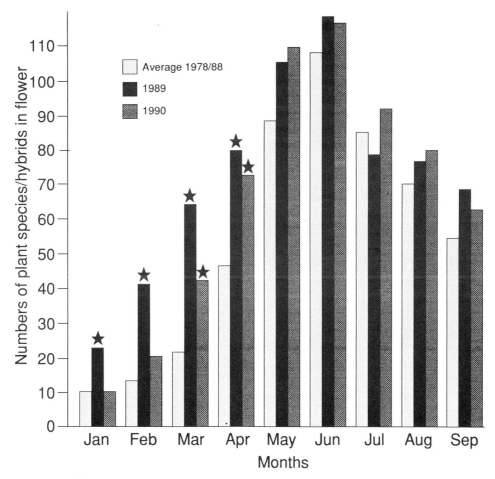

4   Numbers of garden plant species/hybrids in flower at Longniddry, East Lothian in 1989 and 1990 compared with the average for 1978–88. Stars indicate that 1989 and 1990 values differed from the 1978–88 average by more than two standard deviations.

Table 2: First flowering (weeks after 1 January) of selected species in 1989 and 1990 compared with those in 1978/88 (= average) in a garden in East Lothian.

	First flowering (weeks after 1 January)		
	1978/88	1989	1990
I. Species/varieties that usually started to flower in January-February (weeks 5 and 6)			
Snowdrop	5.5	2	3
Crocus (Dutch var.)	5.8	2	3
Anemone blanda	6.0	2	6
Cowslip	6.7	−14* †	9
AVERAGE	6.0	−2 ‡	5.3
II. Species/varieties that usually started to flower in April (weeks 15 and 16).			
'Responsive'			
Rhododendron racemosum	15.0	7*	11
Forsythia	15.0	11*	9*
Euphorbia robbiae	15.6	3*	6*
Rhododendrom keiskeis	15.6	5*	11*
Skimmia japonica	15.7	6*	9*
Euphorbia Griffithii	15.7	6*	16
Japonica	15.8	8*	12
Fritillaria meleagris	15.9	10*	14
Eccremocarpus scaber	16.4	6*	11*
Leucojum	16.6	6*	12*
Choisya ternata	16.9	5*	12*
Celandine	15.8	10*	12*
'Unresponsive'			
Tulipa tarda	15.0	16	14
Honesty	15.8	14	14
Dicentra formosa	16.3	15	14*
Yellow alyssum	16.7	18	18
Tulipa batalina	16.9	17	15
AVERAGE	15.9	9.6	12.4

* Date of first flowering in 1989 or 1990 differed from that of the mean (1978/88) by more than 2 × S.D. of the mean.
† Flowered in week 38 of 1988.
‡ Average time of first flowering was in week 50 of 1988.

There seemed to be three different responses to the mild winter, bearing no apparent relationship with life form (bulb, woody perennial, herb etc.) (Last *pers. comm.*):

i) flowering was premature and of normal duration (e.g. *Rhododendron* "Praecox"; grape hyacinth (*Muscari* spp.));

ii) flowering started early and was more prolonged than normal (e.g. leopard's bane (*Doronicum* spp.); Mexican orange (*Choisya ternata*)); and

iii) both the timing and duration of flowering were as in previous years (e.g. honesty (*Lunaria annua*); apple, (*Malus sylvestris*)).

Table 2 shows the dates of first flowering of selected species. Among the early vernal species, snowdrop and crocus flowered early in both 1989 and 1990, but *Anemone blanda* and cowslip flowered early only in 1989. Among the species that normally start to flower during the first two weeks in April (weeks 15 and 16), *Forsythia*, *Rhododendron* spp. and *Choisya ternata* flowered early in both 1989 and 1990 and can be termed 'responsive

species'. Unresponsive species such as *Tulipa tarda*, honesty and yellow alyssum flowered on about the same date in 1989 and 1990 as in previous years.

In 1989, apple trees flowered around 20 May in Longniddry, close to the 16 year mean. Dates of full bloom of Cox's apple have been recorded in Kent since 1936. Full bloom occurred on 5 May in 1989, the same day as in 1988 and 1987. Thus the flowering date of this important fruit tree was unaffected by the mild winter of 1989.

In general, the data showed that early flowering species responded most to the mild winters while the phenology of late flowering species was less affected. The 1990 season was later than 1989 at Longniddry, but was still significantly earlier than the 1978–88 average. Also, some species flowered consistently early in both 1989 and 1990, whereas others seemed to be insensitive to early warm temperatures and flowered on about the same date in all years.

2.1.4 Herbaceous flora in central England

PREDICTIONS

The British flora appears to be broadly divisible into species which grow rapidly during the cold conditions of spring (and often autumn as well) and those exploiting the warmer summer months (Wells, 1971; Al-Mufti *et al.*, 1977). A physiological mechanism has been suggested for this phenological separation (Grime and Mowforth, 1982). This hypothesis is based on the observation that many species which grow early in spring have large cells and a high nuclear DNA amount (e.g. bluebell (*Hyacinthoides non-scripta*), DNA per nucleus 42.4 pg). By contrast, plants exploiting summer conditions have small cells and low DNA contents (e.g. rosebay willowherb (*Chamaenerion angustifolium*) 0.7 pg).

A mild winter may be expected to result in much early growth irrespective of DNA content. However, not all groups of species will be equally favoured by mild winters. It was predicted that:

1) species with high nuclear DNA amounts would expand their foliage earlier but would show little increase in overall biomass production since the amount of tissue produced is predetermined and relies upon the expansion of cells which have already divided during the previous summer;

2) species which are both winter-green and have a low nuclear DNA amount would benefit greatly. The growth of these species, which occurs mainly during warm periods, involves both cell division and cell expansion. Thus, an increase in number of days conducive to cell division would produce real increases in biomass production and may result in a competitive advantage over species of high nuclear DNA amount;

3) the effect of mild winters on species which combine low nuclear DNA amount with frost sensitivity would

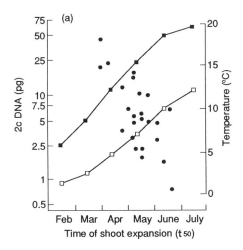
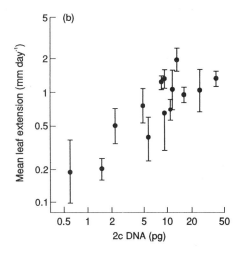

5 (a) The relationship between DNA amount and the time of shoot expansion (date to the nearest quarter month at which 50% of the maximum shoot biomass was obtained) in 24 plant species commonly found in the Sheffield region (redrawn from Grime and Mowforth, 1982). Temperature at Sheffield is expressed as the long-term average for each month of daily minima (□) and maxima (■) in air temperature 1.5 m above the ground.

(b) The relationship between DNA amount and the mean rate of leaf extension over the period 25 March–5 April in 14 grassland species coexisting in the same turf (redrawn from Grime, Shacklock and Band, 1985). 95% confidence limits are indicated by vertical lines.

vary. In response to unusually high air or soil temperatures in spring following a mild winter, shoot growth is likely to commence earlier. In some species, and at warmer sites, the shoots may become larger and more competitive because of this extended growth period. In other species, and in colder situations, the early shoots may suffer frost damage.

FIELD OBSERVATIONS OF SHOOT PHENOLOGY

The relationships between nuclear DNA amount and phenology during a normal year are illustrated in Figure 5. As expected, species of high nuclear DNA content have shoots which expand rapidly in early spring while for species with low DNA amounts shoot expansion is delayed.

Using a rapid survey technique, the extent of cool season growth during the mild winter of 1988/89 was assessed in fifty species of flowering plants growing near Hathersage in North Derbyshire. For each species, estimates were obtained by measuring the area of the largest leaf encountered within prescribed sample areas of 0.5 ha during the last week in March and comparing this with the area of the largest leaf developed by the same species in April/May.

The results, given in Figure 6, illustrate that the leaves of most species with a high nuclear DNA amount, were well-expanded by late March but that those of many species with low DNA amounts were not. This accorded with theoretical expectations. However, superimposed upon this relationship was a tendency for early growth in virtually all species. Thus, early development was a feature of vernal woodland species of high DNA (e.g.

lesser celandine, *Ranunculus ficaria*, DNA 34.3 pg, flowering in January rather than March as is more usual), those of low DNA (e.g. dogs mercury, *Mercurialis perennis*, DNA 4.7 pg, also flowering two months early) and winter annuals (e.g. thale-cress, *Arabidopsis thaliana*, DNA 0.5 pg, more robust than usual and flowering in March instead of April). Extensive cool-season growth was also apparent in species of both high ($\geqslant$ 10 pg) and low DNA amounts (< 10 pg); 34% (12 species) of low DNA and 47% of high DNA species had grown leaves with a surface area (one side) of > 1000 mm² by the end of March. The capacity for species with low DNA to produce extensive cool-season growth is further illustrated in Table 3 and is in accord with observations of the unusually robust early growth of common roadside species such as cow parsley (*Arthriscus sylvestris*), dock (*Rumex obtusifolius*), dandelion (*Taraxacum officinale*) and goosegrass (*Galium aparine*).

Table 3: The species which had produced the largest young leaves by March 31st 1989 at Hathersage, Derbyshire.

	Leaf size mm²	Nuclear DNA amount (pg)
Cow parsley (*Anthriscus sylvestris*)	13642	4.2
Sweet cicely (*Myrrhis odorata*)	13146	1.7
Broad-leaved dock (*Rumex obtusifolius*)	11946	3.0
Butterbur (*Petasites hybridus*)	10142	1.8
Ramsons (*Allium ursinum*)	8826	35.7
Cuckoo pint (*Arum maculatum*)	6680	21.8
Dandelion (*Taraxacum officinale*)	6398	2.6
Hogweed (*Heracleum sphondylium*)	3547	3.8
Branched bur-reed (*Sparganium erectum*)	2463	1.1
Creeping buttercup (*Ranunculus repens*)	2386	20.8

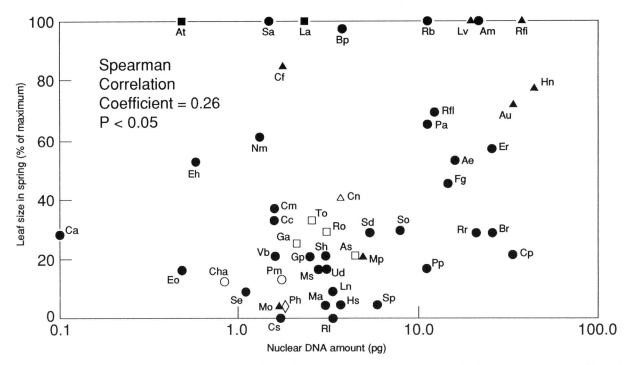

6 The relationship between (a) leaf size at the end of March 1989 as a percentage of leaf size in April/May 1989, and (b) nuclear DNA amount. Data collected from around Hathersage, North Derbyshire.

Ae, *Arrhenatherum elatius*; Am, *Arum maculatum*; As, *Anthriscus sylvestris*; At, *Arabidopsis thaliana*; Au, *Allium ursinum*; Bp, *Bellis perennis*; Br, *Bromus ramosus*; Ca, *Cardamine amara*; Cc, *Carex caryophyllea*; Cf, *Cardamine flexuosa*; Cha, *Chamaenerion angustifolium*; Cm, *Conopodium majus*; Cn, *Centaurea nigra*; Cp, *Caltha palustris*; Cs, *Calystegia sepium*; Eh, *Epilobium hirsutum*; Eo, *E. obscurum*; Er, *Elymus repens*; Fg, *Festuca gigantea*; Ga, *Galium aparine*; Gp, *G. palustre*; Hn, *Hyacinthoides non-scripta*; Hs, *Heracleum sphondylium*; La, *Lamium album*; Ln, *Lysimachia nemorum*; Lv, *Leucanthemum vulgare*; Ma, *Mentha aquatica*; Mo, *Myrrhis odorata*; Mp, *Mercurialis perennis*; Ms, *Myosotis scorpioides*; Nm, *Nasturtium microphyllum*; Pa, *Phalaris arundinacea*; Ph, *Petasites hybridus*; Pm, *Plantago major*; Pp, *Poa pratensis*; Rb, *Ranunculus bulbosus*; Rfi, *R. ficaria*; Rfl, *R. flammula*; Rj, *Reynoutria japonica*; Ro, *Rumex obtusifolius*; Rr, *Ranunculus repens*; Sa, *Stellaria alsine*; Sd, *Silene dioica*; Se, *Sparganium erectum*; Sh, *Stellaria holostea*; So, *Stachys officinalis*; Sp, *Succisa pratensis*; To, *Taraxacum officinale*; Ud, *Urtica dioica*; Vb, *Veronica beccabunga*.

Most species are denoted by a closed circle (●). However, species whose phenology was markedly abnormal are indicated as the following symbols:

☐ Shoots abnormally large by end of March.
○ Above-ground shoots not normally produced until late April – early May.
△ Foliage overwintering in species whose shoots normally die back in late autumn – early winter.
▲ Early flowering observed in the period January to March; onset at least one month earlier than normal.

Some species (*e.g. Lamium album*) are identified by two symbols.

A preliminary analysis comparing leaf area at the end of March as a percentage of the maximum value with published values for biomass in April as a percentage of the maximum (calculated from Al Mufti *et al.*, 1977, who also carried out the studies in Central England), suggested that the measurements collected had a real predictive value (Spearman correlation coefficient = 0.67, P = 0.10, number of species in comparison 11).

The sites visited in 1988/89 were resampled in 1989/90. To ensure that results were comparable, the sampling dates differed by no more than 1 day for the early spring and by no more than 2 days for the early summer sampling. As in 1989, there was a tendency for early

growth in virtually all species. However, in 1990 the relationship between the extent of leaf expansion in early spring and nuclear DNA content was weak, being statistically significant at only the P > 0.1 level. This latter result contrasted with the results for 1989 which showed that the leaves of most species with a high nuclear DNA amount were well-expanded by late March, but those of many species with low DNA were not.

It is possible that the drought of 1989 reduced the amount of cell division, and hence "stored growth", for species of high nuclear DNA amounts. If so, a succession of dry summers followed by mild winters could lead to an even more rapid competitive suppression of vernal (early spring) species such as bluebells with high nuclear DNA amounts, in hedgerows and woodlands, than had previously been thought.

EFFECTS OF THE MILD WINTER ON OTHER FACETS OF LIFE HISTORY

The seeds of many species require chilling and a very mild winter could theoretically prevent germination in certain of these plants. This does not appear to have been a problem during the winters of 1988/89 and 1989/90 in north Derbyshire where seedlings of a variety of herbs e.g. hogweed (*Heracleum sphondylium*), hedge mustard (*Alliaria petiolata*) and cow parsley (*Anthriscus sylvestris*) were observed during the late winter and early spring.

Seedlings of a variety of tree species were also observed in north Derbyshire in the spring of 1989 and 1990. However, at Plymouth in S. Devon, no seedlings of mountain ash (*Sorbus aucuparia*) were observed during the spring of 1990 almost certainly the consequence of the unusually mild winter (K Thompson, *pers. comm.*). The possibility that species with a prolonged chilling requirement for seed germination may become less common in areas of England should mild winters become normal, deserves study.

Some unusual effects of the mild winter on developmental processes were apparent. Butterbur (*Petasites hybridus*) normally expands its flowers before the leaves. In 1989 and 1990, many individuals produced foliage and flowers simultaneously and in some cases the inflorescence was overtopped by large leaves. Some species (e.g. black knapweed (*Centaurea nigra*)) whose foliage normally dies back in Central England, persisted throughout the winter as a rosette of leaves. The effects of such changes in growth patterns and growing periods on the performance and competitive ability of these species is not known.

EFFECTS OF FROSTS ON SPRING GROWTH

Frosts occurred in several parts of the UK in April and May 1989. In Derbyshire two episodes of heavy late frost were observed. The first occurred at the beginning of April just after the spring recording of leaf size. Despite its severity no frost damage was observed in any of the fifty species examined. However, severe frosts at the end of May had a much more devastating effect and a number of species where above-ground shoot expansion is delayed until late spring were effected. The species which experienced widespread frost damage included Japanese knotweed (*Reynoutria japonica*), and ferns, particularly bracken (*Pteridium aquilinum*). The widespread and severe frost damage to the fronds of limestone fern (*Gymnocarpium robertianum*) contrasted with the apparent tolerance of the related but more northern oak fern (*G. dryopteris*) suggesting that the severity and timing of frosts during mild winters may play an important role in determining competitive interactions and plant distribution.

In 1990, widespread frost damage to herbaceous foliage was not observed in Derbyshire. However an early frost episode in March caused widespread damage to elder (*Sambucus nigra*) and hawthorn (*Crataegus monogyna*) (see A2.1.5).

Observations for 1989 and 1990 suggest that, although the timing of spring frosts will affect the performance and even the survival of species, their impacts on the local flora are difficult to assess. In 1990, some early-growing species received a check to their growth, while in 1989 later-growing species were more severely affected.

2.1.5 Impacts on forestry

SPRING FROSTS

Many trees and shrubs flushed early in 1989 and 1990 following the previous mild winters and were thus very vulnerable to the spring frosts which occurred in areas of the UK in both years.

In 1989, minimum air temperatures of below −5°C were recorded in many areas of Scotland and northern England in late April. Damage was reported on individuals or small groups of Sitka spruce (*Picea sitchensis*) in southern Scotland and northern England. Frost damage in larch (*Larix* spp.) leading to death of 1988 shoot tips and browning of 1989 foliage was a feature of several plantations in western Scotland early in the growing season (Gregory *et al.*, 1991).

In Derbyshire, an early frost episode in March 1990, caused damage to elder and hawthorn. In April 1990, temperatures of below −4°C occurred widely in central and southern England. Many oak trees lost their flowers and leaves. Refoliation was completed by early June and subsequent acorn crops were very light. Ash (*Fraxinus excelsior*) and beech (*Fagus sylvatica*) were conspicuously affected in some areas and the foliage and flower buds of a number of ornamental species were also damaged. However recovery was good in many cases (J. Gibbs *pers. comm.*).

SURVIVAL OF TRANSPLANTED CONIFER SEEDLINGS

Each autumn, tree seedlings stop growing, set buds, become frost hardy and their buds become dormant in response to a combination of shortening daylengths, falling temperatures and frosts. In the mild winter of 1988/89 this process of "hardening off" was delayed and/or did not occur to the same extent as in normal winters.

Fully "hardened" seedlings of Sitka spruce are normally well able to regenerate new roots after lifting and transplanting in January-March, i.e. they then have a high "root growth potential". In January-March 1989, the root growth potential of Sitka spruce seedlings was 30–50% lower than normal (W L Mason, *pers. comm.*). Many conifer seedlings are lifted in November-December and held over winter in cold stores at about 0°C before being planted in the spring. Seedlings survive and maintain high root growth potentials in cold storage only when they are fully "hardy". In 1988/89 some 2–3 million conifer seedlings died in cold storage, apparently because they were not sufficiently hardy when they were lifted from the nurseries and placed in storage (W L Mason, *pers. comm.*). Many of those 2–3 million seedlings (transplants) that died were Sitka spruce of southerly provenance (from Washington or Oregon, rather than from British Columbia), and were destined for planting in south Wales and southwestern England. Ironically, the use of more southerly provenance material was part of a deliberate policy of the Forestry Commission to use trees adapted to mild climates for planting in southern Britain.

If mild winters are expected, transplant deaths can be partly avoided by not putting southerly origin material into cold storage and by altering the winter schedules for lifting and transplanting. These measures were taken in 1989/90 and fewer transplant deaths occurred in that season.

OUTBREAKS OF GREEN SPRUCE APHID

Mild winters are generally associated with outbreaks of the green spruce aphid (*Elatobium abietinum*) on Sitka and Norway spruce. This insect overwinters as wingless, viviparous, parthenogenetic females, which are killed in significant numbers only when temperatures fall to $-8°C$ (Carter, 1972), but which otherwise multiply overwinter to reach a population maximum in spring.

In the late winter and spring of 1989 there was a major outbreak of this pest, which feeds on older needles, causes defoliation and checks tree growth. In parts of south Wales, for example, both Sitka and Norway spruce trees 20–30 years old were completely discoloured by aphid needle damage in the winter (Carter, 1989). In most cases, the trees survived, but growth may have been checked for 2–3 years, and in some areas there was a risk that the trees would go into 'decline', especially following the hot, dry summers of 1989 and 1990. There were outbreaks of the green spruce aphid (*Elatobium abietinum*) in the spring

1990, but these were not as serious or widespread as in 1989. It is unusual for a serious outbreak to occur on the same trees in successive years even in the event of a further mild winter, because (i) there may be a build-up of natural enemies and (ii) the trees have fewer old needles and the trees may build up defences.

Casual observations suggest that the northern tree species, bird cherry (*Prunus padus*), was more prone to defoliation by caterpillars at the southerly end of its distributional range during the spring and early summer of 1990. The possibility that the geographical range of some species will become modified because of the greater capacity of insect pests to overwinter deserves study.

[1] CATASTROPHIC WINDTHROW ON 25 JANUARY 1990

On 25 January 1990 a great storm occurred across southern England, gusting to 172 km/h, which blew down approximately 1.3 million m^3 of timber over an area of about 4,800 ha. The land area that was affected by this storm was three times the area affected by the "hurricane" on 16 October 1987, but only about one third as much timber volume was blown down (Table 4).

2.1.6 Conclusions

1. A major impact of the 2 mild winters was on plant phenology. Observations of up to 17 native plant species at 6 ITE stations, and of over 200 garden plants in East Lothian, showed that most plants that normally flower before April, flowered several days or weeks earlier than normal in 1989 and 1990. Comparisons were presented with long-term (> 10 year) mean dates of flowering in the Royal Meteorological Society Phenological Records (1895–1947) and with East Lothian garden records since 1978.

The phenology of late flowering species was less affected; although both mild winters stimulated earlier

---

[1] Although this event was not a feature of the mild winters it reminds us of the large impacts of single extreme events relative to the impacts of unusual seasons and gradual shifts in climate.

Table 4: Catastrophic storm events affecting British forests since 1945 (from Quine, 1991)

Date of storm	Area affected by 100 km/hr gusts (sq km)	Max gust recorded (km/h)	Area blown down (ha)	Volume windthrow (millions m^3)	Percentage of growing stock windthrown in the areas affected
31. 1.53	370 NE Scotland	180	–	1.8	10–25
15. 1.68	510 Central Scotland	189	8337	1.6	15–30
2. 1.76	890 Central England & Wales	169	–	1.0	<5
16.10.87	220 SE England	185	16500†	3.9*	13–24
25. 1.90	690 S England	172	4805	1.3*	1.3

* Including non-woodland trees
† Area clear (not all blown down)

flowering among some species that normally flower between April and June, few records were broken. Not all species responded to early warming, probably because their phenology was controlled by daylength and/or winter chilling.

It is important to note that the phenology of both garden aliens and wild plant species important in semi-natural vegetation, were affected by the mild winters. While garden aliens may be useful indicators of climatic trends, they are of limited value in calculating the costs of such trends to the natural environment.

2. Observations on the size of the leaves of 50 species in Derbyshire in late March 1989 confirmed an expected positive relationship between early leaf expansion and nuclear DNA content. This relationship was not significant in 1990. The unusually vigorous growth of species such as goosegrass with low nuclear DNA content, suggested that a succession of mild winters could lead to the competitive suppression of vernal species with high nuclear DNA amounts (such as bluebell) in many hedgerows and woodlands.

3. The seeds of many species require chilling prior to germination and mild winters could prevent germination in some species. Although seedlings of a variety of herbaceous and tree species were observed in north Derbyshire in the springs of 1989 and 1990, no seedlings of mountain ash were observed in the spring of 1990 at Plymouth.

4. Many species suffered frost damage in late spring of 1989 and 1990, although the damage was not as severe as expected. In the event of regular mild winters, the timing of spring frosts will affect the performance and survival of individual species. However the overall impact on local plant communities is difficult to assess.

5. Several indirect effects of mild winters were more damaging to vegetation, particularly trees, than the more obvious direct effects. For example, the lack of hardening of Sitka spruce seedlings in forest nurseries in 1988/89 led to the death of 2–3 million transplants in cold storage and a similar number after planting out.

Trees were also indirectly damaged by the increased capacity of insect pests to overwinter in the mild winters. In spring 1989 a major outbreak of green spruce aphid on Sitka and Norway spruce resulted in defoliation of whole mature trees in some areas probably leading to long-term growth check. The northern species, bird cherry, also suffered defoliation (by caterpillars) at the southern end of its range during 1990.

6. In the event of continued mild winters, changes in species composition may occur in a number of ways. Change may be caused directly e.g. absence of prolonged chilling requirement, or may be indirect,

such as the competitive suppression of vernal herbaceous species in hedgerows and woodlands, and increased capacity for insect pests to overwinter.

7. However the impacts of these gradual progressive changes in vegetation must not be over-emphasised. A storm on 25 January 1990 blew down 1.3 million m^3 of timber over an area of 4,800 ha, representing not only a loss of stock but also the loss of much woodland habitat.

A2.2 IMPACTS ON ANIMALS

2.2.1 Introduction

In the UK animals are adapted to survive low winter temperatures. For foraging animals the amount of rain, frozen ground or snow cover are also important factors.

An important aspect of overwintering strategy is the contrast between species which are ectotherms (cold-blooded) or endotherms (warm-blooded). Typical examples of ectotherms are lizards and snakes which become torpid and hibernate as soon as the temperature falls below critical levels for the species. Insects are similarly dependent on the external temperature for activity. Mammals and birds are endotherms and are able to maintain body heat in ordinary circumstances, although, in winter, some mammals and birds enter a state of torpor, or hibernation, when the body temperature is lowered, metabolism slowed and energy consumption reduced. Other species avoid the effects of winter cold and lack of food by migration.

Winter conditions undoubtedly affect the abundance of organisms, but while severe winters may markedly reduce populations, mild winters do not necessarily result in increased populations. In order to separate the impact of mild winters (or indeed hot summers) from that of numerous other factors which control the abundance of species, it is necessary to have long runs of reliable population census data. In the absence of such data, quantitative information from natural history observations and experimental studies must suffice.

2.2.2 Invertebrates

APHIDS

Many aphid species pass the winter as eggs and are not responsive to mild winter temperatures. Those that respond most to mild winters are the "anholocyclic" species, i.e. those that pass the winter in all stages of development and which are parthenogenetic. The effects of mild winters on these species have been summarized by Bale (1989) (Table 5).

In 1989 and 1990, the first migrations of aphids were early, as shown by results from the Rothamsted Experimental station suction traps (Harrington, *pers. comm.*).

Table 5: Effects of mild and severe winters on anholocyclic aphids (after Bale, 1989).

Severe winter	Mild winter
Low survival	High survival
Delayed spring increase	Early increase in spring
Crowding delayed	Early crowding
Winged migrants late	Winged migrants early
Migration late	Migration early
Arrive on well-grown crops	Arrive on germinating and early crops
No damage	Potential outbreak

The numbers of the peach potato aphid (*Myzus persicae*) were correlated with the mean temperatures from January to April and showed that the first appearance of this species was the earliest for 24 years in 1989, and second earliest in 1990 (Figure 7a). Many other species were also trapped, and the number of species caught in 1989 was greater than in previous years. In 1990, out of 17 common, and mostly economically important species, nine showed the earliest ever first record for the last 23 years, and all

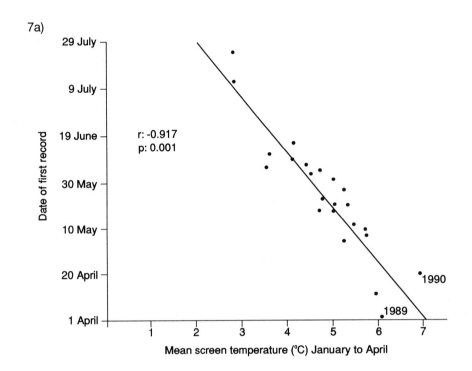

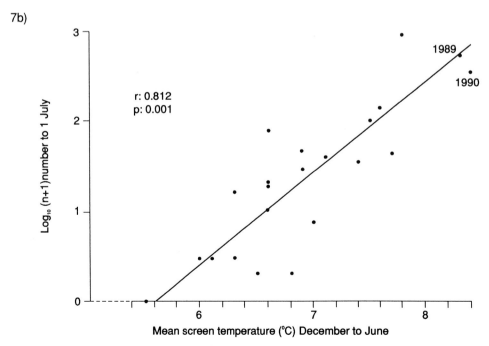

7 (a) Correlation of mean January-April temperatures with the first record of the peach-potato aphid (*Myzus persicae*) in the suction trap at Rothamsted, and

(b) correlation of mean December–June temperatures with numbers of aphids in the suction trap by 1 July (from Harrington, 1990, unpublished report).

except *Myzus ascalonicus* and green spruce aphid (*Elatobium abietinum*) were ranked in the first 1–3 years out of the 23 recorded. The English grain aphid, (*Sitobion avenae*), (anholocyclic) is also usually caught early and in larger numbers in spring following mild winters in southern England (Walters and Dewar, 1986). Conversely the rose aphid (*Metopolophium dishodum*) is more likely to increase after severe winters which delay the autumn sown cereal growth, giving more day degrees for increase in abundance before the crop becomes unsuitable (Howard and Dixon, 1990).

Numbers of aphids later in the summer are also correlated with temperatures in winter and spring, and statistics from Rothamsted for peach-potato aphid showed that numbers on 1st July 1989 were the second largest for 24 years. Numbers were third largest in 1990 (Figure 7b). However there is no correlation for numbers of *Sitobion avenae* caught up to the end of the flowering period of wheat and the peak number per tiller earlier in the year (Dixon *et al.* in Cavallora and Sunderland, 1988). (The subject is further discussed under hot summers in Chapter B2.2.1).

The food web involving aphids is complicated, making it difficult to interpret the effect of weather. Thus, the condition of the food-plant affects the aphids, while the build up of predators and parasites is slower than than of the aphids. At the same time, the ichneumonid and braconid wasps which parasitize the predators will also be favoured by good weather and high populations of prey. The system is therefore quite heavily buffered. The number of ladybirds and hoverflies which prey on aphids was large in 1990, especially the 7-spot ladybird (*Coccinella septempunctata*). These species had built up and survived the mild 1989/90 winter well.

In some places aphids were so abundant early in 1989–90 that they caused direct damage to crops and garden plants (Jackson, ADAS *pers. comm.*), but more problems were caused by the vectored spread of viruses, e.g. in potatoes and sugar beet by peach-potato aphid, and barley yellow dwarf virus in cereals by bird cherry aphid (*Rhopalosiphum padi*). Reports by Carter (1989) and Morrison and Spense (1989) on aphid impacts on agriculture and horticulture are discussed in Chapters A4 and B4 and the outbreak of green spruce aphid is discussed in Chapter A2.1.5.

MOTHS

The winter of 1988–89 was exceptional for activity of moths in the winter and spring, especially in northern England and Scotland, where the largest anomalies in temperature occurred. The winter and spring 1989/90 was less unusual in this respect.

The Rothamsted Insect Survey run by Rothamsted Experimental Station provides long term records of moths caught in many light traps. Four examples are 14 years

at Yarner Wood (Devon), 23 years at Geescroft (Hertfordshire), 13 years at Kielder (Northumberland) and 11 years at Beinn Eighe (Wester Ross). In the first five weeks from 1 January to 11 February 1989 there were 5 catches of moths at the two northern sites which were among the four largest ever, and 3 such catches at the two southern sites (Woiwodd *pers. comm.*). This winter activity coincided with unusual records of bats flying in early 1989. Bats are important predators of moths.

An examination of data for seven spring-flying moth species showed only one exceptionally early first record over the long-term for Yarner Wood, none for Geescroft, 3 for Kielder and 5 for Beinn Eighe. Exceptionally early appearances of these moths were also recorded by Dunn (1989) in Gloucester, Durham and Cromarty. The appearance of the common quaker (*Orthosia stabilis*) and clouded drab (*Orthosia incerta*) at Durham was the earliest for 37 years.

Figure 8 examines the total catch in 1989 of one moth species, Hebrew character (*Orthosia gothica*) compared with previous years. At Geescroft, the entire catch for 1989 was about a week early and the catch was earlier for most of the time at the two northern sites; however, there was no evidence for Yarner Wood (Devon) that the entire flight period had been shifted.

Where the entire flight period was shifted there was a possibility that additional generations could have been completed (in multivoltine species) and/or that emergence was not synchronous with the growth of food plants (Strong *et al.* 1984).

At ITE Furzebrook (Dorset) a light trap was run from 27 January to 20 April 1989 to compare numbers of spring-flying moths with records obtained over the 5 years from 1972–76. Twenty species were caught earlier than the previous average date of their first appearance, some species several weeks earlier (Figure 9a). Thirteen of the 25 species caught were recorded earlier than in any of the previous 5 years of records, one species equalled the previous earliest date and the others were later (Figure 9b).

On the Isle of Wight, Knill-Jones (1991) recorded early spring emergence of 38 macromoths in 1989–91 at a mercury vapour light. Of 14 species occurring in all three years in January-March, 4 were earliest in 1989, 7 in 1990, but only 2 in 1991. Common quaker, oak beauty (*Biston strataria*) early grey (*Xylocampa areola*) and early thorn (*Selenia dentaria*) which all over-winter as pupae, were more advanced in 1989 and 1990 than in 1991.

BUTTERFLIES

Butterflies occasionally emerge from hibernation and fly on warm days in winter (Archer-Lock, 1989). During the winters of 1988/89 and 1989/90, there were many sightings of hibernating species of butterflies, like the brimstone

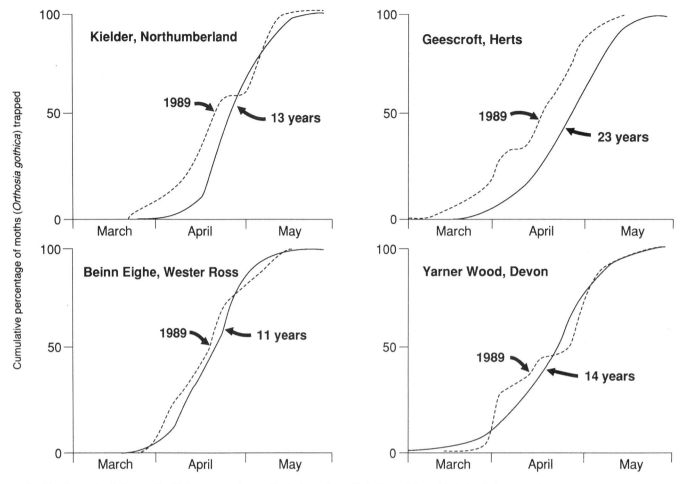

8   Total catch of the moth, Hebrew character, *Orthosia gothica* (L.) (Lep. Noctuidae) in light traps in 1989 compared to the mean for all the previous years of trapping. Data from the Rothamsted Insect Survey.

(*Gonepteryx rhamni*), small tortoiseshell (*Aglais urticae*), peacock (*Inachis io*) and comma (*Polygonia c-album*). One sighting was of a brimstone at Furzebrook, Dorset on 21 January 1989 (the 3rd earliest record in the 1900–1924 Dorset Natural History Society). Another sighting was of a small tortoiseshell in Warwick in 27 December 1988 on a mild sunny day with a maximum temperature of 11.5°C (Herron, 1989). The 1989/90 season was apparently less exceptional with fewer sightings than in 1988/89, probably because the 1989/90 winter was wetter. Early appearances of some of these hibernating species could be deleterious if body food reserves are used up before nectar or food plants are available. Such species also fall prey to birds. There was a large decrease in the number of small tortoiseshell butterflies recorded between the autumn of 1987 and spring 1988, possibly owing to unseasonal activity in the mild winter of 1987/88 (Pollard, 1988).

The sighting of a few red admirals (*Vanessa atalanta*) in the winter and spring of 1988/89 and 1989/90 was particularly interesting (e.g. on 22 January in Cornwall (Tremewan, 1989)). A few painted lady butterflies (*Cynthis cardui*) were seen in March 1989 in Dorset, after an early migration from the continent. This butterfly was also recorded very early in February and March in the south of England in 1988 (Pollard, 1988). In 1989 and 1990, a few red admirals and painted ladies may have survived overwinter and bred in this country instead of being solely migratory, as they have been in most years (Thomas, *pers. comm.*). Normal migration was noted in late March in Purbeck in 1989, but was not noted until June in 1990 (Dorset Environmental Records Centre).

Those species that overwinter as pupae, and undergo development before emergence, may be better indicators of longer periods of warmer temperature in winter. Speckled wood (*Pararge aegeria*) and orange tip (*Anthocharis cardamines*) butterflies emerged considerably earlier than normal in 1990 in Dorset. Similarly, larval development was speeded up and the meadow brown (*Maniola jurtina*) had an earlier flight period in May and June (Pollard and Yates, 1990).

BEES, WASPS AND ANTS

Most of the social bees and wasps overwinter as adults and may become active in periods of warm weather. Many bees and bumble bees were seen in January and February 1989 as far north as Banchory, Kincardineshire and there were reports of increases in the abundance of bumble bees (e.g. in the Pennine moorlands) (*pers. comm.*

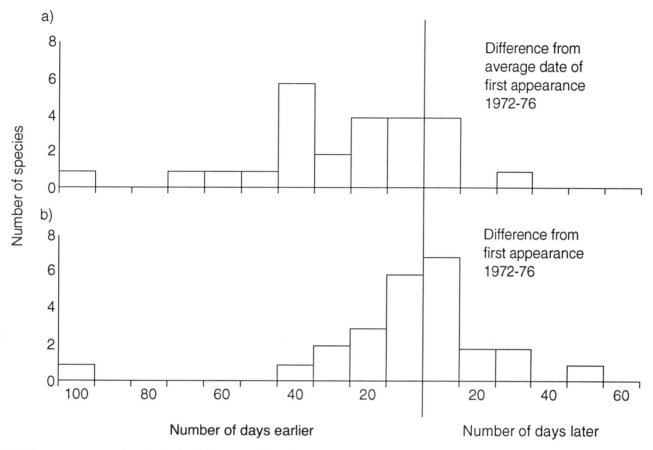

9 First appearances of moths in the light trap at Furzebrook in Dorset in 1989: (a) first appearance contrasted to average date of the first appearance for all records from 1972–76, (b) first appearance contrasted to all records from 1972–76.

Coulson). Both honey and bumble bees are known to forage in quite cold weather (Alford, 1975). Queen wasps were observed at Furzebrook, Dorset on 7 January. These queens can be roused from hibernation and may move to new hibernation sites (Spradbery, 1973). Brian and Brian (1952) showed that the first appearances of the wasp *Dolichovespula sylvestris* is correlated with temperature in May in Scotland.

SLUG POPULATIONS

There were many observations that pest species of slugs remained active during the 1988/89 winter and caused damage to cereals, potatoes and other crops eg ADAS at Bristol (Jackson, *pers. comm.*) reported that slugs were a serious problem on winter cereals, and that numbers were probably higher than for the previous 10 years. Molluscicides became in short supply, farmers had to repeat doses, and in bad cases had to re-drill.

Slugs had apparently built up in numbers during the wet summer of 1988, were active during the mild winter of 1988/89 and continued feeding overwinter on the slow growing winter cereals. Also, during the summer of 1988 the harvest was late and crop canopies were present longer, which provided a favourable habitat for slugs. In 1988, damage was greater on the early drilled crops, which also indicated an autumn build-up of populations.

There is relatively little published work on the quantitative effects of climatic factors on slug populations. South (1989a and b) found that cold weather delayed development of slugs in permanent pasture, the growth of the early infantile stages of *Arion intermedius* being especially affected. Few other effects of cold weather on slug numbers were found. Conversely, Hunter (1966) in a more restricted study, found that immature slugs on arable land were killed in considerable numbers by frost. Generally, therefore, in a mild wet winter little or no mortality of young stages of slugs would be expected and the rate of development may be increased. This could lead to increased reproductive success and hence population growth. However, reproductive success is also affected by the weather at other times of the year – dry weather in summer being particularly deleterious.

CONCLUSIONS ON INVERTEBRATE POPULATIONS

It is clear that the mild winter affected invertebrates, particularly their phenology, with many species being recorded much earlier than usual. There are a number of effects, or likely effects on invertebrate populations:

i) Species with active stages in the winter, e.g. slugs and many aphids, increased in number following the mild winters.

ii) Other species, such as red spider mite, which begin

reproduction early and have a short generation time, were likely to have benefitted from the mild winters, although no quantitative data are available.

iii) Some normally migrant species, e.g. humming bird hawk moth (*Macroglossum stellatarum*), may have been able to overwinter successfully in this country and to reproduce in spring.

iv) For many butterflies and other insects, rainfall and summer temperature are just as, or more, important than winter temperatures. Some butterflies, which have various patterns of winter diapause, may even have been adversely affected by the mild winter. Beirne (1955) thought that good butterfly years from 1864 to 1952 followed severe winters, but Pollard (1988) using multiple regression analysis on the relatively short run of years in the BMS data, could not prove any correlation. The adverse effect of mild winters on small tortoiseshell numbers was attributed to increased bird predation.

v) Increasing populations caused by mild winters/hot summers are buffered by predators and parasites, although there may be time-lags in numbers.

2.2.3 Amphibia and reptiles

FROGS AND TOADS (AMPHIBIA)

Breeding was early in frogs and toads in 1989 and 1990. Both groups hibernate underground or in mud at the bottom of ponds. The common frog emerges from hibernation when air temperatures reach about 4°C, and 2–3 days later they spawn (Frazer, 1983). The date of frog spawning was one of the events selected for detailed recording in the earlier part of the century by the Royal Meteorological Society. Savage (1961) concluded from the Phenological Reports that the date of spawning was correlated with temperature and rainfall in the previous month.

The Royal Society for Nature Conservation ran a Frogwatch Survey in 1984, 1985 and 1988/89 (Morrison, 1989). In 1988/89 spawning occurred in December and January in southern Scotland, Wales and England, whereas in 1984 and 1985 spawning did not begin until February and spread from southwest England to Scotland (Figure 10). Cummins (*pers. comm.*) confirmed that frog spawning in Dartmoor and southwest Scotland was 2–3 weeks earlier in 1989 than in the previous 7 years.

Toads move from hibernation when air temperatures reach 7–10°C and spawn when water temperatures reach about 9°C (Frazer, 1983). In Dorset, Reading (*pers. comm.*) found that in 1989 and 1990 the start of toad reproductive behaviour, and the actual date of spawning, were earlier than in any of the previous 9 years (Figure 11). Reading also found a significant negative correlation between winter temperature and the survival of old male toads (n = 15, r = −0.7) but no such relationship existed for young or female toads. In the Huntingdon area toads were also early in spawning (fourth week of March) and so were closer in date to frogs which were spawning later than usual in late February (Cooke, *pers. comm.*). Sometimes, when this occurs toads and frogs may become mixed in pairing couples, resulting in wasted reproductive effort.

The natterjack toad does not seem to have been affected by the mild winters (e.g. at Ainsdale NNR, Lancs, and other coastal reserves, Wheeler (*pers. comm.*)). It emerges late and does not spawn until May or June, and the spawning date is related to rainfall and water table levels as much as to temperature (see Chapter B2.2).

REPTILES

Reptiles hibernate underground and in sheltered places, and lose about 10% of their body weight during a normal

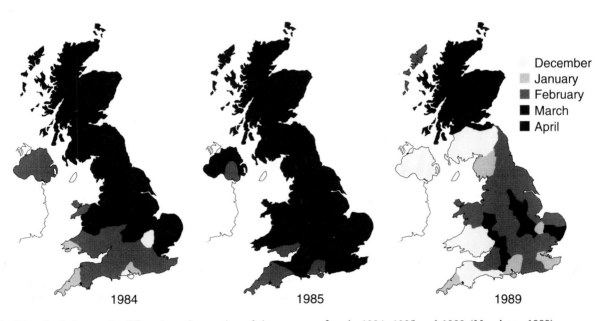

December
January
February
March
April

1984   1985   1989

10   Phenological records of first date of spawning of the common frog in 1984, 1985 and 1989 (Morrison, 1989).

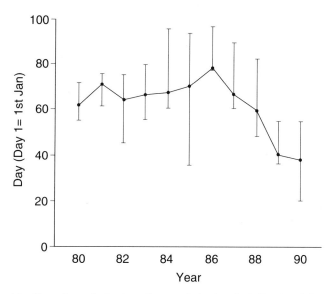

11 Duration of the breeding periods (vertical lines) of the common toad in Dorset 1980–89. (Reading, pers. comm.). ● – first spawn laid.

Table 6: Date of emergence of male sand lizards from hibernation in Dorset

1986	27 February
1987	1 March
1988	28 February
1989	8 February
1990	8 February

British winter (Gregory, 1982). When temperatures rise they seek warm places to bask.

In Dorset, male sand lizards emerged early from hibernation in 1989 and 1990 (Table 6) (Mills, *pers. comm.*). The temperature threshold for activity was about 10°C. Early emergence was followed by a spell of wetter weather in 1990, and the males then needed to disperse in order to feed. When the females emerged, mating and egg laying were apparently less successful than in other years. Weather in May is an important factor in the reproductive success of this species.

At Ainsdale NNR, Lancs. (where there is a conservation management programme for sand lizards) about a third of the captive sand lizards that emerged in February 1989 died in the subsequent cool March weather, when temperatures may have dropped too fast for them to reach safe hibernation burrows. Premature activity was again harmful in 1990 when lizards were caught by a sharp late frost (Wheeler, *pers. comm.*).

Adders emerge when their underground hibernation sites reach about 8°C. They are occasionally seen in winter, but in 1989 unusually large numbers were seen. On Studland Heath in Dorset, one adder was seen on 10 December 1988, 5 adders on 9 February 1989 and 6 adders on 26 February 1989. There were very few sightings before the end of February in the previous 20 years (Cox *pers. comm.*), or in 1990, when although warm, the weather was also rather wet.

2.2.4 Birds

INTRODUCTION

British bird populations are monitored using a variety of measures including estimates of the breeding population size (or density), breeding success, autumn populations (e.g. game bags) or winter populations (at specific sites such as lochs or estuaries). It was anticipated that mild wet winters would mainly affect bird survival through to the following spring and hot dry summers would affect their breeding success. More complicated relationships are possible – eg. a hot dry summer may help trees set seed in abundance and this can provide more food for birds enhancing their survival through the following winter or in subsequent years – but the initial search was for effects on overwinter survival in 1988/89 and 1989/90 and breeding success in 1989 and 1990. Overwinter survival is rarely measured; usually it is merely implied by a high breeding population the following year.

Of the 200 or so bird species commonly breeding in Britain, the breeding populations and success of about 130 are monitored regularly (Marchant *et al.*, 1990), but probably for less than 50 of these are estimates accurate enough to detect other than large (› 10%) changes from year to year. Similarly, of the 190 or so species regularly wintering in Britain, only about 60 are counted frequently and about 30 given an annual winter population index. Only a handful of species in restricted localities are the subject of long-term intensive study. Most of the quantitative information on nationally monitored populations in 1989 and 1990 was not available at the time of writing so published reports in "popular" articles have had to be taken at face value.

THE 1988/89 WINTER

Bird movements are often less in mild winters than in severe winters (Baillie *et al.* 1986). Thus, in the 1988/89 winter, about 100 eiderducks roosted at Studland Heath NNR (usually only 30) and 14 long-tailed ducks (usually none) (Cox, *pers. comm.*). At Yarner Wood NNR, about 100 pied wagtails and 150 meadow pipits passed through in December on their way north instead of roosting (Page, *pers. comm.*). Fewer waders came from the north as far south as Poole Harbour as in previous winters.

Of the 57 resident species monitored using Common Birds Census techniques, 15 showed population decline from 1988 to 1989, 12 remained the same but 30, mostly passerines, increased. Fourteen of these changes were statistically significant – tawny owl and skylark declined, whereas kestrel, stock dove, collared dove, meadow pipit,

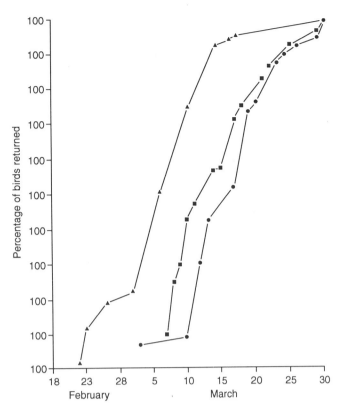

12 Percentage of marked oystercatchers which returned to Banchory, Kincardineshire during February and March in 1987 (●, n=42), 1988 (■, n=60) and 1989 (▲, n=67) (from Picozzi, pers. comm.).

wren, dunnock, robin, song thrush, goldcrest, long-tailed tit, tree creeper, and linnet increased (Marchant and Whittington 1990). The species that increased most, (goldcrest and long-tailed tit) were the lightest in body weight, which are those expected to survive well during a mild winter.

Birds returned to their summer nesting places sooner in 1989 than in previous years. Picozzi (*pers. comm.*) found that ringed oystercatchers returned from overwintering estuaries to Banchory, Kincardineshire about 10 days earlier in 1989 than in previous years (Figure 12). There was no relationship between distance from the overwintering site and dates of return to Banchory.

Numerous observations were made of full breeding behaviour in the winter 1988/89 (Glue, 1989a and 1989b). Thus, well grown barn owls at nesting sites in central southern England during November were clearly from the second brood. Breeding probably continued because small mammals remained active and available as prey. Woodpigeon and collared doves also incubated clutches and fed young in December in the home counties, and feral pigeons continued to breed into the New Year in parts of both England and Scotland. On Tring Reservoirs, great crested grebes began nest building on 11 January, and one-week-old young were recorded on 26 January at Frimley in Surrey. A brood of fledgling ravens was found in southwest Scotland on New Year's day, while blackbirds were found incubating eggs in January.

Records made on the last few days of January and early February included nest building by heron, dipper, magpie, jackdaw and blue tit, with sightings of mallard, moorhen and mistle thrush with young. Several passerines, owls, pigeons and freshwater aquatic species completed successful nesting attempts. On Salisbury Plain, lapwings began laying about 10 days earlier (15 March) in 1989 than in the three previous years (Pearson, *pers. comm.*). However, there was late snow in March and early April in Scotland, and on some higher ground in England and there were widespread losses among water fowl and waders while rook, dipper, woodlark and others also suffered (Glue, 1989c).

THE 1989/90 WINTER

It would be expected that a mild winter would favour those species traditionally viewed as vulnerable to severely cold weather (Marquiss and Newton, 1990). The populations of grey herons and kingfishers should be higher than usual, as well as those of small insectivorous residents such as wrens, goldcrests and stonechats. Forty-four resident species were monitored between the two breeding seasons, 1989 and 1990, using Common Birds Census techniques (Marchant *et al.* 1991). Seven of these species showed little change between years, 17 showed some increase and a similar number (20) some decrease. However only 5 of these increases, and 7 of the decreases, were statistically significant at the 5% level with no obvious pattern existing that might suggest a mild winter affect. Thus there was no suggestion of a general increase in small bird populations as apparently occurred following the previous winter. Such changes as did occur between 1989 and 1990 seemed more likely to be associated with other factors.

A report on the 1990 breeding season in Scotland (da Prato, 1990) stated that kingfisher, wren, song thrush and stonechat numbers were high (see also Chapter A3.4.4), though no data were given. For the first time in many years, a stonechat was recorded well inland, at high elevation in the Cairngorms (*pers. obs.*). Nest counts at 7 heronries in 1990 showed an average increase of 6% on counts in 1989 (S.C. Bryan, J. Mitchell and *pers. obs.*) suggesting a high overwinter survival. Overwinter survival of sparrowhawks (estimated directly from ringed bird recaptures) was high compared with previous years, but this was probably due to relaxation in the persecution of adults rather than to the mildness of the winter (I. Newton *pers. comm.*).

A large number of seabird carcasses were washed up on beaches in eastern Scotland during the 1989/90 winter, suggesting a high mortality, particularly of razorbills and guillemots (Bourne, 1990). The cause could have been poor foraging due to winter gales or a shortage of small sprat as prey.

An outstanding feature of the winter 1989/90 was the large population of winter thrushes and seed-eating

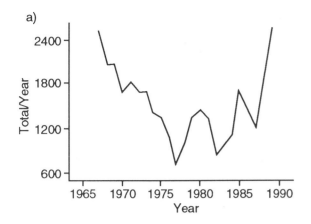

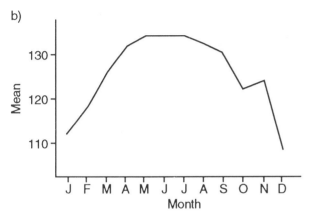

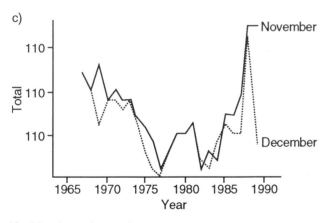

13 Numbers of rat infestations recorded by Ealing District Council 1967–89. (a) Total numbers per year; (b) mean monthly total; (c) numbers recorded in November (——) and December (. . . .) in each year.

finches inland in northern Britain. Fieldfares and red-wings usually arrive there in autumn passing rapidly through to overwinter further south. In 1989, they stayed on in very large flocks feeding on the bumper crop of rowan berries (*pers. obs.*, A Watson, *pers. comm.*). On mild days well into November, they were also observed foraging for invertebrates in grassy fields. By January, the rowans were stripped of berries and the thrushes were gone. Similarly, large flocks of redpolls and siskins fed throughout the winter on the huge crop of birch seed. Feeding at first in the trees then later on the ground, these flocks did not disperse until spring 1990. This was

not so much the effect of the mild winter as of the previous hot dry summer, which promoted seed production. More crossbills bred in Scotland in 1990 than in the previous two springs (R. Rae and E. Duthie, *pers. comm.*, and *pers. obs.*). This, together with an influx of continental immigrants in summer 1990 led, to a peak in the crossbill population.

CONCLUSIONS

In this review of effects on bird populations that could be ascribed to the two mild wet winters, the largely 'anecdotal' evidence suggests that some major changes could have occurred. However, in the absence of published quantitative information, there is only evidence for a significant impact of the mild winters of 1988/89 and 1989/90 on some populations of small insectivorous passerines, and on the timing of the spring arrival and breeding of some wading birds.

A2.2.5 Mammals

RATS

Rat numbers increased during the late 1980s and were the subject of a special report by the Environmental Health Officers in 1989. Numbers remained high in 1990 as reported by Rentokil and by district councils.

Ealing District Council recorded infestations of rats at the end of each month from 1967 (Higgins, *pers. comm.*). The total for each year shows that numbers in 1989 were the highest they had ever been (Figure 13a), and that they had risen sharply in the previous 3 years. The mean totals per month of numbers of infestations of rats (reflecting activity) are normally higher in summer than winter (Figure 13b), but exceptionally high figures were reported in 1989 for November and December, and in 1990 for November (Figure 13c). This indicated that rats were active in these milder winters.

The reasons for fluctuations in rat numbers are complex. Certainly, there was better control in the mid-1970s, reducing numbers to low levels by 1980. The increase in numbers in the 1980s may be attributed to greater food supplies (e.g. litter from takeaways and output from waste disposal units), and the state of sewers, as well as to mild winters and hot summers.

WOOD MICE AND VOLES

The small mammals survey of the Mammal Society (Flowerdew 1989, 1990) showed variable numbers of wood mice and bank voles at different sites, with no national trend (Figure 14). Sites with good acorn crops had large numbers of wood mice, whereas on dry grassland sites numbers of voles and woodmice were low. The dependence of population levels on food supplies and predation would tend to mask effects of the weather.

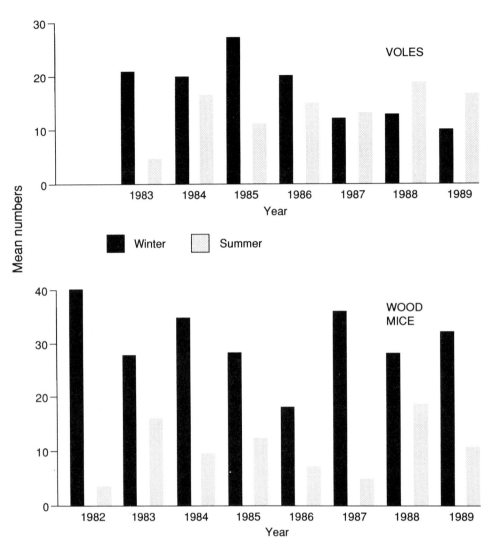

14 Mean catch of bank voles and wood mice trapped in winter (November/December) and summer (May/June) at 10 standard woodland sites recorded by the Mammal Society, National Small Mammal Survey (Flowerdew, 1989; 1990 and pers. comm.).

Observations by Churchfield (*pers. comm.*) of mice and shrew numbers in grassland at Silwood Park, Ascot since 1985 showed no consistent impact of the two mild winters. Numbers of mice and shrews decreased during the winter as normal.

SQUIRRELS

Studies of the population dynamics of red and grey squirrels in deciduous woodlands in southern England since 1982 (Kenward, *pers. comm.*) showed that pre-breeding spring populations were high following good mast crops (tree seed) and cold winters with little snow or rain. The numbers of spring young produced is dependent upon the food supply and lack of rain between January and March. Rainfall from October to December is the most important factor influencing survival of young red and grey squirrels. Unusually good survival of young red squirrels on Furzey Island during 1989 was most probably due to the dry weather in late summer, since food supplies were poorer than in the previous year (Kenward, 1990). The dry weather in 1990 generally promoted survival of young grey squirrels.

DEER
1989/90

During the 1980s, numbers of red deer in Scotland rose from about 30,000 to 45,000. During the winter of 1988/89, natural mortality was very light in eastern Scotland and the Central Highlands. However, in the western Highlands and Islands there were pockets of heavy mortality owing to high winds, driving rain and a period of frost and snow in April when the body condition of the deer is poorest (Staines, *pers. comm.*). The autumn, winter and spring rainfall were anomalously high in northwest Scotland, in contrast to the rest of Britain (see Chapter A1.2). While the wet winter and spring was the primary cause of death, a contributory factor was the inability of the deer to put on sufficient fat reserves in the late summer and autumn of 1988 (McCulloch, 1989). It is interesting that mortality was high in the absence of prolonged snow lie, which is normally related to deaths of red deer (Clutton-Brock and Albon, 1989).

An explosion in numbers of introduced muntjac in parts of eastern England and the Midlands occurred in the late

1980s resulting in severe damage to the natural vegetation. At Monks Wood NNR (Huntingdon) muntjac was first recorded in 1980, but increased extremely rapidly to 1985. Walks at dusk commonly produced counts of 15 animals per hour, and even up to 44 per hour (Cooke, *pers. comm.*). The damage was such that deer were excluded from sensitive areas by electric fencing. These large numbers certainly pre-dated the mild winters at Monks Wood; nevertheless, because this species reproduces for seven months of the year, warmer weather is likely to have improved breeding. Also, mild winters will have increased survival.

HEDGEHOGS

Hedgehogs were seen more commonly in both the 1989 and 1990 mild winters, although in fact their populations were probably lower than previously. More were reported as road casualties than usual during the winters (Wildlife Hospitals Trust, Aylesbury). During the summer of 1989, fewer hedgehogs were counted than usual on a measured length of road, suggesting that numbers were reduced during the winter (P. Morris, *pers. comm.*).

BATS

Bats are especially sensitive to temperature because their long membranous wings have a large heat loss and a large energy requirement. The threshold temperature for flight for some pipistrelle bats is 9°C (Avery, 1984). At this temperature moths, which are an important food, were active and recorded in traps (section A2.2.2) in the winter of 1988/89. Bats are often seen in flight in winter in southern England, but sightings seem to have been unusually frequent in 1988/89 although there are no quantitative data. However, the mild winter probably had little effect on the population ecology, which is greatly influenced by human disturbance (Stebbing and Griffith, 1986).

2.2.6 Conclusions

1. The activities of animals are greatly affected by higher temperatures, whether in winter or summer, and these effects are greater on cold-blooded species like insects, amphibia and reptiles. In the higher winter temperatures insects and other animals were moving about and feeding more actively. The phenology of many species was altered and various life events occurred earlier, especially the temperature dependent developmental/growth events or reproductive behaviour.

2. It is clearly difficult to separate the effects of weather from other factors that determine the abundance of organisms, in the absence of good or long term population data.

   The information received in this chapter includes some long term data together with shorter term experimental evidence and anecdotal observations. The conclusions to be drawn from this information must necessarily be tempered with caution.

3. Some of the best data sets are for pest species such as aphids. The Rothamsted suction trap data showed that aphids were active early in 1989 and 1990. Near record numbers were caught up to 1 July 1989, but numbers caught up to 1 July 1990, although high, were not quite as high as expected, because aphid predator numbers (ladybirds and hoverflies) had built up during 1989/90.

   There was a major outbreak of green spruce aphid in the spring of 1989, but lesser outbreaks in spring 1990. There was also widespread aphid damage on oak, and mite damage on lime.

4. Long term data sets also exist for moths and butterflies. Moths were unusually active in March-April 1989 and 1990. The Rothamsted and ITE light traps recorded some exceptionally early appearances, in some cases for the entire flight period from March to May. The humming bird hawk moth overwintered in the UK in 1989/90. Red admiral and painted lady butterflies, which are normally migratory, overwintered successfully in both 1988/89 and 1989/90. Many butterflies were active during both winters but fewer sightings were made in 1989/90 than during the 1988/89 winter when it was drier.

5. Early appearance of some hibernating species could be deleterious if food reserves are used up before nectar or food plants are available. Species that overwinter as pupae and undergo development before emergence are better indicators of long periods of warm winter temperatures, e.g. speckled wood and orange tip butterflies emerged earlier than normal in Dorset in 1990.

6. The climatic effects on species which have a full range of parasites and predators are normally buffered by corresponding changes in populations of natural enemies. In rapidly reproducing species, such as aphids, populations can outstrip natural enemies temporarily but predator numbers can then build up. In 1988/89, aphid numbers were high but predatory ladybirds also increased and by the winter of 1989/90 hugh populations of ladybirds had built up only to be themselves parasitised later by parasitic wasps.

7. Insects such as bees and wasps were active in the warm weather and slug populations were higher than for about 10 years, owing to 2 mild winters (1987/88 and 1988/89), a wet summer and autumn in 1988, and continued growth of vegetation and crops in the mild 1988/89 winter.

8. The common frog spawned several weeks or months earlier than in previous years in England and southern Scotland. Common toads spawned about 20 days

earlier than normal in Dorset, but the natterjack toad was unaffected.

Reptiles (lizards, snakes etc.) were active during the 2 winters. Sand lizards were adversely affected by cool weather in March, but otherwise there is no evidence that population sizes were affected.

9. There was anecdotal evidence that some major changes could have occurred in bird populations as a result of the mild winter of 1988/89. These changes included the enhanced survival of some species, birds wintering further north than was usual, some birds returning to their breeding grounds earlier than usual and some unseasonal breeding. The best substantiated of these effects involved the enhanced survival of small insectivorous passerines, and early return dates of oystercatchers.

There was no good evidence for substantial effects of mild weather on birds in the 1989/90 winter. The outstanding feature of this winter was the occurrence of large populations of fruit and seed-eating birds in northern Britain, attributed to a bumper crop of berries and seed – an effect of the 1989 hot summer rather than the 1989/90 mild winter.

10. Climatic effects on small mammal populations are normally buffered by changes in predator populations of predators (e.g. owls, hawks, weasels, foxes) and this may account for the lack of consistent evidence for a change in the populations of voles, mice and shrews.

11. Hedgehogs were active during both mild winters which may have been responsible for the increased numbers of road casualties recorded. Bats were also active but populations are unlikely to have been affected by the mild winters due to the overriding influence of human interference.

12. Rat populations were high in 1988/89 and 1989/90 but the mild winter temperatures were only one contributory factor.

13. The population dynamics of larger mammals such as red deer are affected in many ways by climatic variables. In 1988/89, red deer mortality was high in western Scotland because of wet windy weather from autumn 1988 to spring 1989. Muntjac deer in eastern England and the Midlands, on the other hand, benefitted from the long mild breeding season and absence of severe winters and reached pest proportions in some woodlands.

APPENDIX

Number of days difference in flowering and leafing dates between (1) long-term means and 1989 (2) long-term means and 1990 (3) 1989 and 1990. Negative values indicate earlier days, positive values indicate later days.

	Furzebrook			Monks Wood			Bangor			Merlewood			Edinburgh			Banchory		
	1	2	3	1	2	3	1	2	3	1	2	3	1	2	3	1	2	3
Hazel		−20		−3	−17	−14	−4	28	32	−10	−18	−8	20	12	−8		−49	
Coltsfoot				−18	−25	−7	−15	2	−18	−20	5	25	8	3	−5	4	5	−9
Lesser celandine	−27	−7	20	−1	1	2	−17	1	18	−22	5	27	5	3	−2	−24	−18	6
Wood anemone	−23	0	23	−11	−7	4		−15		8	16	8	−5	−19	−14	2	−5	−7
Horse chestnut 1f	−27	−38	−11	−13			−34	−24	10	−26	−21	5	−12	−13	−1	−39	−37	2
Blackthorn	−4	−19	−15	−19	−29	−10	−18	−13	5	−45	−36	9				−95	−45	50
Sycamore 1f			1			−12			9			3			−15			−11
Garlic mustard	−12	−16	4	−8	−16	−8	5	−22	−27	3	0	−3	13			0	−6	−6
Oak 1f			−4			−19			−7			−3			−8			−4
Beech 1f			−13			−4			−5			−4			−4			−8
Hawthorn	0	−9	−9	−2	−28	−26	−8	−12	−4	−2	−11	−9	0	−9	−9	−9	−23	−14
Ash 1f			−8			18			7			−9			−8			0
Horse chestnut	0	−2	−2	−6	−5	1	0	−6	−6	−11	−11	0	5	−4	−9	−10	−29	−19
Lilac	3	−5	−8	−1	−11	−10	5	−4	−9	0	−7	−7				−10	−29	−19
Laburnum	2	−5	−7	2	−7	−9	0	0	0	5	0	−5	17	4	−13	−9	−17	−8
Rowan			4			−8						−7			−5			−11
Ox−eye daisy	−7	−20	−13	−15	−26	−11	−18	−14	4	−12	−13	−1	13	−5	−18	0	6	6
Elder	−14	−29	−15	−8	−17	−9	−22	−24	−2	−7	−11	−4	−1	−8	−7	−13	−19	−6
Dog rose				−11	−23	−12	−1	−12	−11	−5	−11	−6	32	−13	−45	−5	−20	−15
Harebell				13			8	3	−5	−11	−10	1				5	15	10
Lesser Knapweed					19		−19	10	29	9	18	9				3	12	9
Hedge bindweed				−11	−12	−1	20	−4	−24	−5	−6	−1	4	−11	−15			

Chapter A3
Impacts on Freshwater Systems

A3.1 INTRODUCTION

In this chapter, the impact of the mild winter of 1988/89 and the warm wet winter of 1989/90 on freshwater ecosystems in the UK is assessed with particular reference to the effects of temperature. The effects on river flows and water supply are considered in the hydrology section in Chapter A1.2. This chapter has largely been compiled from published sources and from material prepared by colleagues within the Institute of Freshwater Ecology. The chapter is divided into three sections covering the physical, chemical and biological aspects of the mild winters. The physical section includes data from several sites in the UK, whereas the biological section is largely based on long-term studies in the English Lake District.

A3.2 PHYSICAL ASPECTS

Year to year variations in winter temperature can influence both the survival and growth of freshwater organisms. River temperatures respond in a direct way to changing air temperatures (Smith, 1981). Lake temperatures reflect the combined effects of air temperature, solar heating and wind-induced mixing and, at some sites, the incidence of surface ice and snow.

3.2.1 River temperatures

The processes influencing the transfer of heat into river systems are many and varied, but air temperature is usually the major controlling factor. Crisp and Howson (1982) showed that the average water temperature in streams of varying size could be directly related to the average air temperature. At most sites, the relationship between the average air and water temperatures remained linear from −5 to +15°C (Figure 1a). In some high altitude streams, however, the relationship between the average air and water temperature became non-linear when the air temperature fell below zero (Figure 1b). Crisp (1988) excluded these sub-zero observations from his linear prediction equations and assumed that the rivers would then have been frozen over.

In Figure 2, the predictive equations derived by Crisp (1988) have been used to reconstruct a twenty year "winter temperature" record for the River Tees at Tees Bridge and the River Tyne below Kielder Reservoir. Figure 2 also shows the predicted winter temperatures for Black Beck in Cumbria (Crisp & Howson, 1982) and the measured winter temperatures for the River Frome in Dorset (Dawson personal communication). In all cases the "winter temperature" is the average for January,

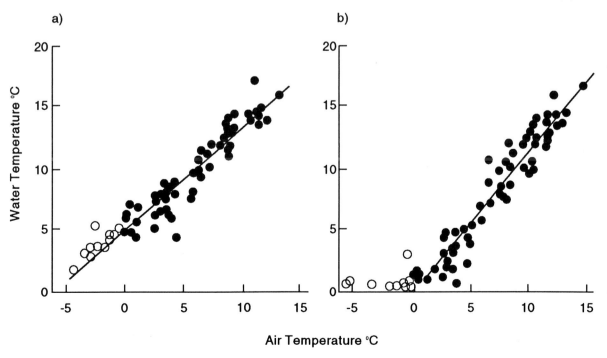

1   Plots of 5-day mean water temperatures against 5-day mean air temperatures for (a) Black Brows Beck in Cumbria and (b) Mattergill Sike in the Pennines. (From Crisp and Howson, 1982).

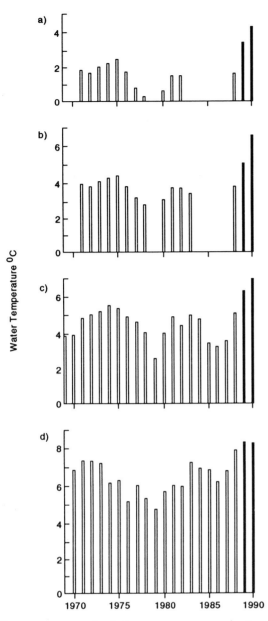

2 Twenty year records of winter water temperatures in (a) the River Tees, (b) the River Tyne, (c) Black Brows Beck, and (d) the River Frome. The plotted temperatures are the average of daily readings in January, February and March.

February and March. This differs from the definition of the "short" winter in Chapter A1.1, but water temperatures are invariably a lagged function of average air temperatures. At all four sites, the water temperatures in 1988/1989 and 1989/90 were the highest in the series. The deviation from the twenty year average was greatest on the Tees (+3 to +4°C) and least on the Frome (+ 1.3°C). The Tees is a surface fed river in the northeast of England where air temperature anomalies of +3.0°C and +2.0°C were recorded in the winters of 1988/1989 and 1989/90 respectively (see Chapter A1.1). The Frome is a partly spring fed river in Dorset where the air temperature anomaly in 1989 was less than 2.5°C.

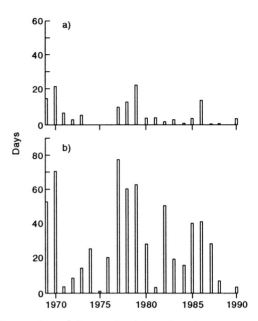

3 The number of days each winter when there was some ice cover on: (a) Windermere, Cumbria; and (b) Loch Leven, Fife.

3.2.2 Lake ice cover

Kuusisto (1989) suggested that changes in lake ice at high latitudes could well provide the first unambiguous evidence of global warming. In Figure 3 the daily record of ice cover from Windermere, Cumbria and Loch Leven, Fife are compared. Windermere (Figure 3a) is a deep lake that seldom freezes over in winter but some ice usually forms in the more sheltered bays. No significant ice cover was reported in 1988/89 nor 1989/90 but the mild winters of 1974, 1975 and 1976 were also reported as ice free. Loch Leven (Figure 3b) is a shallow lake that invariably freezes in winter. The twenty year record shows that this loch was free of ice in 1988/89 but froze for four days in 1989/90.

The timing and extent of winter ice cover can influence the pattern of phytoplankton succession much later in the year (Lund, 1959, Mathews & Heaney, 1987). Motile flagellates tend to dominate the phytoplankton under ice. Some non-motile species, such as *Asterionella*, can also grow under ice, but others, such as *Melosira*, sink out of the low turbulence water column. Long-term observations in Windermere suggest that individual ice-free winters have little effect on the phytoplankton, but that a succession of such winters could produce a shift in species composition.

3.2.3 Lake water temperature

Daily temperature readings have been taken in the North Basin of Windermere since the early 1940's. Air temperature records are also available from a meteorological station only a short distance from the lake. Such long term records provide a unique resource that can be used to assess the significance of extreme events. In Figure 4, the average air and water temperatures recorded during

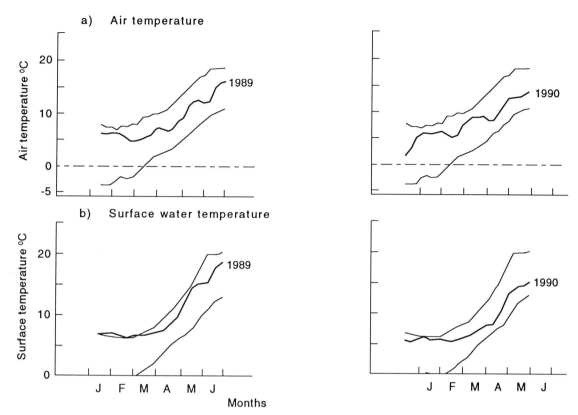

a) Air temperature

b) Surface water temperature

Months

4 The long-term trend in (a) air, and (b) surface temperatures at Windermere in 1989 and 1990 compared with the range recorded between 1943 and 1987. All values were smoothed with a three point, centre weighted running average.

the first half of 1989 and 1990 are compared with the ranges recorded between 1943 and 1987. (1988 was deliberately excluded from the historical series since this year was also exceptionally mild.) The air temperatures recorded in the first six months of 1989 and 1990 all fell within the historical range (Figure 4a). However the water temperatures recorded over the same period were unusually high (Figure 4b). The most pronounced deviations were recorded in January and February 1989 when the weekly measurements all fell outside the forty-four year range.

A3.3 CHEMICAL ASPECTS

3.3.1 The influence of road salt on water chemistry

The concentration of most ions in surface waters is determined by the inputs in rain and the type of rocks and soils in the catchment. The concentration of sodium and chloride can, however, also be influenced by the leaching of de-icing salt used on the roads. Sutcliffe & Carrick (1983a) analysed the various sources of sodium and chloride in Cumbria and found that some streams and lakes received large quantities of road salt. In the Borrowdale region, headwater streams that do not receive drainage from roads have a mean sodium concentration of 124 μ equivs 1^{-1} (range 86–189) and a mean chloride concentration of 129 μ equivs 1^{-1} (range 79–204). Headwater streams that receive drainage from mountain

roads gave average sodium concentrations of 1153 μ equivs 1^{-1} and average chloride concentrations of 1198 μ equivs 1^{-1}. Most of the salt washed down the streams eventually finds its way into the larger lakes. In the south basin of Windermere, Sutcliffe & Carrick (1983b) estimated that the use of road salt resulted in a 27% increase in the concentration of chloride over a twenty year period. The average concentration of sodium and chloride in these waters is still well below the upper limit recommended for drinking water and the maximum levels are unlikely to have a deleterious effect on the fauna. However high levels could form a potentially damaging "reservoir" of salt in the soil if heavy road salting were to continue.

In the winter of 1981–1982 ca 2000 tonnes of salt were applied to the roads in Cumbria. By contract in 1988/89 only 25 tonnes was removed from store (and much of this salt was left stockpiled by the roadside), and similarly small amounts were used in 1989/90. Thus, mild winters are likely to reduce sodium chloride levels in freshwaters.

3.3.2 The winter concentration of nitrate in rivers and lakes

In recent years, there has been a steady increase in the concentration of nitrates in many of our rivers and lakes. Much of this increase is due to the increased use of nitrogenous fertilisers, but there is also a significant input

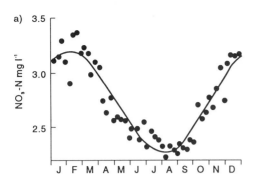

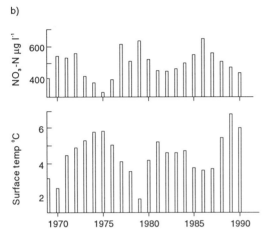

5 (a) Means of weekly nitrate concentrations in the River Frome plotted against time of year for the period 1965–1975. From Casey and Clarke, 1979.

(b) The twenty year trend in winter nitrate levels and water temperatures in Windermere.

from domestic drainage. Nitrate concentrations are always much higher in winter than in summer, but the seasonal pattern of change is also influenced by short term changes in the weather. Casey & Clarke (1979) used a simple periodic model to describe the average seasonal variation in the concentration of nitrates in a southern chalk stream. The weekly mean nitrate concentrations (Figure 5a) peaked in early February and followed a cosine wave that was strongly correlated with the mean weekly discharge. The seasonal nitrate concentrations were, however, less closely correlated with discharge, and the cosine model produced poor predictions when the summer was unusually dry. In 1976, low river flows and high water temperatures gave rise to very low summer concentrations of nitrate but very high winter concentrations were recorded when it finally rained in the autumn. 1989 was also exceptionally dry in the southwest but summer nitrate concentrations were higher than in 1976 and proportionately less nitrate was leached from the catchment in the winter of 1989/90. The release of nitrate from the catchment is, however, influenced by the temperature as well as the rainfall.

The concentration of nitrates in most lakes and reservoirs is strongly influenced by weather related changes in the rate of leaching from the catchment. In Windermere, the highest concentrations of nitrate are typically recorded in

cold winters. When winters are mild, microbial processes in the soil tend to recycle much of the nitrate before it reaches the main drainage channels. The time series in Figure 5b shows that winter nitrate levels in 1989 and 1990 were relatively low, despite recent increases in the amount of nitrogenous fertilisers applied to pastures in the catchment.

A3.4 BIOLOGICAL ASPECTS

3.4.1 Lake phytoplankton

Increases in winter temperature can, theoretically, hasten the spring growth of phytoplankton and influence the pattern of succession later in the year. In many lakes, however, factors such as washout and changes in the underwater light climate have such a pronounced effect on the growth of phytoplankton that the direct effects of temperature are of little practical significance.

For many slow growing species, the size of the overwintering population is determined partly by the population density at the end of the growing season and partly by losses due to winter washout (Canter et al. 1990). In 1989, the winter in the northwest was wetter than average (Chapter A1.2), but the increased flushing rate appears to have had little effect on the dynamics of the phytoplankton. The situation in the dry southeast of England may, however, have been very different. With the reorganisation of the water industry, individual authorities were reluctant to release any biological records. It is suspected, however, that "bloom" conditions may have been encountered much earlier in the year in 1989 in some shallow reservoirs. In shallow lakes, the spring growth of diatoms is strongly influenced by increases in temperature and variations in flow-through. Spring diatom maxima, normally recorded in March, could have appeared as early as February because the winter was both warm and dry.

Temperature and dilution effects are much less obvious in deep valley lakes like those in the English Lake District. In these lakes, winter phytoplankton growth is regulated primarily by daylength and by the response of phytoplankton to wind-induced mixing. A critical factor is the proportion of illuminated and "dark" water in the mixed water column. Phytoplankton suspended in "dark" water cannot grow because their respiratory losses are greater than their gross photosynthesis. When they are physically transported into "light" water, (the euphotic zone) this balance is redressed and their "average" growth rate is then related to the intensity of wind mixing. Figure 6a shows the typical limits of "light" and "dark" water in four English lakes in the month of April (Talling, 1971). The general trend is towards a larger ratio of total lake volume to euphotic zone volume in the deeper basins, the morphometric/mixing factor clearly being far more important in the deep basins of Windermere than in the relatively shallow waters of Esthwaite and Blelham. Figure 6b shows the effect of the morphometric/mixing

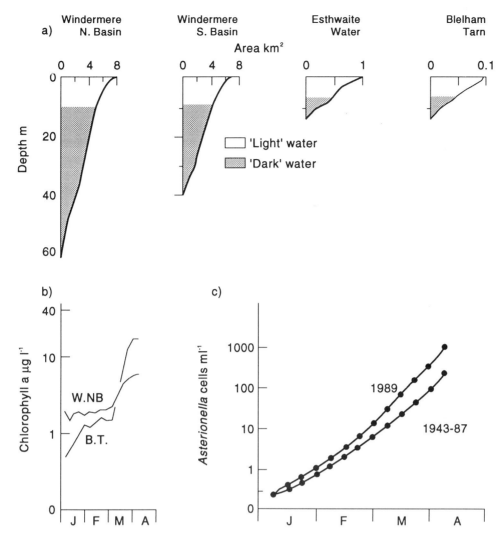

a) Windermere N. Basin, Windermere S. Basin, Esthwaite Water, Blelham Tarn — Area km²

Depth m

'Light' water
'Dark' water

b) Chlorophyll a µg l⁻¹

W.NB

B.T.

J F M A

c) *Asterionella* cells ml⁻¹

1989

1943-87

J F M A

6 (a) Typical limits of "light" and "dark" water in four lakes of different depths in April, showing the morphometric/mixing factor.

(b) The spring increase in chlorophyll in a relatively shallow lake (Blelham Tarn), and a deep lake (the North Basin of Windermere).

(c) Growth simulations of the diatom *Asterionella* in Windermere. The lower curve shows the predicted growth in an "average" year, the higher curve the predicted growth in 1989 (Figures (a) and (b) are taken from Talling, 1971).

factor on the growth of phytoplankton in the South Basin of Windermere and Blelham Tarn (Talling, 1971). At the time of sampling, the average temperature in the two basins was practically identical but the phytoplankton grew very much faster in the shallower lake.

In Figure 6c a simple simulation model has been used to quantify the effects of temperature on the growth of *Asterionella* in Windermere during the first three months of 1989. The input variables to the model are temperature, day-length, mixed depth and a series of species specific variables that describe the organisms photosynthetic behaviour (Reynolds, 1989). The two curves show the predicted growth of *Asterionella* in Windermere in an "average" year and in 1989. The spring growth of *Asterionella* was slightly faster in 1989, but the final crop densities only differed by a factor of two after three months of active cell division.

3.4.2 Aquatic invertebrates

Temperature and food are considered to be two of the most important factors controlling the abundance of aquatic invertebrates. Temperature frequently controls growth and hatching rates, while the availability of food affects the fertility of females and the survival of their offspring. In nature, it is often difficult to distinguish between the direct effect of low temperature and the indirect effect of insufficient food. Laboratory experiments with well fed populations can, however, be used to highlight the temperature component in population growth.

Populations of the water flea *Daphnia* are often used as "model" invertebrates. The animals reproduce asexually, carry their eggs in brood pouches, and the time taken for the eggs to develop is largely a function of temperature.

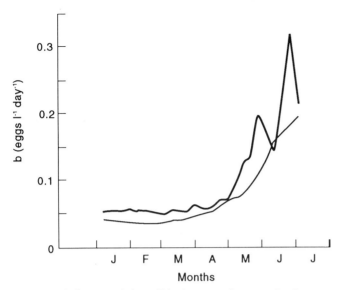

7   The influence of the mild winter on the reproductive rate of *Daphnia*. The lower curve shows the standardised birth rate in an "average" year (see George *et al.*, 1990). The upper curve shows the predicted birth rate in Windermere during the first six months of 1989.

Edmondson (1960) developed a single egg ratio model to describe the temperature dependent birth rate of *Daphnia*. In Figure 7, this technique was used to quantify the effect of the mild winter on the growth and development of a hypothetical *Daphnia* population. The thin line shows the change in the birth rate expected in an "average" year, and the heavier line shows the predicted changes in 1989. It is clear that the quite substantial difference in winter temperature between an average year and 1989 (Figure 5b) had relatively little effect on the reproductive potential of the *Daphnia* population. Such a response is typical of many aquatic invertebrates and reflects the fact that their rate of development is an inverse linear function of temperature (Edmondson & Windberg, 1971). The fluctuations in the 1989 curve also show that some of the "gains" in January and February were later "lost" in May and June.

3.4.3 Freshwater fish

Different species of fish have very different thermal responses (Elliott, 1981), and there are lower as well as upper temperature limits for feeding and growth. Many species lay their eggs in the colder months of the year, so that an increase in winter temperatures can potentially bring about a significant change in their annual pattern of reproduction.

The most temperature sensitive fish in the UK are the whitefish (*Coregonus* sp.) and charr (*Salvelinus alpinus*). Both have an upper thermal limit of 8°C for their egg stage, so would not have been adversely affected by the 2–3° rise in winter lake temperature in 1988/89 and 1989/90. The high winter temperatures may, of course, have influenced their subsequent development rate, but no growth rate data are yet available for whitefish populations in the UK.

Brown trout (*Salmo trutta*) usually lay their eggs in November and the young fish hatch in February and March. No field comparisons are yet available for 1989, but Weatherly & Ormerod (pers. comm.) have been able to estimate some hatching and emergence dates for their trout populations in south Wales. The models used were those developed by Elliott (1975) and Crisp (1981, 1988b). The driving variables were the winter/spring temperatures recorded in 1985/86, 1986/87 and 1988/89 at a series of sites in south Wales. The wet weight on emergence from the gravel was assumed to be 0.17g and the simulations were run for two fertilisation dates (1 November and 1 December).

Table 1 summarises the results of these simulations at one station in the upper Tywi. Hatching dates were forty days earlier in 1989 than in 1986 and 1987. Emergence dates were also forty days earlier in 1989 and the growth simulations suggest that this could have resulted in a two-fold weight gain by the end of May.

These models are, however, simplistic and do not take account of all the temperature related factors that influence the growth and survival of trout. Trout eggs that develop in warmer water typically produce small fry that are then less likely to survive short periods of starvation. Mild winters may well encourage early emergence, but cold periods in the spring can check both the feeding rate and the growth rate of the young fish.

In many river systems, early emergence coupled with rapid growth can greatly enhance recruitment if other conditions are favourable. However, some trout populations are regulated by internal rather than external factors. For example Elliott (1985, 1989, 1992) was able to show that the annual recruitment of trout in a Cumbrian stream

Table 1:   Simulated hatching and emergence dates for brown trout in a south Wales stream. In each case, the simulated weight on 31 May is given.

Fertilization date	Hatch date	Emergence date	Wet weight (g)
1.11.85	28.1.86	1.5.86	0.28
1.11.86	21.1.87	13.4.87	0.43
1.11.88	15.1.89	18.3.89	0.53
1.12.85	21.3.86	24.5.86	0.20
1.12.86	17.3.87	9.5.86	0.27
1.12.88	15.2.89	20.4.89	0.42

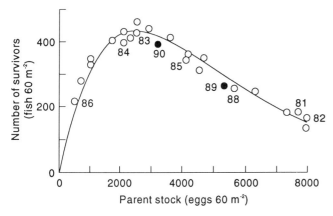

8 Survival of juvenile sea trout in a Lake District stream between 1966 and 1990. The curve shows the strong "density dependent" relationship between the number of survivors and parent stock (number of eggs), apparently unaffected by the mild temperatures in 1989 and 1990.

Table 2: The mean catch per hour of ringing effort of Welsh river birds (1986–1989). The values are based on 84–117 visits per year, and are presented ± standard error.

| Year | SPECIES | | |
	Kingfisher	Grey wagtail	Dipper
1986	0.11 ± 0.03	0.18 ± 0.05	1.57 ± 0.20
1987	0.32 ± 0.08	0.22 ± 0.06	2.29 ± 0.28
1988	0.36 ± 0.08	0.15 ± 0.06	1.18 ± 0.15
1989	0.87 ± 0.17	0.59 ± 0.14	1.10 ± 0.16
1990	0.77 ± 0.14	0.12 ± 0.06	1.16 ± 0.19
1991	0.32 ± 0.10	0.11 ± 0.06	1.05 ± 0.20

was primarily related to the parent stock (number of eggs) and not to any year-to-year changes in the weather. This density dependent relationship can be illustrated graphically by means of a two parameter Ricker curve (Ricker, 1954). Figure 8 shows the Ricker curve drawn by Elliot (1992) for the survival of sea trout fry in Black Brows Beck, Cumbria. The mild winters of 1989 and 1990 appear to have had little effect on the survival of fry in this low-lying stream (but winter spates can have a serious effect on trout recruitment in some upland streams).

3.4.4 River birds

Several species of river birds are clearly dependent on rivers for food (Ormerod & Tyler, 1987a). In Wales, the breeding performance of the Dipper (*Cinclus cinclus*) and Grey Wagtail (*Motacilla cinerea*) has been monitored in some detail since 1978 and the densities and age structures of these species together with those of the Kingfisher (*Alcedo atthis*) have been assessed every autumn since

1986 using standardised ringing on the basis of "catch-per-unit-effort". This index gives a good indication of population size (see Ormerod *et al.* 1988).

The median date of egg laying by Grey Wagtail is closely correlated with the mean air temperature in March (Ormerod & Tyler, 1987b). In 1989, the median laying date was day number 118, (April 29), but equally early egg laying has been recorded three times in the past 11 years (range of medians, 106–132).

Year-to-year survival in both Grey Wagtails and King-fishers is strongly influenced by the severity of winter conditions. Table 2 shows the result of recent censuses in south Wales (Ormerod *pers. comm.*). The number of Kingfishers increased markedly following the mild winters of 1988/89 and 1989/90. The number of Wagtails also increased in 1989 but fell off again in 1990 and 1991. Dipper numbers declined following both wet (1988) and very dry summers (1989, 1990). Thus mild winters favoured the Kingfisher and Grey Wagtail (see Chapter A2.2.4), but the two consecutive dry summers of 1989 and 1990 seem to have adversely affected the numbers of Grey Wagtail and Dipper.

A3.5 CONCLUSIONS

1. During the winters of 1988/89 and 1989/90, water temperatures were about 2°C higher than average, and many lakes and rivers that normally freeze were ice-free throughout the winter.

2. We may presume that there were smaller inputs than normal of salt from roads, and in some cases, relatively low winter nitrate levels.

3. Populations of phytoplankton were probably little affected by the increase in temperature *per se* being more affected by periods of heavy rain in shallow lakes, and by the timing and intensity of wind mixing in deep lakes.

4. A population model of *Daphnia* suggested that the warm winter temperature in 1988/89 and 1989/90 probably had little effect on numbers of many freshwater invertebrates.

5. The mild winters led to earlier hatching and emergence of fish such as Brown trout, but the mild temperatures probably had little effect on fish numbers, which are regulated by other factors such as egg numbers.

6. The survival of some river birds was favoured by mild winter temperature, but they suffered during the summer droughts.

Chapter A4
Impacts on Agriculture and Horticulture

A4.1 INTRODUCTION

This chapter provides a general overview of the effects of two mild winters on agriculture (main arable crops, grassland and livestock) and horticulture in the United Kingdom. The chapter contains sections on individual crops, livestock, pests and disease based on extensive discussions with farmers, research scientists, and university and college staff, as well as on reviews on contemporary reports in the farming press.

General aspects of the impact of the mild winter on pests and weeds are discussed first because they influenced so many of the cropping and livestock activities reviewed later. The effects of sharp frosts which occurred in March and April 1990 are also described (4.6).

A4.2 PESTS

4.2.1 Birds

There is evidence to suggest that during the two mild winters, more bird pests than usual survived. However, because adequate natural food supplies were available throughout the winter, crops did not suffer as much bird damage as in a severe winter, and in 1988/89 pigeon damage was generally less than normal. In contrast, rooks were a nuisance in autumn-sown crops late in 1988. In the Midlands especially, rooks were reported to be pulling up cereal plants in a search for soil-living organisms such as leather-jackets (ADAS).

In 1990, widespread pigeon and/or crow damage was reported to arable crops during the winter and spring. This may have been due to a high population of birds, but may also have occurred because several spring (1990) sown crops exhibited poor emergence due to dry soils.

4.2.2 Rodents

In 1989 and 1990, there were widespread reports of damage due to rodents. This may have indicated a lack of winter kill, both of the animals and of their food supplies. However, mild conditions may have stimulated activity, which could partially account for more sightings even if populations did not increase.

Many growers reported unusually large amounts of damage to emergent crops by mice. Sugar beet and legume crops were especially affected. There are conflicting reports as to whether the lack of winter kill caused an increase in the rabbit population, as the number of rabbits had been increasing for some time (MAFF).

4.2.3 Slugs

The mild winter temperatures meant that crops were advanced and presented a good food supply to slugs, which continued feeding throughout the winter. Soft fruit and vegetable crops particularly suffered. However, slug damage in winter 1989/90 (drier) was less than that in winter 1988/89 (wetter) when damage was so severe in newly emergent crops that resowing was necessary in some fields (see Chapter A2.2.2).

4.2.4 Aphids

Weather conditions over the mild winter 1988/89 and the following spring were conducive to the overwintering of aphids (see Chapter A2.2.2) (and their host plants), and consequently encouraged early activity. For example, large numbers of blackfly eggs overwintered in 1988/89 on spindle trees, contributing to the largest blackfly population for 10 years (Big Farm Weekly 8 June 1989).

Aphids are vectors of viruses, in particular those affecting cereals (Barley Yellow Disease Virus), sugar beet (Virus Yellows) and potatoes. Overwintering and the early build up of large numbers of active aphids due to the mild temperatures meant that aphid-borne diseases were transmitted early in 1989. Generally, young immature plants are more susceptible to virus disease attack than are older more mature plants. Autumn-sown crops, which were more advanced in their growth than normal, therefore suffered less damage than did spring-sown crops. However infected autumn-sown crops provided a pool of innoculum for the infection of spring-sown crops. Often, spring-sown crops were also under stress from drought, and, where infection was not prevented by the use of aphicidal sprays, the characteristic chlorotic symptoms later became evident. Despite control with aphicides, aphid numbers were so high in the spring 1989 that fresh waves quickly established themselves between sprays. The unusually large numbers of aphids also posed direct threats to crop plants via feeding damage and sheer weight. These new threats warranted the use of aphicides after plants had reached the growth stage where it was no longer considered worthwhile to spray against virus infection.

With so much demand for aphicides, some agrochemicals were frequently sold out, and farmers used what they could get when they could get it (whether or not it was ideal for the biological system). Consequently it is possible that the wide usage of aphicides in 1989 has added to the development of resistant biotypes. This would mean that future aphid control could be less successful and that crops losses due to aphid-transmitted diseases could be greater.

Aphids were again present on most crops throughout the autumn and winter 1989/90. Observations (courtesy of A Mills) at Gleadthorpe EHF showed that 2.5 times as many aphids were present in a winter barley crop at the end of October 1989 (25 per plant) than at the same time in 1988 (10 per plant).

Despite an abundance of host plant material which overwintered in 1989/90, aphid numbers were lower in 1990 than in 1989. The mild winter may have allowed a greater level of activity of predators/pathogens, and may have facilitated the build up of an unusually active complex of different predators.

Aphid numbers were also reduced over the 1989/90 winter during periods of unsettled weather, and especially in the gales of December-February. Aphids find it difficult to cling on to host plants in wet and windy weather and are easily drowned. Because of potentially high aphid numbers in the summer, farmers were strongly advised to destroy old fodder beet clamps to lessen the number of "safe" environments for aphids over the winter. The occasional frosts, particularly the sharp frosts in March and April probably further curtailed the reproductive activity/numbers of aphids.

A4.3 WEEDS

Weeds responded in various ways to the mild winters. Germination was early and often continued throughout both winters; a large percentage of weed seedlings survived and weeds grew vigorously competing with crop plants. In contrast, some early-sown winter cereals and oil seed rape were so far advanced that they out-competed the weed species, and herbicide usage was lower than in previous years. Weeds, and more importantly, volunteers (i.e. plants germinating from seed left from a previous crop), acted as "green bridges", allowing the carry-over of pathogens from the previous season. In the 1988 season, there was considerable disease, particularly cereal rust, and, due to the 1988/89 mild winter, large numbers of pathogens survived on the volunteer hosts, from which they moved to infect more recently sown crops.

In the 1989/90 winter, as in that of 1988/89, the size of weeds and the lack of frost meant that weeds were difficult to kill. Because crop plants sown in the mild winter exhibited lush growth, there was some danger of them being scorched by herbicide applications, and care was required over the timing and mixing of herbicides. Also, due to the rapid development of weeds through herbicide susceptible stages, the "window of application" was narrow. Many herbicides "weaken" weeds and the final kill is made by frost. It is possible that weeds which survived the initial herbicide application developed some degree of resistance to subsequent applications. The mild winter, and consequent higher than usual soil temperatures,

may have resulted in some weed species, especially black-grass and wild oats, germinating from greater soil depths than usual. It is also possible that the rate of degradation of systemic herbicides in the soil was increased at higher temperatures, making them less effective and reducing the duration of their activity (ADAS).

A4.4 EFFECTS ON AGRICULTURAL CROPS

4.4.1 Cereals

Mild conditions over the 1988/89 winter had a profound impact on cereal crops. The primary effect was the unusually early growth and development of autumn-sown cereals. The timing of crop management practises, such as the application of fertiliser and growth regulators had to be altered. Experimental evidence from Newcastle University suggested that the application of early nitrogen to winter barley increased the risk of eyespot and other stem based diseases in 1989 (Murphy, unpublished data). There were few reports of crops suffering from nitrogen deficiency, possible because: (i) the mild winter tempera-tures increased rates of N mineralisation, and (ii) the absence of heavy rainfall early in the year reduced leaching of nutrients. ADAS recommended that cereal crops, following high residue crops on light and chalky soils, required 25 kg/ha less nitrogen fertiliser than normal in spring 1989. However, the rapid rate of plant growth resulted in susceptible soils becoming depleted of manga-nese earlier and to a greater extent than usual (ADAS).

Vigorous crop growth warranted the widespread use of growth regulators to prevent lodging later in the season. Growth regulators were applied to more cereal crops in 1989 than in 1988. In some cases, crop development was so far advanced that the point at which normal growth regulator application ceases to be effective had passed before there were opportunities for action; in these instances alternative regulators which could be applied later were used. In general, however, the frequency of lodging was low, partly because of dry, still weather in late spring and summer.

A secondary effect of the mild winter was the survival of large numbers of pests and diseases which would normally be controlled by winter cold kill. Severe damage was sustained by some crops, especially from mildews, which thrived during the mild winter, yellow rust, which overwintered on host cereal volunteers, and barley yellow dwarf virus (BYDV) which is transmitted by an aphid vector (see Appendix).

In some cases, the vigorous growth of autumn sown crops actually helped to reduce damage from pests and diseases. For example, attack by cereal bulb fly, which can cause considerable damage in young cereal crops, was minimal in 1989, probably because crops were able to "grow away" and recover rapidly from injury (ADAS). Such benefits of early growth were not the case with spring-sown

Table 4.1: Development of winter wheat, cv Avalon in four growing seasons near Newcastle-upon-Tyne.

Season	Sowing Date	No of days to terminal spikelet	No of days to flag leaf emergence
1985/86	28 October	202	231
1986/87	28 October	184	219
1987/88	4 November	176	211
1988/89	18 November	153	188

Table 4.2: Growth and development of two cultivatars of winter barley in 1987/88 and 1988/89 near Newcastle upon Tyne. Sowing dates were 28 September 1987 and 18 September 1988, and the measurements were made in January each year.

	SEASON			
	1987/88		1988/89	
Cultivar	Magie	Marinka	Magie	Marinka
Dry matter (g m^{-2})	19.5	20.7	40.8	41.4
Shoot density (m^{-2})	730	1020	1150	1440
Number of leaves on main stem	4.1	4.6	6.1	6.7

cereals, which is some areas did not have a good start, and were especially susceptible to yellow rust, brown rust and BYDV. Because of the mild winter, spring seed beds were sometimes of poor quality and emerging crops were often stressed by lack of available soil moisture, especially in the South West. The poor condition of many spring-sown cereal crops also meant that they were particularly susceptible to diseases introduced to them from winter cereals. However, on heavier soils where droughting was not such a great problem and where disease control had been effective, spring cereals performed well.

WINTER WHEAT

Germination and pre-emergent development depend on sowing date and temperature (Walker and Hay 1989). Temperatures late in 1988, when winter cereals were sown, were not so mild as to inhibit vernalization (the requirement for a period of cold exposure to trigger developmental phases), and so development was not seriously disrupted. Germination and emergence in autumn 1988 were reported by some farmers to be typically about one week earlier than normal. The percentage of seed which germinated was also reported to be good, although some fields suffered damage from mice, birds and slugs (see 4.2). Post-emergent development is very much influenced by temperature, and early growth is largely controlled by available soil water and nutrients. At the beginning of the growing season (i.e. late 1988/early 1989) water and nutrients were not considered to be limiting, and the rapid early development was largely attributed to relatively high temperatures. Post-emergent plants were usually vigorous, and formed dense, well-tillered crops. In early sown crops, the early growth stages (up to about Growth Stage 32, second node detectable), were generally found to be between two and four weeks earlier than usual. Later on in the season the advance in development was less pronounced. This was considered to result from a combination of the photoperiodic control of further reproductive development and below-average temperatures in parts of March and April. By the time of anthesis, crops were only approximately one week to ten days more advanced than usual. Table 4.1 illustrates these points, comparing the development of winter wheat, cv. Avalon, in 1988/89 with that at the same site in the three previous seasons (courtesy of D. Murphy, unpublished data, University of Newcastle).

High post-anthesis temperatures resulted in rapid grain-filling and ripening in 1989. In most areas the high light intensities and temperatures over the ripening period in the summer were ideal. In crops which were free of disease and drought, yields in summer 1989 were good, even with early harvesting.

WINTER BARLEY

As with winter wheat, the rate of growth and development of winter barley was advanced in 1988/89 and much which has already been stated regarding wheat also applies to barley.

An example of forward growth in the early part of the winter in 1988/89 compared with 1987/88 is shown in Table 4.2 for the two cultivars Magie and Marinka (unpublished data, courtesy of D Murphy, University of Newcastle). Plant material was analysed in January.

The relatively rapid rate of leaf emergence observed in 1988/89 may be attributable not only to the mild temperatures, but also to the above-average hours of sunshine.

In Table 4.3 the extent of forward growth in the later part of the winter and spring for the cultivar Igri at Sutton Bonington is shown (unpublished data, courtesy of C.K. Baker, University of Nottingham). In spite of the later sowing date in 1988, plants in spring 1989 were almost twice the size of plants at the same time in spring 1988.

As with winter wheat, the timing of flowering depends on accumulated thermal time *and* photoperiod, and so the rate of early vegetative development was not maintained into the flowering stage. In Scotland, a large range of growth stages was reported at any one time in the crop. At the end of February barleys ranged from between six leaves (just tillering) to third node stage. It appeared that only a proportion of the crops continued to develop in the mild winter, probably owing to site microclimatic differences.

The final harvesting dates for winter barley were about 7–10 ten days early, although in East Anglia some crops

Table 4.3: Dry weight of winter barley, cv Igri, in 1987/88 and 1988/89 at Sutton Bonington, Nottinghamshire. In 1987, sowing was on 25 September and emergence on 12 October; equivalent dates in 1988 were 15 October and 24 October.

1988 Date of sample	3 February	9 March	11 April
Dry weight (mg plant^{-1})	191	248	640
1989 Date of sample	8 February	21 March	17 April
Dry weight (mg plant^{-1})	222	446	1020

Table 4.4: Dates of developmental stages in two cultivars of winter bean (*Vicia faba* L.) in 1987/88 and 1988/89 at Sutton Bonington, Nottinghamshire.

Cultivar	Sowing Date	Developmental stage	
		Early stem extension	Flowering
1987/88			
Alfred	7 November 1987	25 April 1988	13 May 1988
Bourdon	7 November 1987	25 April 1988	25 May 1988
1988/89			
Alfred	28 October 1988	14 March 1989	4 May 1989
Bourdon	28 October 1988	14 March 1989	15 May 1989

were harvested 2–3 weeks earlier than usual (Farmers Weekly, 28 July 1989).

The 1989 early harvest provided ample time for seedbed cultivation and weed eradication; consequently, winter cereals were sown early. As in the previous mild winter, growth was advanced, and by spring 1990 crops had more tillers than usual. This proved beneficial after severe frosts in late March and early April, as surviving tillers could at least partially compensate for frost-damaged tillers (see 4.5).

4.4.2 Oilseed rape

The germination of winter oilseed rape in 1988 was good and many crops were dense as a result. At a site in the west of Scotland on 5 January 1988, rape plants were at the rosette stage, whereas on the same date in 1989 stem extension was already occurring, i.e. plants were about one month forward. This aggressive growth tended to outcompete weeds which were thus not generally a problem. The advanced rate of development was maintained until flowering. On 2 March 1988 at the site in the west of Scotland, flower buds had started to appear, whereas in the following year by 17 March 1989 about 10% of the buds had already flowered (data courtesy of V. Heppel, Scottish Agricultural College). Crops further south at Rothamsted were also advanced by 3–4 weeks.

After both mild winters there was a high incidence of foliage diseases. Pests also proved a problem with cabbage stem flea beetles and mealy aphids being especially active over both winters.

4.4.3 Sugar beet

The mild winters affected the sugar beet crop by influencing the condition of spring seed beds and by allowing the overwintering of aphids which act as disease vectors. As a spring-sown crop, sugar beet was also influenced by the low rainfall in the main growing areas, and by high spring temperatures, which affected the growth of the crop, particularly when late-sown (see also Chapter B4).

4.4.4 Legumes

Winter beans sown in October and November 1988 exhibited good germination and emergence. In some instances the mild weather meant that seedling survival was too good, and post-emergence cultivation was required to lower stand density and reduce the risk of lodging later in the season. Several growers reported seedling damage caused by mice. Weeds however could not compete with the dense, rapidly growing crop and savings were made on herbicides (MAFF).

Table 4.4 compares the rate of early stem extension and flowering of autumn-sown beans in 1988/89 with that in the previous year (unpublished data, courtesy of G. Batts, University of Nottingham). The varieties used are Alfred (a semi-determinate spring bean) and Bourdon (a winter indeterminate bean).

These data show that winter-sown beans were sown and flowered about 10 days earlier in 1988/89 than in 1987/88. At Gleadthorpe Experimental Husbandry Farm (EHF), also near Nottingham, winter-sown beans flowered 2–3 weeks early. Flowering at Gleadthorpe was prolific; the flowering time was shorter than usual and was followed by a high level of pod set. Most winter bean crops were reported to be relatively pest free, the main damage being caused by bean weevils.

Mild winter conditions in 1989 encouraged some growers to sow spring beans as early as February, 2–3 months early. Crops sown at this time did not suffer from water shortage as much as those sown later.

Over the 1989/90 winter many pests survived and spraying against aphids was early and more frequent than usual. Winter bean yields were good, probably as a result of vigorous early growth and relatively little loss to pests and diseases.

4.4.5 Potatoes

There were losses from potato stores particularly unventilated ones with inadequate temperature control. ADAS recommended vigilance over potato stores, and there were several reports of silver scurf, black dot and bacterial soft rots. Often blight was a precursor to these diseases.

Seed potatoes broke dormancy and sprouted early, and, where weather conditions and labour permitted, were planted early.

Aphids migrated into potato crops early in 1989. As these insects can carry debilitating virus diseases which appear in the following season, growers were advised to have homegrown seed tested. Despite this, there were reports that some 1990 crops grown from such seed exhibited virus symptoms. These represented a loss in yield and also a reservoir of infection for 1991 crops. The many groundkeepers which overwintered, also provided a source of infection. Continuing activity and survival of aphids over the 1989/90 winter, and consequent early infestation of potato crops, meant that the risks of saving homegrown seed in 1990 were greater than in 1989. As in 1976, commercial seed produced in Scotland was downgraded in 1990 due to virus.

Blight inoculum survived both mild winters but, in general, the following hot summers were too dry to promote the development of the disease.

A4.5 EFFECTS ON HORTICULTURAL CROPS

Horticultural crops were generally advanced over the winter and spring 1989 and 1990. The relatively warm winter temperatures meant that unrefrigerated stores, especially of onions, started to rot. The problem was exacerbated by periods of low demand for winter vegetables, and only quality produce could command high prices.

The mild winter conditions encouraged the build-up of several diseases which normally would be controlled by cold spells. In the absence of cold, the shelf life of produce was often limited due to disease. The mild weather contributed to the ease of lifting root crops, and harvesting conditions for the labour force were more pleasant than usual.

4.5.1 Brassicas

Brussel sprouts were one to two weeks earlier than normal. In the Midlands, late crops were advanced enough to be picked alongside the mid-season crop. Yields were high and the quality was described as fair. Quality deteriorated later in the season as mild, muggy weather promoted the spread of disease. Diseases which are usually checked by frost, such as light leaf spot, *Altenaria*, ringspot and white blister were common on susceptible varieties. Between November 1988 and February 1989 the wholesale market price of sprouts was down by between 4 and 35% compared with 1987/88 (MAFF).

In Cornwall, spring cabbage was forward by three weeks in March 1989. This led to oversupply in an already depressed market. In other cabbage types the mild conditions promoted overmaturity and overlarge heads, which later began to split, reducing the value of the crop. The warm weather also encouraged the rapid development of ringspot on some crops in December 1988, which necessitated extra trimming. Aphids were also reported on many crops throughout the winter; numbers rapidly built up over the spring to problem levels. In February 1989, stored winter white cabbage began to develop *Botrytis*, and demand was so low that much of the crop ended up as stockfeed or was ploughed in. The amount of wastage of winter cabbage varieties in April 1989 was 21%, compared with 13% in 1988 (MAFF).

Some cauliflower crops in Cornwall were four weeks early, but these did not hold well in the field and led to slight oversupply. There was some damage from mice and ringspot. Elsewhere in the country, crops were advanced by about two weeks. Due to the lack of frost, harvesting of cauliflower in some areas continued through to January in 1989 and 1990, whereas harvesting usually ends in December.

4.5.2 Carrots

Mild weather in early spring provided ideal drilling conditions for the 1989 crop. Some of the early-sown crops were covered with polythene. In February, late-sown 1988 crops continued to fill out, and frost losses were negligible, so that considerable surpluses were expected. In the same month in Cambridgeshire, the high winter temperatures led to deterioration in field-stored crops. The quality of crops under plastic and straw in Norfolk also began to suffer in February due to high temperatures. Premature regrowth under strawed crops, and a black discoloration affecting the crown was also associated with the mild weather. As well as considerable top and lateral regrowth, pests and diseases such as carrot fly, violet root rot and cavity spot were present in some crops. Yields were generally good, but quality was affected by disease, and by crops not keeping well in the soil or under straw. Demand for carrots was poor, and the average wholesale market price between November 1988 and February 1989 was down by between 31 and 52% compared with the previous year (MAFF).

4.5.3 Leeks and Onions

Growing and lifting conditions for leeks on December 1988 were excellent. In Cambridgeshire some crops were showing signs of over maturity and, generally, cold weather would have been welcomed to stabilise the disease situation. Rust and leaf blotch occurred throughout the winter. Leaf diseases in February in the South necessitated leaf stripping before marketing. The mild weather encouraged some crops to bolt, although this was not widespread. Demand for this crop was generally good.

Table 4.5: Dates of maturity of four cultivars of autumn-sown onions in average seasons and in 1988/89 near Cambridge (data courtesy of NIAB).

Variety	Date of Maturity	
	8 yr. mean for 4 sites	1988/89 Cambridge
E E Kaizuka	11 June	26 May
IMAI Yellow Globe	30 June	20 June
Keepwell	28 June	14 June
Senshyo Semi Globe	3 July	22 June

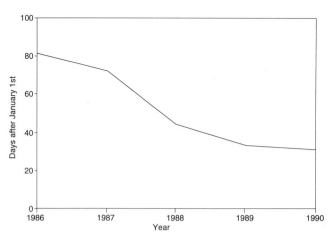

1 Dates when T-SUM 200 was reached at Nottingham University School of Agriculture, Sutton Bonington, Notts. (Data courtesy of N. Sweet). T-SUM is the accumulated day degrees above the base temperature for grass growth.

Winter kill in autumn-sown onions was 1% in 1988/89 compared with 6% in the previous eight years. The maturity of autumn-sown onions was also brought forward by the mild conditions; Table 4.5 summarises the dates of maturity of four cultivars growing near Cambridge (data courtesy of NIAB).

However, warm conditions made storage difficult, and stored onions began to show signs of neckrot and bacterial breakdown as early as December 1988. Regrowth of onions in stores was reported in February. The incidence of disease and regrowth in stores increased throughout the winter and spring in stores. Demand for stored onions was low.

4.5.4 Flowers

As with tomatoes, flower production costs in heated glasshouses were low during the mild winters. Outdoor narcissus in Cornwall were earlier than normal. The dates of peak output of narcissi at Rosewarne EHS were 6 March in 1987, 26 February in 1988, and 10 February in 1989. The continuing mild weather also extended the season. Because of this, the production from the south western and eastern growing regions overlapped. Early eastern-grown flowers provided a bonus for growers in that region at the expense of the western growers.

A4.6 FROST DAMAGE

On 27 March and 4 and 9 April 1990 there were severe night frosts. Due to the particularly mild winter many crops were advanced in their development and were at a cold susceptible stage at the time of the frosts. Some crops, especially the early winter barley variety "Torrent", were at the vulnerable floral initiation stage. Several crops in the southern counties, and some further north, which were in frost pockets were considered lost. These crops were harvested green and usually ensiled. When harvested early enough, some of these crops were replaced with linseed.

The flowers of fruit crops, especially tree fruit, were also early as a result of the 1989/90 mild winter. In some orchards, crops were decimated, especially plum and cherry. However, as only about 5% of flowers need to set fruit to provide an adequate crop, many orchards of top fruit retained the capacity to yield adequately despite substantial flower loss.

A4.7 GRASS GROWTH AND ASSOCIATED ANIMAL PRODUCTION

4.7.1 Grass production

Grass continued to grow throughout the winters of 1988/89 and 1989/90, except in high upland areas where conditions were too severe. T-SUM 200 (a measure of thermal time after which the first application of nitrogen to grassland is recommended) was reached about 2 weeks earlier than normal in both seasons. Figure 1 shows that at Sutton Bonington, Nottinghamshire T-SUM 200 was reached 3 days earlier in 1990 than in 1989. In the north, the 1988/89 winter was milder than the 1989/90 winter. Consequently the 1990 T-SUM 200 was reached 5–10 days later than in 1989, but this was still 10–14 days ahead of the long-term average (Farmers Weekly, 16/2/90).

Grass growth during the mild winter of 1988/89 yielded good silage and hay. However, in the south, later cuts were reduced in quantity due to the effects of the hot dry summer. In some areas, high temperatures in soil exposed by the initial cut were sufficient to damage roots and productivity.

In some regions, especially in the south and west, there was a chronic grass shortage in 1989 and stockfarmers had to resort to feeding with newly cut fodder as well as supplements. In contrast, the wetter weather in the north meant that grass growth was not so restricted and most stockfarmers in Scotland and Northern Ireland did not have to buffer feed at all.

Wet weather in the early autumn 1989 stimulated grass growth and many farmers were able to get an autumn cut. In the early autumn, reseeded pastures were infested

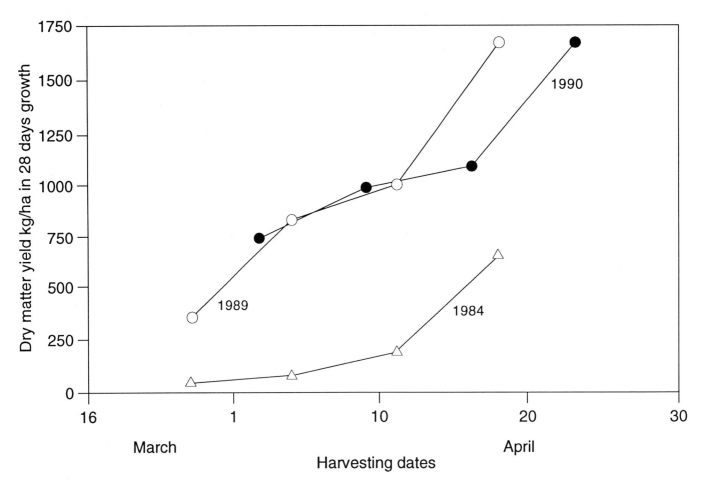

2   A perennial ryegrass sward, var. Cropper was allowed to grow after cutting in November the previous year. Grass was cut again from March onwards at 4 weekly intervals in a staggered sequence. The yields from these clearing cuts are given. (Data courtesy of R.H. Lavender, R. Sheldrick and R. Martyn, IGER North Wyke).

with larger than usual numbers of frit fly. The larvae of these insects caused damage to grass and cereal crops over the following winter and spring when mild temperatures encouraged their activity.

Over the winter period 1989/90 the shortage of fodder meant that many stockfarmers, especially those in the south west, had to buy in feed stuff, leave winter housed stock out until quite late in the year, and/or turn stock out earlier in 1990.

Figure 2 shows data from the North Wyke Research Station of the Institute of Grassland and Environmental Research, indicating the amount of grass growth that took place over the 1989/90 mild winter compared to that in 1988/89 and in a "normal" winter, i.e. one that is close in weather pattern to the 30 year average, in this case 1983/84. The data from this Devon site show how much the mild winter temperatures affected grass growth. The site lies on impermeable soils and is at altitude; droughting was not a severe problem.

4.7.2 Livestock

The mild winters affected stock and stock-keeping in various ways. The extended growing period made extra

grass available quite early in the season. This grass could not often be used because of risks of adverse weather. Stock that were allowed to overwinter outside either performed well or suffered from metabolic disorders when the nutritional quality of the grass was overestimated. For example, low magnesium concentrations in spring grass necessitated the feeding of supplements to prevent hypomagnesaenia in summer calvers. Similarly in sheep, nutritional disorders were responsible for an above-average incidence of pregnancy toxaemia and milk fever in 1989.

Damp, mild conditions in winter resulted in an increased incidence of calf pneumonia. The same conditions are thought to have contributed to silage spoilage, resulting in increased incidences of abortion. (The Veterinary Record, 10 June 1989). The mild conditions also induced an additional threat of lungworm, as not only were some cattle allowed to graze for longer periods over the 1988/89 season, but the activity of the soil-living larvae was not curtailed by low temperatures. Sheep were also reported to have large parasite burdens in 1989 which caused increased incidences of gastroenteritis.

Some stock-keepers and Veterinary Investigation Centres noted that the condition of cattle tended to be too good before calving, possibly because feeding regimes were not adjusted to take the mild temperature conditions into account. The result was overlarge calves and consequent birthing problems.

The amount of grass available over the winter period probably caused a reduction in the costs of producing outwintered and grass-finished beef sucklers. But a cold, wet, late spring meant that dairy cattle were turned out late in 1989 resulting in slightly lower milk yields in April 1989 compared with 1988 (Farming News 2 June 1989).

The mild weather increased the survival rate of newborn lambs resulting in a high number of slaughterings in 1989, especially of finished lambs in the autumn. However, in some cases, good quality grass led to overfat lambs, and a loss of premium.

A4.8 CONCLUSIONS

1. The mild winter conditions led to diverse effects on pests. Pigeon damage was generally less than normal on crops like oilseed rape because alternative food supplies were plentiful. In contrast rocks damaged many autumn-sown crops as they foraged for soil living organisms. Rat and mouse populations were larger than normal and mice damaged emerging sugarbeet and legumes. Slugs were very active; repeated doses of molluscicides and sometimes resowing were necessary. Many black and green aphids survived the winter and despite the use of aphicides new waves of aphids quickly reinvaded crops.

2. Weeds continued to germinate throughout the winter and many survived because of the lack of frosts. Early-sown cereal and oilseed rape crops grew so vigorously that they effectively suppressed the weeds. Volunteer cereals and potatoes readily survived the winter and carried a great deal of pathogen inoculum.

3. In the absence of severe frost since 1986/87, mechanical means were necessary to prepare seedbeds. Warm soil temperatures in 1989/90 increased mineralization by microorganisms, and increased nitrate levels in some soils, thereby decreasing the use of fertilizers.

4. Winter wheat crops were generally more advanced in both seasons. On water retentive soils, rain was adequate to give high yields. Winter barley growth was similarly advanced but effects on development were not so consistent.

Some cereal crops were affected early and severely with mildew, yellow rust, and barley yellow dwarf virus. Unusually large quantities of fungicides and aphicides were used. Brown rust and net blotch were also prevalent on barley. Yields of spring sown cereals were the lowest in some areas since 1976.

5. In potato stores where ventilation and temperature could not be adequately controlled there were increased losses from storage rot and sprouting was also a problem.

6. Autumn-sown beans established well and flowered early and as a result yields were good with relatively little loss to pests and disease.

7. Horticultural crops were generally advanced over the winter and spring of 1989 and 1990. Yields were usually good often leading to an over-supply on a depressed market. Quality of produce was frequently poor due to disease or other damage during storage.

8. In many regions of the UK grass growth continued throughout both winters. Stocks of silage were plentiful in 1988/89. Hay and silage was of good quality, owing to warm, sunny weather, but amounts were less in many areas owing to drought, especially in the southwest.

9. In 1989/90 the winter grown grass reduced costs of overwintering animals. However some farmers over-estimated the nutritional value of the lush grass and failed to feed adequate supplements which led to nutritional disorders.

APPENDIX

Observations on cereal diseases in the two mild winters.

Agent	Survival method	Conditions in 1988/89, 1989/90 Winters	Control	Consequences
Powdery Mildew	Survives on stubble, late tillers, early sown cereals, volunteers and over-wintering weeds.	No frost kill led to reinfection and a problem in crops in early 1989. Winter barley was worst affected, with disease appearing as early as October 1988. Worst year ever for this disease on barley. In 1989/90 the disease was controlled and not as damaging as in the previous wetter winter.	Up to 3 sprayings of fungicide were required in areas where none are normally applied.	Reduced yield.
Yellow rust	Survives on stubble, late tillers, early sown cereals, volunteers and over-wintering weeds.	Wheat was mainly affected particularly high yielding varieties such as "Slejpner". The disease was reported as early as February in Wiltshire, and East Anglia suffered the worst epidemic for 20 years. In 1989/90 the disease was less severe due to drier condtions.	1–2 extra applications of fungicide were required. Growers were advised to use fungicide-treated seed when sowing susceptible varieties in autumn 1989 and to reduce the use of susceptible varieties.	Protected crops yielded well in 1989.
Brown rust	"	This rust is favoured by hot dry conditions. In 1989 it was reported to be the most damaging foliar disease of winter barley.		Estimated cost of loss of yield in 1989 was £12.2M.
Barley yellow Dwarf virus	Crops are infected by aphid vectors. Winter crops and volunteers provide a source of disease and vectors.			

Section B

Impacts of the Hot Summers 1989 and 1990

Chapter B1

The Climate

B1.1 TEMPERATURES AND SUNSHINE DURATION

1.1.1 Introduction

This chapter compares average temperatures and sunshine duration over the United Kingdom during May to October in 1989 and 1990 with previous years. The conventional definition of summer, June to August, and the extended summer, May to October are considered.

Temperature comparisons are made using data from the Central England series (see Chapter A1.1.1) and regional meteorological stations. Sunshine duration during 1989 and 1990 is compared with previous years using the UK Meteorological Office Sunshine record which began in 1909.

Special attention is given to the exceptional warm period in August 1990.

1.1.2 Central England temperatures during May to October 1989 and 1990

MONTHLY TEMPERATURES IN THE CENTRAL ENGLAND SERIES

The mean monthly temperatures for the six months May to October 1989 and 1990, together with the 1961–80 average are listed in Table 1. The mean summer temperatures for June to August (conventional definition of summer) in 1989 and 1990 were 16.5°C and 16.2°C, 1.3°C and 1.0°C, respectively, above the 1961–80 average, making the 1989 summer the equal 22nd, and the 1990 summer the equal 39th, warmest since 1659.

The warmest summer ever recorded in the Central England time series was 1976. This summer had a mean temperature of 17.8°C, 1.3°C warmer than in 1989. Further details of the 1976 summer and its associated

impacts are discussed by Doornkamp *et al.* (1980). Other recent warm summers occurred in 1947 (17.0°C), 1959 (17.0°C), 1975 (16.9°C) and 1983 (17.2°C).

When the six month period from May to October is considered, the extended summers of 1989 and 1990 are a much rarer occurrence. For this six-month period, 1989 was 1.3°C above the 1961–80 average. This is the equal fourth warmest such season, 0.4°C cooler than the warmest which occurred in 1959. The six-month summer in 1947 and 1976 were 0.2°C and 0.1°C warmer respectively, than 1989. The May to October periods in 1949 and 1826 were of equal warmth to the period in 1989.

None of the individual months during May to October 1989 broke any records. July was the most anomalously warm month with 18.2°C (1961–80 anomaly 2.4°C). Even this month was 1.3°C cooler than the warmest July month ever recorded in the complete Central England Temperature series, which occurred in July 1983.

The extended summer of 1990 was 0.4°C cooler than 1989 and only the equal 17th warmest. The most anomalous month of the entire six month season was August which was 2.3°C above the 1961–80 reference period. This was the sixth warmest August recorded since 1695, 0.7°C cooler than the warmest ever August in 1975.

Figure 1 compares the temperatures during 1976 with those in 1989 and 1990. As can be seen, 1976 was clearly exceptional during June, July and August. When the six month extended summer is considered, however, the near normal months of September and October 1976 lower the temperature for this period to only slightly above the 1989 value. In 1989, all six months were almost 1°C above the 1961–80 average, with the exception of June. The relative coolness of June was caused by the first week of the month which was exceptionally cool. Temperatures in 1990 only just exceeded 1976 during May, August and October.

Table 1: Monthly mean central England temperatures (°C). May to October 1989 and 1990.

Month	1961–80 average	1989 mean temperature	1990 mean temperature	1989 Anomaly	1990 Anomaly
May	11.2	13.0	12.6	+1.8	+1.4
June	14.2	14.6	13.6	+0.4	−0.6
July	15.8	18.2	16.9	+2.4	+1.1
August	15.7	16.6	18.0	+0.9	+2.3
September	13.6	14.7	13.2	+1.1	−0.4
October	10.7	11.7	11.9	+1.0	+1.2
June–August	15.2	16.5	16.2	+1.3	+1.0
May–October	13.5	14.8	14.4	+1.3	+0.9

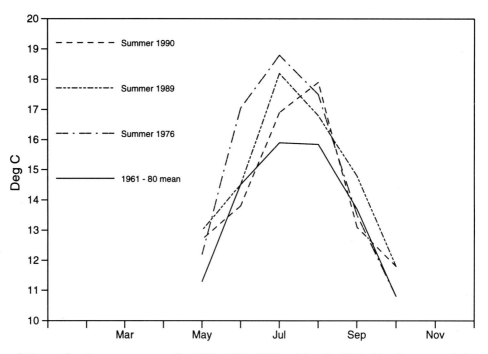

1   Comparisons of May to October temperatures for 1990, 1989, 1976 and for the 1961–80 reference period.

DAILY TEMPERATURES FROM THE CENTRAL ENGLAND SERIES

The daily Central England temperature series enables the number of extremely warm days above a specific threshold to be calculated. The series is of **mean** daily temperatures, hence it is not possible to consider **maximum** daily temperatures. Here, the number of days each month when the mean daily temperature was above 20°C were counted. The counts, along with the average values for 1961–80, are given in Table 2.

Table 2: Number of days with mean temperatures above 20°C over Central England, May to October 1989 and 1990.

Month	1961–80	1989	1990	1989 Anomaly	1990 Anomaly
May	0	0	0	0.0	0.0
June	0.60	3	0	+2.40	−0.60
July	0.85	7	3	+6.15	+2.15
August	0.95	0	6	−0.95	+5.05
September	0.05	0	0	−0.05	−0.05
October	0	0	0	0.0	0.0
June–August	2.40	10	9	+7.60	+6.60
May–October	2.45	10	9	+7.55	+6.55

During the summers of 1989 and 1990, there were 10 and 9 days, respectively, with average temperatures above 20°C. Since 1845, twelve summers have had 10 or more days above 20°C (Jones and Hulme, 1990). In 1989, all such days occurred in June and July, and six of the days in July occurred in succession from July 20 to 25. In 1990, all days above 20°C occurred in July and August and warmest day of the 1990 summer was 3 August with

an average daily mean temperature of 24.4°C in the Central England series. This made the 3rd August 1990, the warmest August day and the 4th warmest of all days since 1845. The warmest three days were 29 July 1948 (25.5°C), 4 July (24.7°C) and 3 July 1976 (24.6°C).

1.1.3 Temperatures over the United Kingdom during May to October 1989 and 1990

In the previous section, the summers of 1989 and 1990 were compared with the long monthly and the shorter daily historic record of Central England temperatures. In this section, the regional variations that occurred across the country are considered. Fifteen sites were chosen for which data are readily available both for the extended summer period and for the 1961–80 reference period. The

Table 3: Locations of the 15 meterological stations over the United Kingdom.

Station	Height (m)	Latitude (°N)	Longitude (°W)
Aldergrove	68	54°39'	6°12'
Durham	102	54°46'	1°35'
Dyce	65	57°12'	2°12'
Elmdon	98	52°27'	1°45'
Eskdalemuir	242	55°19'	3°12'
Gatwick	59	51°09'	0°11'
Kirkwall	26	58°57'	2°54'
Long Ashton	51	51°26'	2°40'
Oxford	63	51°46'	1°16'
Plymouth	27	50°21'	4°07'
Ringway	75	53°21'	2°16'
Santon Downham	24	52°29'	0°41'E
Shawbury	72	52°48'	2°40'
Stornoway	15	58°13'	6°19'
Valley	10	53°15'	4°32'

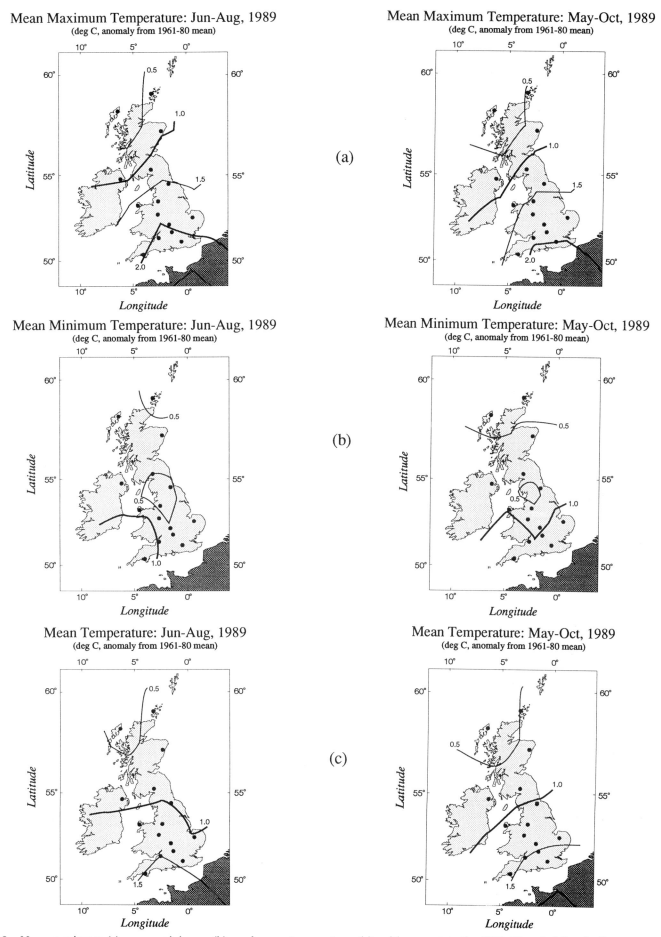

2 Mean maximum (a), mean minimum (b), and mean temperatures (c), with respect to the 1961–80 period for the June to August 1989 and the May to October 1989 seasons.

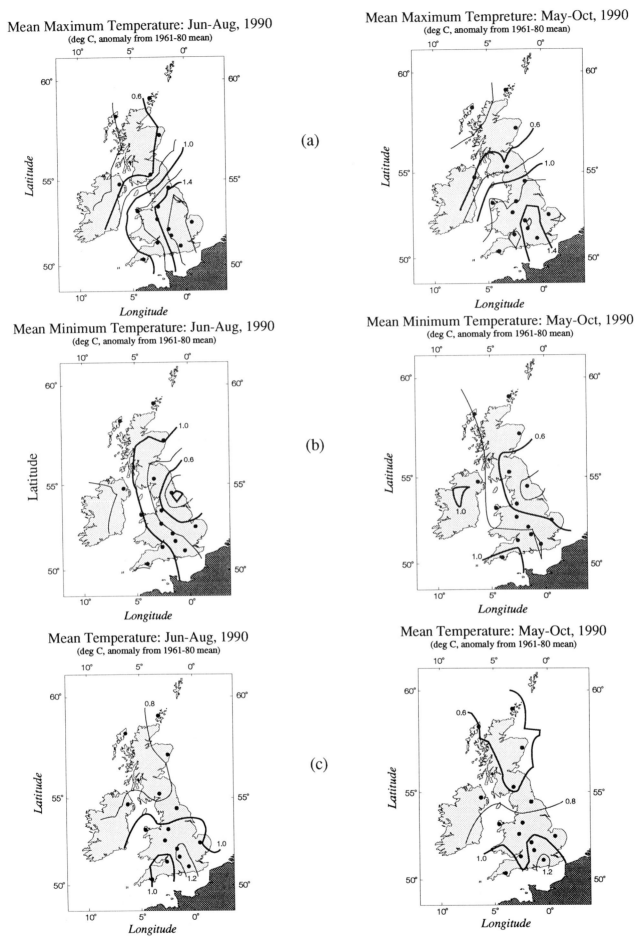

Mean Maximum Temperature: Jun-Aug, 1990
(deg C, anomaly from 1961-80 mean)

(a)

Mean Maximum Tempreture: May-Oct, 1990
(deg C, anomaly from 1961-80 mean)

Mean Minimum Temperature: Jun-Aug, 1990
(deg C, anomaly from 1961-80 mean)

(b)

Mean Minimum Temperature: May-Oct, 1990
(deg C, anomaly from 1961-80 mean)

Mean Temperature: Jun-Aug, 1990
(deg C, anomaly from 1961-80 mean)

(c)

Mean Temperature: May-Oct, 1990
(deg C, anomaly from 1961-80 mean)

3 Mean maximum (a), mean minimum (b), and mean temperatures (c) with respect to the 1961–80 period for the June to August 1990 and the May to October 1990 seasons (contour intervals 0.2°C).

locations of the stations are listed in Table 3 and are shown as the large dots on figures.

MAXIMUM, MINIMUM AND MEAN TEMPERATURES

Figures 2 and 3 show maximum, minimum and mean temperature anomalies for the two summer seasons, the conventional June to August and the extended summer from May to October 1989 and 1990. In 1989, the anomalies for both seasons were of a similar magnitude (about 2°C for maximum and 1°C for minimum temperature anomalies) as reflected in the Central England anomalies and were greatest in the south of England. Mean temperature anomalies were centred towards the south west of England during the conventional summer season, but during the extended summer season, were marginally greater in southeast England. In 1990, the anomalies were greatest for maximum temperatures, with the greatest anomaly of 1.5°C being located over southern and eastern England. Minimum temperature anomalies (about 1.0°C) were greatest over the western coastal regions of Britain and Ireland. Mean temperature anomalies were dominated by the maximum anomalies and were thus greatest over the southern third of England and Wales. The shorter conventional summer season was more anomalously warm than the extended summer season.

DAYS ABOVE TEMPERATURE THRESHOLDS

The apparent warmth of a summer is not only reflected in the mean temperatures but also in the number of very warm days. In Figures 4 and 5 two different warm day thresholds are examined. The first threshold follows the

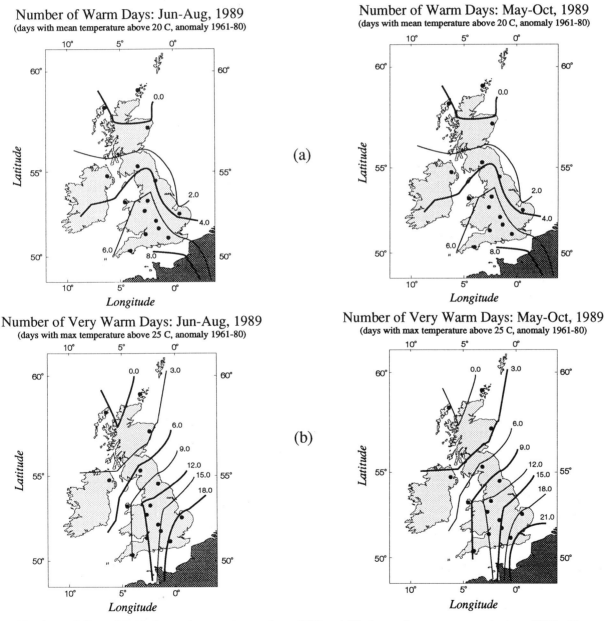

4   Numbers of days with (a) the mean temperature above 20°C and (b) the maximum temperature above 25°C with respect to the 1961–80 period for the June to August 1989 and the May to October 1989 seasons.

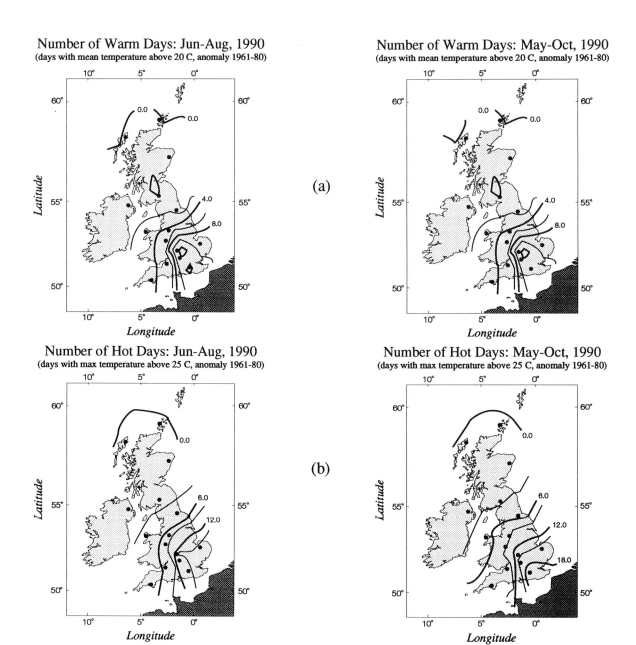

Number of Warm Days: Jun-Aug, 1990
(days with mean temperature above 20 C, anomaly 1961-80)

(a)

Number of Warm Days: May-Oct, 1990
(days with mean temperature above 20 C, anomaly 1961-80)

Number of Hot Days: Jun-Aug, 1990
(days with max temperature above 25 C, anomaly 1961-80)

(b)

Number of Hot Days: May-Oct, 1990
(days with max temperature above 25 C, anomaly 1961-80)

5   Number of days with, (a) mean temperature above 20°C (contour intervals 2 days) and, (b)maximum temperature above 25°C (contour interval 3 days) with respect to the 1961–80 period for the June to August 1990 and May to October 1990 seasons.

previous Central England temperature analysis and selects the number of days with a mean temperature greater than 20°C. The second selects the number of days with a maximum temperature greater than 25°C. In selecting these thresholds, some compromises have been made, particularly in Scotland. The north-south temperature gradient across the country means that both extremes occurred in most summers in southern England but were somewhat rare in Scotland. At Kirkwall and Stornoway, neither threshold was exceeded in 1989 and 1990 nor in the reference period 1961–80. It is not surprising therefore that the greatest number of anomalous warm and hot days occurred in southern Britain.

The pattern and magnitude of anomalies for both thresholds were similar in both years. For warm days with mean temperatures above 20°C the greatest anomalies were located over southwestern England in 1989

(Figure 4a) and over southeastern Britain in 1990 (Figure 5a). The pattern of anomalies for hot days (above 25°C) was almost identical in 1989 and 1990, with the greatest anomalies in southeastern England (Figures 4b and 5b). The absolute magnitude was, however, about 3 days less in 1990 than in 1989, when maximum temperatures over 25°C were recorded in southeastern England on over 25 days compared with than the 1961–80 average of 5 days.

1.1.4 Sunshine hours during May to October 1989 and 1990

The most anomalous feature about the 1989 summer was the considerably greater than normal number of sunshine hours. The Meteorological Office have developed a series that is representative of the average sunshine conditions over England and Wales. Figure 6 shows time series plots for sunshine duration for the two seasons, June to August

UK Met Office EW sunshine record for Jun-Aug season, 1909-1990

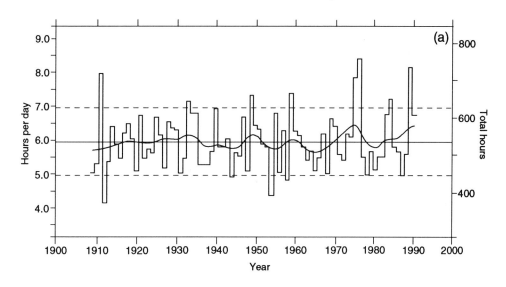

UK Met Office EW sunshine record for May-Oct season, 1909-1990

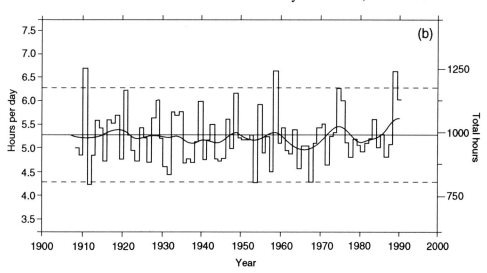

6   Number of sunshine hours per day and seasonal totals for the June to August (a) and May to October (b) periods. The dotted lines are one hour per day deviations from the 1909–1990 average. The smooth lines are ten year Gaussian filters fitted through both series.

and May to October for 1909–1990. For the June to August season, 1989 had the second highest number of sunshine hours, exceeded only in 1976. A similar number of sunshine hours to 1989 was recorded during 1911 and 1975. For the May to October season, 1989 recorded the highest ever number of sunshine hours, just exceeding the totals for 1911 and 1959.

Although not as sunny as 1989, the 1990 summer was still one of the sunniest on record (Hulme and Jones, 1991). The May to October 1990 period was the seventh sunniest such period since 1909. For the shorter June to August season, 1990 was less extreme because of an extremely cloudy June. All other months from May to October were sunnier than normal. The two years 1989 and 1990 were remarkable for their sunshine both in the

summer and the winter half year periods. Over those two years sunshine totals were well below normal only in June 1990. The sunshine total for the calendar years 1989 and 1990 made those years the sunniest and second sunniest, respectively, recorded since comparable records began in 1909.

Figure 7 shows the anomalous number of sunshine hours per day in 1989 for the June to August and the May to October periods. Over southern and central England and South Wales there were at least 2 hours more sunshine per day than was the average for 1961–80. For the longer summer season the same region and most of northeastern England had at least 1.2 hours more sunshine per day than average.

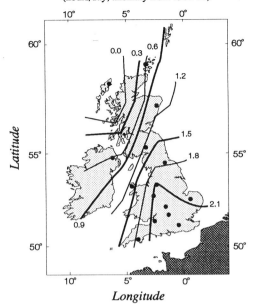

Bright Sunshine: Jun-Aug, 1989
(hours/day, anomaly from 1961-80)

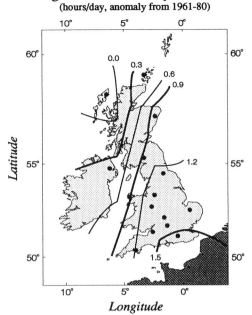

Bright Sunshine: May-Oct, 1989
(hours/day, anomaly from 1961-80)

7 Number of anomalous sunshine hours with respect to the 1961–80 period for the June to August 1989 and the May to October 1989 seasons.

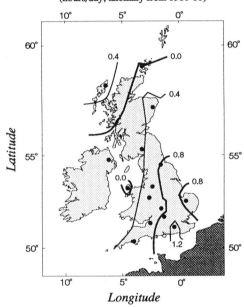

Bright Sunshine: Jun-Aug, 1990
(hours/day, anomaly from 1961-80)

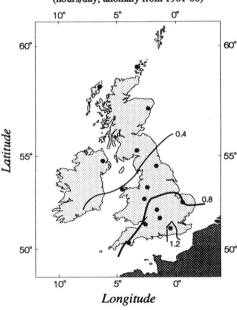

Bright Sunshine: May-Oct, 1990
(hours/day, anomaly from 1961-80)

8 Number of anomalous sunshine hours over the United Kingdom with respect to the 1961–80 period for the June to August 1990 (left) and the May to October 1990 (right) seasons (contour intervals 0.4 hours/day).

In 1990 the greatest sunshine anomalies in both seasons tended to occur over southern and eastern England (Figure 8). Many regions recorded departures in excess of 0.8 hours per day for both seasons.

1.1.5 *The heat wave of early August 1990*

The most anomalous feature of the 1990 summer was the very warm spell which occurred over the four days, 1 to 4 August. Although there are problems comparing the maximum temperatures on those days with temperatures measured during the nineteenth and early twentieth

century because of changes in screen design (Brugge, 1991), it is evident that many sites recorded their warmest ever temperature during this spell. The warmest day of the spell was 2 August over extreme western Britain and Ireland, the 3 August over most of central and eastern Britain and the 4 August over coastal areas of southeastern England and the Isle of Wight region.

Figure 9 shows the distribution of absolute maximum temperatures recorded at 171 stations between 2–4 August. Figure 9a shows that a maximum temperature exceeding 30°C was recorded almost everywhere in

Absolute maximum temperature, Aug 2-4 1990
(deg C)

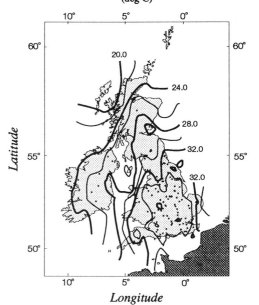

Absolute maximum temperature, Aug 2-4 1990
(deg C)

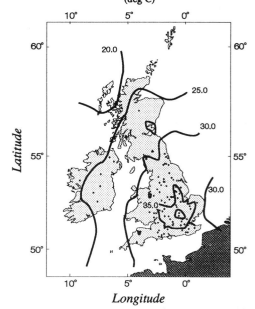

9   Absolute maximum temperature occurring during the hot spell of August 2–4 1990. The dots show the locations of the 171 stations used. (a) Contoured at 2°C intervals to show finer detail. (b) Contoured at 5°C intervals for comparison with Brugge (1991).

Table 4: Maximum temperature records broken between 2–4 August 1990.

Site	Temperature (°C)	Previous record (°C)	Date	Records began
Oxford	35.1	34.3	26/7/76	1853
Ross-on Wye	35.0	33.7	9/8/11	1877
Sheffield	34.3	33.5	9/8/11	1882
Bradford	32.2	31.1	22/6/41 & 12/8/53	1908
Scarborough	31.4	31.1	28/8/33	1930
Cranwell, Lincs	35.2	32.9	26/6/76	1930
Rothamsted, Herts	33.8	33.8	19/8/32	1930
Elmdon (B'ham)	34.9	32.9	3/7/76	1930
Ilfracombe	32.4	30.0	22/8/55	1930
Durham	32.5	30.6	31/7/43	1930
Cambridge	36.5	35.6	19/8/32	1931
Heathrow	36.5	34.2	8/8/75 22/7/89	1949
Tynemouth	31.9	28.1	16/7/69	1957
Marham, Norfolk	34.8	33.9	26/6/76	1957
Wyton, Cambs	35.4	33.4	3/7/76	1957
Silsoe, Beds	35.0	34.9	27/6/76	1957
Watnall, Notts	34.6	33.8	8/8/75	1957
Hurn, Bournemouth	34.1	33.8	28/6/76	1957
Lyneham, Wilts	34.9	33.5	4/8/75	1957
Rhoose (Cardiff)	33.5	32.2	3/8/75	1957
Jersey Airport	34.5	31.9	28/6/76	1957

Note: all maximum temperatures were recorded on 3 August, with the exception of Hurn which was recorded on the 4th.

England and Wales during the three day spell. The highest absolute temperatures were recorded in the southwest Midlands area (37.1°C at Cheltenham on 3 August), in the lower Thames Valley (36.5°C at Heathrow on 3 August) and in the Fenland area (36.5°C at Cambridge on 3 August). Figure 9b shows the same data plotted with a 5°C contour interval for comparison purposes with some of Brugge's (1991) figures. The cooling effect at coastal locations is evident here, because the 35°C contour is restricted to interior locations in southern England.

Table 4 lists the sites with relatively long records where new maximum temperature records were set on 3 or 4 August 1990. At numerous other sites with shorter time series, 3 or 4 August also broke records. At 26 of these sites with data back to 1959 new absolute maximum temperature records were also set. Some temperature records were only just beaten, but many of the previous records which generally occurred in the summers of 1975 and 1976 were beaten by between 1 to 2°C. Tynemouth exceeded its previous warmest day by 3.8°C. Of the sites over England and Wales with records extending back to the last century only Southampton did not break its record; there, the 1976 maximum was 2°C above the 33.6°C recorded on 3 August 1990.

It is evident from Figure 9, and more particularly from Table 4, that the heat wave of 1 to 4 August 1990 was clearly the warmest and most widespread hot spell of the last 100 years. The spell was, however, rather short in contrast to many previous hot spells. Brugge (1991) has made comparisons with similar events in the Augusts of 1906 and 1911. Other notable hot spells are evident from Table 4 in August 1932, August 1933, August 1975, July and August 1976 and July 1989. The hottest day in the daily Central England temperature record (29 July 1948) does not appear as an extreme in any of the site records listed in Table 4, because this record is one of mean daily temperatures. Minimum temperatures during the late July 1948 warm spell were extremely high (Anomymous, 1949), probably because the weeks before had been wetter than normal.

1.1.6 Conclusions

1. Overall, the May to October period in 1989 was the equal fourth warmest such period since the Central England temperature record began in 1659. The average temperature was 1.3°C above the 1961–80 reference period. All months were warmer than normal, especially July and May.

2. During most months the greatest temperature anomalies in 1989 were located over southern England. Maximum temperature anomalies were greater than +3°C over all of southern Britain during May and July.

3. If the more usual definition of summer is used, then the June to August period in 1989 was less exceptional (1.3°C above the 1961–80 average), being exceeded 21 times since 1659. This period was 1.3°C cooler than the warmest June to August period, which was recorded in 1976.

4. The most notable feature of the May to October period in 1989 was the number of sunshine hours. Using the Meteorological Office representative sunshine series for England and Wales, the May to October 1989 period recorded more sunshine hours (~1250) than any other such period since 1909, just exceeding by a few hours the totals for 1911 and 1959. For the July to August season the 1989 total was the second highest (~740) exceeded only slightly in 1976.

5. In 1990, the May to October period, was the equal 17th warmest since 1659. The average temperature was 0.9°C above the 1951–80 reference period. All months except June and September were warmer than normal. Spatially, the summer was very similar to 1989 with the warmest temperatures over southern Britain. Maximum temperatures in August were over 4°C warmer than normal over southeastern England.

6. The most unusual feature of the 1990 summer was the warmth of the spell 1–4 August, particularly with regard to maximum temperatures. The maximum temperature recorded during this period was 37.1°C and occurred on 3 August at Cheltenham. This was the warmest maximum temperature recorded in Britain for at least 100 years and probably since the development of properly screened thermometers. Almost all regions of England and Wales, except for the extreme north and some coastal areas, recorded a temperature in excess of 30°C. A large region of central and southern England and southeastern Wales recorded a temperature in excess of 35°C. Using the average mean daily Central England temperature, 3 August was the 4th warmest day since comparable records began in 1845.

7. The 1990 summer was not as sunny as in 1989 because of a cloudy June in 1990. It was, however, still the 7th sunniest May to October period since 1909.

B1.2 HYDROLOGY

1.2.1 Introduction

In this section, the hydrological characteristics of the hot summers of 1989 and 1990 are discussed and compared with previous hot summers. Clearly the impact of the mild winters of 1988/89 and 1989/90 (described in Chapter A1.2) cannot be discounted and some overlap between this section and section A1.2 is inevitable.

The various data sources for this section are acknowledged in A1.2.1. In addition to discussion of rainfall, evaporation and soil moisture, ground water levels and river flows, attention is given to water management responses during the two hot summers.

1.2.2 Rainfall

SUMMER 1989

Following a relatively wet spring, May 1989 was unusually dry. For example the London Weather Centre recorded only 2% of the May average. Over England and Wales as a whole, May was the driest since 1896, with only 33% of the 1941–70 average. Interestingly, May 1990 was also exceptionally dry, recording only 37% of the long term average. In Scotland too, a run of dry Mays occurred with 1989 and 1990 having 64% and 60% of the long term Scottish average, respectively.

The following summer months (June to August) produced warm and dry conditions throughout England and Wales. Figure 10 plots England and Wales rainfall against the Central England Temperature from 1766, for the June to August period. In general, the warmer the summer the less the rainfall, and 1989 proved no exception. The summer 1976 is also plotted to highlight the extreme conditions of that year in comparison to 1989. In June

Table 5: 1989 rainfall in millimetres and as a percentage of the 1941–70 average.

		May	Jun	Jul	Aug	Sep
England and Wales						
North west	mm	37	82	33	116	29
	%	45	99	32	93	24
Northumbrian	mm	22	51	19	77	20
	%	34	84	25	76	25
Severn Trent	mm	25	53	40	44	38
	%	39	95	62	54	57
Yorkshire	mm	19	61	43	41	20
	%	31	119	61	46	28
Anglian	mm	14	56	41	35	30
	%	30	114	72	55	58
Thames	mm	14	39	37	44	28
	%	25	75	62	63	45
Southern	mm	5	41	28	29	37
	%	9	82	47	40	52
Wessex	mm	21	32	37	43	49
	%	31	59	60	52	62
South West	mm	12	40	31	62	107
	%	14	62	37	61	103
Welsh	mm	25	67	48	91	62
	%	27	82	51	76	50
Total	mm	20	55	38	58	41
	%	30	90	52	65	49
Scotland						
Highland	mm	68	90	65	222	118
	%	66	82	51	150	75
North east	mm	59	57	25	84	55
	%	77	81	27	79	63
Tay	mm	42	58	30	140	83
	%	44	70	29	119	72
Forth	mm	36	64	27	144	69
	%	43	85	28	124	64
Clyde	mm	46	90	63	252	120
	%	47	87	48	177	69
Tweed	mm	43	51	23	113	47
	%	57	75	26	99	51
Solway	mm	35	71	42	176	77
	%	38	79	38	135	51
Total	mm	53	76	49	184	96
	%	58	83	44	143	70

1989, only modest drought conditions existed in some southern and western districts (Table 5). By the end of August, moderate to severe drought conditions existed in all but the far north west of Scotland. April-August 1989 ranked as second driest in the England and Wales rainfall series that begins in 1766 (Anon, 1990).

Considering Scotland alone, the overall picture was somewhat different. The 1989 summer rainfall total was 325mm, 98% of the 1941–70 average, but this percentage hides a large variability within Scotland. The north and west received up to 150% of average with only about 60% falling in the east. Thus for the three month summer, Ayr received 31% more than the 1941–70 average, whilst Aberdeen received 34% less. Annually, the figures for 1989 at those sites showed that, while Ayr received rainfall marginally above average, Aberdeen experienced the second driest year this century, some 38% below average. Only 1921 had been drier. For Scotland as a whole the 1989 total was a little above average.

SUMMER 1990

The three month summer (June, July and August) of 1990 was also dry, although not spectacularly so. The three months produced a rainfall total of 152mm for England and Wales and 322mm for Scotland, corresponding to 68% and 97% of the 1941–70 averages, respectively. Table 6 shows how these figures hide great monthly variability. June throughout Britain was wet, with 118% of normal rainfall in England and Wales and 139% in Scotland. July and August were both drier than average, especially in England and Wales where falls were less than 50% of the average. Heathrow recorded only 6.9 mm, the lowest July total since 1931 and Southend (Essex) experienced a run of 37 days with no recorded rainfall starting on 7 July (Eden, 1991). In Figure 10, 1990 plots well into the warm and dry quadrant (despite the wet and cool June) but is less extreme than either 1989 or 1976.

Over the period from May to October 1990, rainfall was 77% of the average, (with only June and October

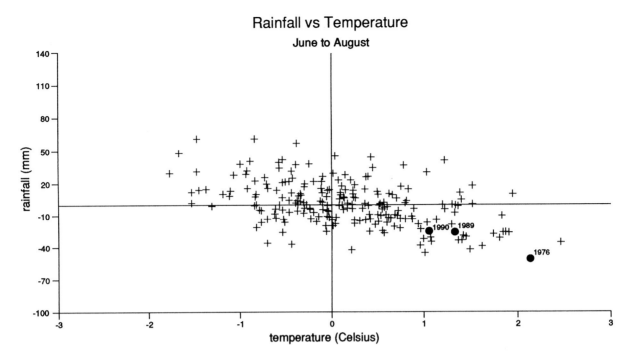

Rainfall vs Temperature

June to August

Rainfall = difference from 1941-70 average
Temperature = difference from 1961-80 average

10   Comparison of temperature and rainfall in England and Wales in summer (June to August). The data extend back to 1766.

recording above average rainfall) in England and Wales. Large areas of southern England received under 5mm of rainfall in May, with some districts recording less than 1mm, the driest May for 100 years (Eden, 1991). Scotland as a whole received about 104% of average for the same period with June and October again being particularly wet. The nine months from March to November 1990 produced a rainfall only 68% of the long term average in England and Wales (with an estimated return period of 60–80 years), which is drier than the equivalent period in 1989. This period in 1976 was somewhat wetter owing to the exceptionally high rainfalls of September and October. The fact that a dry 1990 followed a dry 1989, with only a ten-week wet period during the 1989/90 winter meant that some particularly severe water resource problems occurred during the summer of 1990.

SPATIAL VARIATION IN RAINFALL

The spatial variation in rainfall was large in both 1989 and 1990. Tables 5 and 6 list the rainfall (as monthly totals and as a percentage of the 1941–70 mean) for each of the National Rivers Authority (NRA) regions and the River Purification Board region of Scotland for the two summers. In the summer 1989, some areas received below average rainfall in every month, for example eastern Scotland, and both north east and south east England. Anglia and Thames NRA received below average rainfall in all of the nine months between March and November, whilst the Highland River Purification Board region recorded below average rainfall only in May, July and October.

Figure 11 illustrates the 10 month period in 1990 (February to November) for each month for the 188 MORECS boxes, and compares the results with 1989 and 1976. What is immediately evident is the similarity between 1989 and 1990, with a very dry May followed by a cool and wet June. July was basically a dry month throughout Britain, whereas during August Scotland and the North West turned wetter in both years. September was predominantly dry, with October slightly wetter than normal and November again turning drier than the average. The principal difference between the two years was that rainfall was low in England and Wales during March and April in 1990 but was quite high in 1989. By contrast, 1976 saw a very dry winter, spring and summer, with the (meteorological) drought ending abruptly in September. The 1975/76 drought achieved an unprecedented intensity within a 16-month time frame; the 1989/90 event was different in character, being less intense, but of a more notable duration, albeit punctuated by several hot episodes. In retrospect, it may be seen that the very dry early winter of 1988/89 heralded a prolonged period (> three years) of rainfall deficiency which was without parallel this century (Marsh and Bryant, 1991).

SEASONAL RAINFALL DISTRIBUTION

On average, rainfall in the UK as a whole is fairly evenly distributed throughout the year, and for England and Wales, the ratio of winter (October to March) to the following summer (April to September) rainfall is generally close to one. Figure 12 plots the time series of this ratio for England and Wales for every year since 1766

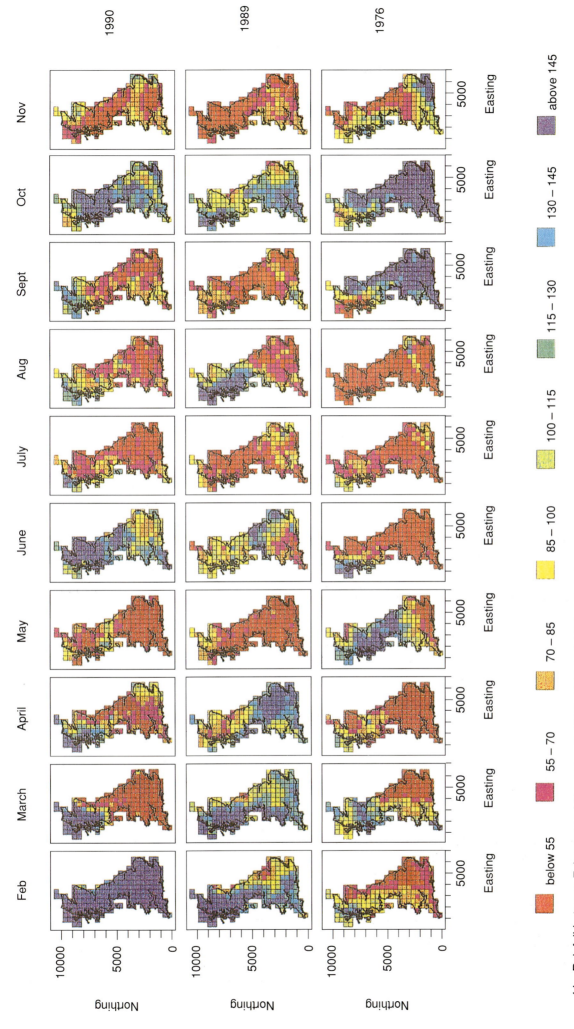

11 Rainfall between February and November in 1990, 1989 and 1976, expressed as a percentage of the 1961–80 average.

Table 6: 1990 rainfall in millimetres and as a percentage of the 1941–70 average.

		May	Jun	Jul	Aug	Sep	Oct	Nov
England & Wales								
North west	mm	49	99	58	73	86	175	73
	%	60	119	56	58	70	148	60
Northumbrian	mm	51	69	40	53	53	107	61
	%	80	113	52	53	67	143	65
Severn Trent	mm	19	63	27	37	46	93	52
	%	30	113	41	46	59	143	66
Yorkshire	mm	29	83	32	47	40	92	55
	%	47	143	46	52	56	133	62
Anglia	mm	16	45	21	31	32	51	53
	%	24	92	37	48	61	98	85
Thames	mm	7	47	17	35	34	58	34
	%	12	90	28	50	55	91	47
Southern	mm	10	61	13	33	38	105	63
	%	18	122	22	45	53	135	67
Wessex	mm	12	62	31	41	49	87	51
	%	16	115	50	50	62	106	53
South west	mm	25	99	61	59	69	128	106
	%	30	152	73	58	66	113	79
Welsh	mm	34	98	53	64	85	152	112
	%	37	119	56	54	68	118	78
TOTAL	mm	25	72	35	46	53	103	67
	%	37	118	48	51	64	124	69
Scotland								
Highland	mm	54	140	93	156	234	225	147
	%	52	127	73	105	148	121	87
North east	mm	49	110	43	75	86	136	95
	%	64	157	47	70	99	140	92
Tay	mm	44	128	38	73	68	186	63
	%	46	154	37	62	59	153	53
Forth	mm	39	125	49	83	68	194	56
	%	46	167	50	72	63	183	52
Clyde	mm	57	138	96	151	172	301	94
	%	59	134	74	106	98	165	56
Tweed	mm	46	106	52	61	69	159	53
	%	60	156	58	53	74	181	51
Solway	mm	76	121	74	106	81	218	77
	%	83	134	67	81	54	151	53
TOTAL	mm	54	128	75	119	149	213	102
	%	59	139	67	92	109	143	72

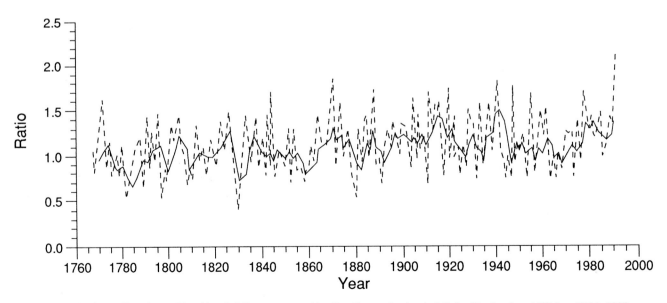

12   Ratio of winter (October – March) rainfall to summer (April – September) rainfall for England and Wales, 1766–1990.

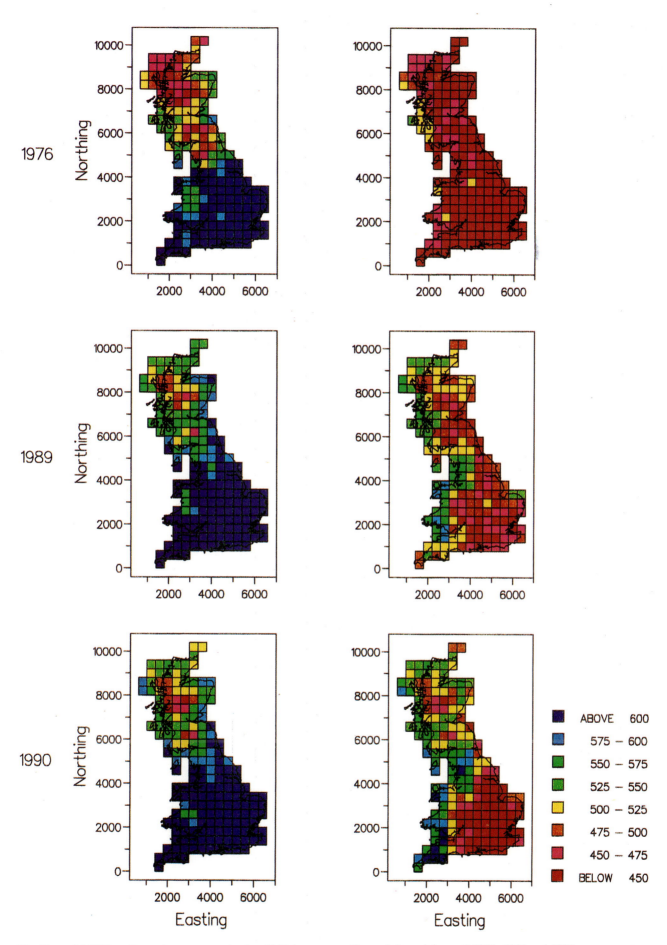

13   Potential (PE) and actual evapotranspiration (AE) in summer (June, July and August) 1976, 1989 and 1990 as a percentage of the 1961–80 average. MORECS data.

and a tendancy for the ratio to increase from around 1960 may be recognised. This tendancy achieved an extreme expression in 1989/90 when, for the first time, rainfall over the winter half-year was more than twice that of the ensueing summer half-year (Anon 1991). This exaggeration in the seasonality of rainfall was an important factor contributing to the water resources and ecological stress experienced over the latter half of 1990.

Although the total rainfall for 1990 was not far from average, its concentration in a relatively short winter period was very unusual and more characteristic of a Mediterranean climate regime.

1.2.3 Evaporation and soil moisture

During the summers of 1989 and 1990, (June to August) the high temperatures and record sunshine totals produced potential evapotranspiration rates well above the 1961–80 average over the entire country, apart from a small area of north west Scotland in 1989 and a large area of northern Scotland in 1990. Actual evapotranspiration, however (taking into account the poor availability of water) exhibited an almost reversed pattern. Areas of southern and central England and the eastern seaboard recorded below average rates in the summer of 1989 and below 65% of the 1961–80 average rates in 1990, reflecting the lack of rainfall and the exceptionally dry soil conditions. Wales, the north west and much of Scotland recorded greater than average evaporative losses in both summers, because the rainfall was sufficient to meet these high evapotranspiration demands.

The summer of 1976 provided an interesting comparison with the summers of 1989 and 1990 (Figure 13). In 1976, and 1990 to a lesser extent, there was a far more obvious north west/south east pattern than in 1989. In 1976, south east England experienced potential evapotranspiration losses of more than 30% above the long term mean over a much wider area than in 1989 and 1990 (Figure 13a,c,e). However, the south west, large areas of northern England, and Scotland recorded higher potential evapotranspiration in 1989 than in 1976. In 1990, potential evapotranspiration rates higher than 1976 also occurred in the south west and areas of northern England, but in Scotland potential rates were similarly low in 1990 and 1976.

The actual evapotranspiration over the entire country was higher during the summers of 1989 and 1990 (Figure 13d,f) than in the summer of 1976 (Figure 13b) because of the greater availability of water. But in 1990, actual losses were nearly as low as in 1976. The pattern of actual, like potential evapotranspiration in 1976 and 1990, exhibited a north-west/south-east trend. In 1976, an area of actual transpiration totals less than 65% of the 1961–80 mean occurred over almost all of England south of Yorkshire. In 1990, this area was only slightly smaller, and in the south-east losses due to actual evapotranspiration were some of the lowest on record, with only the totals for June to August 1976 being lower. The north

and west of England and Scotland recorded actual evapotranspiration totals above the average in 1976 and 1990, highlighting the areas with relatively little water stress. In 1989, these areas occurred much further south.

The shortfall of actual, relative to potential evapotranspiration is an indication of water stress and hence is of hydrological significance. In 1989 and 1990, shortfalls in summer were commonly in excess of 140mm throughout lowland England, the northeastern seaboard and the south west. In some areas, shortfalls in excess of 260mm were recorded. Such figures have been exceeded only in 1976.

As evaporative losses (typically peaking in June and July) exceed the rainfall, soil moisture deficits (SMDs) begin to build up. North west Scotland (represented by MORECS box 41) showed summer SMD values that were not obviously different from any of the previous four years. It may be observed, however, that both potential and actual evapotranspiration rates were slightly higher in 1989 and 1990 and this is seen to be true of every MORECS box selected. The rapid decrease in the amount of rainfall from west to east Scotland produced very different SMD patterns. The east coast is represented by MORECS box 38.

In January 1989, deficits built up in eastern Scotland following the mild and dry winter. These deficits were removed during the more sustained rain in February. With the very dry and warm conditions of the summer, deficits reached 100mm in many boxes in eastern Scotland by July. This area saw the most anomalously low rainfall of the winter 1989/90, which coupled with very high potential evapotranspiration rates, meant that SMDs were maintained throughout the winter. This pattern in eastern Scotland was repeated in most of eastern, southern and central England, where many areas maintained deficits throughout the February 1988 to January 1990 period. In some districts of Northumbria and the extreme south east of England SMDs were not fully replenished through the winter of 1989/90. The method of calculating SMDs within the MORECS model puts the maximum possible deficit for grass at 125mm. During the summer of 1989, 55 of the 188 MORECS boxes reached a deficit of 125mm for at least one month, and many of these maintained this maximum between July and September.

In 1990, the west-east gradient in rainfall normally seen in Scotland was not apparent in June and soil moisture returned briefly to field capacity at the end of June in MORECS box 41 and box 38. Moving south into England, a slightly different picture emerged. Unlike the previous year, and due to the wet winter of 1989/90, all areas had reached field capacity by the end of February. With a warm and dry spring leading on to a dry summer, evaporative losses were very high and deficits began to build during April and rose quickly in all areas. An important feature of the SMDs during 1990 was not only their magnitude, but also the period of time for which a certain deficit was maintained. There were 70 MORECS

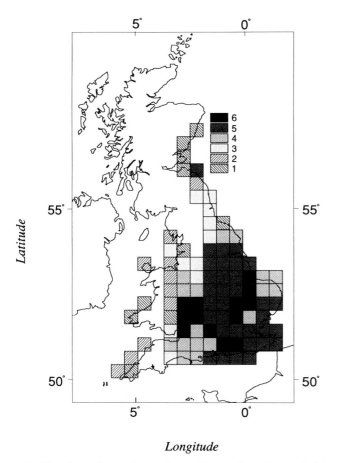

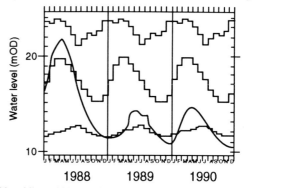

Site name: DALTON HOLME - East Yorkshire

National grid reference: SE 9651 4530   Well number SE94/5
Aquifer: CHALK AND UPPER GREENSAND Measuring level: 33.50

Max, Min and Mean values calculated from years 1889 to 1987

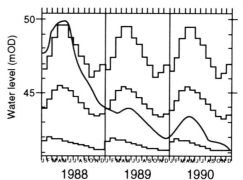

Site name: WASHPIT FARM - Lincolnshire

National grid reference: TF 8138 1960   Well number TF81/2
Aquifer: CHALK AND UPPER GREENSAND Measuring level: 80.20

Max, Min and Mean values calculated from years 1950 to 1987

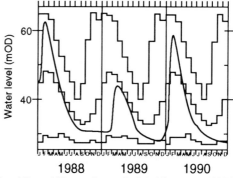

Site name: COMPTON HOUSE - Sussex

National grid reference: SU 7755 1490   Well number SU71/23
Aquifer: CHALK AND UPPER GREENSAND Measuring level: 81.37

Max, Min and Mean values calculated from years 1894 to 1987

14 Number of months ending with a soil moisture deficit greater than 100 mm in 1990.

squares (out of 188) that recorded a deficit greater than 80mm for at least 20 weeks of the year: in some parts of the Thames basin, Cambridgeshire, Lincolnshire and Humberside this level of deficit was maintained for over 30 weeks. There was also a large area (51 squares out of 188) that experienced deficits in excess of 100m for longer than 20 weeks. Figure 14 shows the spatial pattern of the 95 squares in the south and east that recorded at least one month finishing with SMDs greater than 100mm: nine of these recorded this deficit for six months. In an average year, only three squares (around the Thames estuary) record deficits greater than 100mm, and that is for only one month.

1.2.4 Groundwater

Recharge of groundwater storage generally takes place in winter, commencing once rainfall rises above potential evapotranspiration and finishing some time in spring when potential evapotranspiration again rises above rainfall (as described in Chapter A1.2). Groundwater levels decline through the summer, with the lag between recharge and groundwater level response depending on aquifer properties. Summer groundwater levels represent storage in the aquifer, and are therefore an integration of winter recharge and summer drainage over a number of years. The situation is more complicated in some

15 Ground water levels in three wells in the chalk aquifer in 1988, 1989 and 1990.

well-fissured aquifers and aquifers close to the surface which may also be recharged during summer.

Figure 15 shows groundwater level traces during 1988, 1989 and 1990 at three wells (located in Figure 16). The

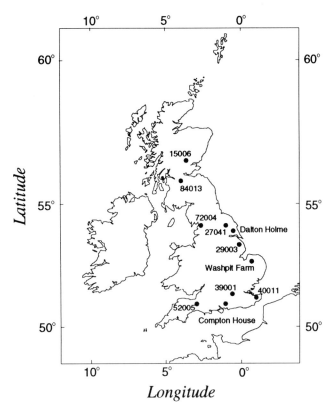

16   Location of sites shown in Figures 15 and 17.

low recharge in the winter of 1989/90 in the eastern Chalk is illustrated by the Dalton Holme and Washpit Farm records, which were typical of patterns in wells in the chalk across much of Yorkshire, East Anglia and Kent.

The winter of 1988/89 was dry, but infiltration during the spring of 1989 boosted groundwater recharge at a time when levels are more usually falling and groundwater levels across most of Britain were close to average at the start of summer. Only in the Chalk in eastern and parts of southern England (Yorkshire, Kent and a portion of Sussex) were groundwater levels in May 1989 considerably below average, approaching levels recorded in 1976 (in some regions, such as in parts of east Devon, groundwater levels were low as a result of a combination of the dry winter and high groundwater abstraction). Through the summer of 1989 groundwater levels remained higher than those recorded in 1976 across most of Britain.

Recharge during the winter of 1989/90 was apparently above average for most UK aquifers, but there were a number of unusual features. Recharge was below average for a second year in those groundwater areas which had below average rainfall; recharge was also below average in some areas which had high winter rainfall during 1989/90 and where recharge during the winter of 1989/90 built upon the very low levels which had been reached by the end of autumn 1989.

Following the very early onset of the seasonal decline in groundwater levels in 1990 and exceptionally steep recessions in the late spring, groundwater levels continued

to fall throughout the summer of 1990, and by October were everywhere below average and generally lower than in 1989. Levels in the Yorkshire Chalk (at Dalton Holme) were lower than levels recorded at the same time during the 1976 drought by June. Recessions continued during October, and the usual seasonal upturn only began in November and December 1990. By November 1990, levels in many wells in the Chalk of eastern and southern England were below the minimum levels recorded at the end of the 1976 drought. At Dalton Holme, levels had declined by the end of the autumn below any recorded in a continuous 102–year series. Notably depressed levels were also registered throughout a broad zone from the Yorkshire Wolds to Kent.

Low groundwater levels during 1990 built upon the low levels inherited from 1989, and this is shown particularly clearly in the Washpit Farm record in Figure 15. Recharge during 1987/88 was considerably higher than average across large parts of the UK, and groundwater levels at the beginning of the 1988/89 recharge season were high: the high volume of storage remaining in the aquifer at the end of spring 1988 lessened the impact of the low recharge during 1988/89, and helped to maintain levels during the summer of 1989. This inheritance was not available during 1990.

1.2.5 River flows

River systems in the United Kingdom are heavily managed, and this management is particularly intense during dry periods. River flows may be augmented by pumping from other catchments or from groundwater, and may be reduced as further amounts are extracted for supply: alternatively, licences for abstraction of water may be revoked. It is possible, however, to find a subset of catchments with either natural records or minimal influences which can be used to estimate natural river runoff patterns during the summers of 1989 and 1990.

Four key points emerge from an analysis of river flows during the summers of both 1989 and 1990: first, the recession from high spring flows was very rapid in many catchments; secondly, variations in rainfall deficits across the UK in 1990, combined with variations in catchment geological and soil moisture conditions, produced very significant regional and local differences in drought impact; thirdly, long-term runoff deficits built up in a number of catchments; fourthly, low flow conditions persisted well into the winter of 1990/91 and beyond.

Figure 17 shows the departure from average monthly runoff in 6 catchments from October 1988 to December 1990. Although river flows were generally very high in February 1990 (Chapter A1.2), river flows fell rapidly from March through the whole of summer. Runoff rates were especially depressed in lowland rivers sustained principally (or largely) from groundwater. For instance, flows in the Lud, Stour and Tone were particularly low during the summer of 1990, and indeed in the Lud

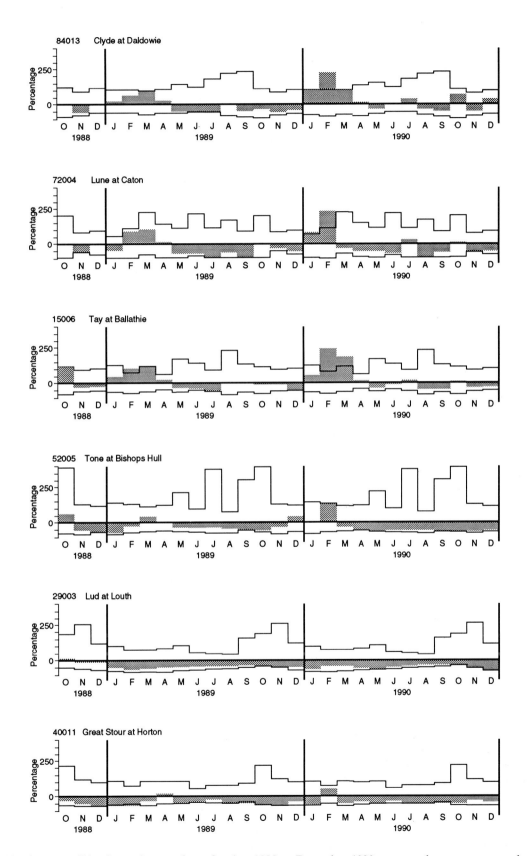

17   Monthly river runoff in six catchments from October 1988 to December 1990, expressed as a percentage departure from the long-term monthly mean.

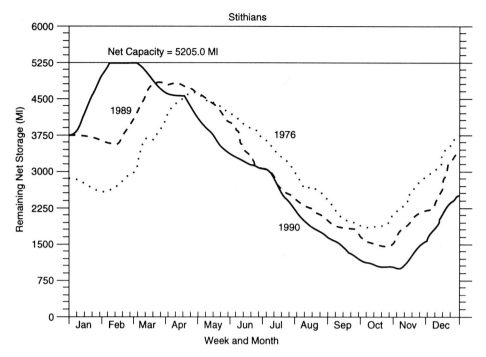

18   Reservoir contents for Stithians Reservoir, South West Water, in 1976, 1989 and 1990.

remained lower than average during the winter of 1990/ 91. Flows were more than 60% lower than average by late summer in several catchments in the north and east of the UK, and around 50% below average in late summer across much of the south and east. Figure 17 also shows that flows were very close to average during the summer of 1990 in catchments in the west of the United Kingdom (the Lune and the Clyde) and catchments draining the Scottish Highlands (the Tay).

Figure 18 shows the content, during 1989 and 1990, of a reservoir operated by South West Water Services. Although the reservoir filled in 1990 – unlike in 1989 – its contents declined rapidly in the dry spring and, by April, was below the corresponding contents in 1976 (when the reservoir failed to reach capacity but stocks increased gradually into the late spring). By the summer, the reservoir contained less than the previous year. This example shows that surface water storages, like groundwater stores, suffer from an early cessation of replenishment, and that if only a little recharge is to take place, it is better later in winter rather than sooner.

The spatial distribution of departures from the mean during summers 1989 and 1990 is shown in Figure 19 which contains data from 34 catchments. The contrast between the high flows in the north and west and the low flows in the east and south are clear: the map shows below average flows in three eastern catchments even in February 1990. Runoff was at least 25% below average across most of southern and eastern Britain during the summer of 1990. A comparison of rainfall and runoff in October 1990 (see also Figure 11) shows that, whilst rainfall was generally above average, river flows remained below average across virtually the whole of England and

Wales because the rainfall had to replenish large soil moisture deficits.

There are two reasons for the different behaviour of different catchments during the summers of 1989 and 1990. First, there were regional variations in the rainfall deficit and increased evapotranspiration, as indicated in the previous sections. Secondly, superimposed on this regional-scale variation were the more local effects of catchment geology. Large parts of lowland Britain are underlain by aquifers, with Chalk being the most widespread. River flows in such areas are largely sustained by groundwater discharge, and summer flows reflect groundwater storage in the catchment at the end of the winter recharge season. Groundwater-dominated catchments therefore have a long "memory", and summer flows may be dependent on the amounts of recharge received over several winters. River flows would be little affected by a summer drought which followed a wet winter, but it was unfortunate that in both 1988/89 and 1989/90 the areas of Britain with the greatest reliance on groundwater-dominated rivers were amongst those which had the least winter rainfall. Flows in the Lud (draining chalk in Lincolnshire) fell below average in November 1988, and had not risen above average even by February 1991. The Yorkshire Derwent (the headwaters of which drain the limestones of the North York Moors) had below average flows from September 1988 through to December 1990. Winter rainfall in these northern groundwater regions was only slightly higher than average in 1989/90.

Figure 19 also allows a comparison to be made between flows during 1990, 1989 and 1976. In general, flows in the summer of 1990 were lower than those in the summer of 1989 in many catchments, particularly in lowland

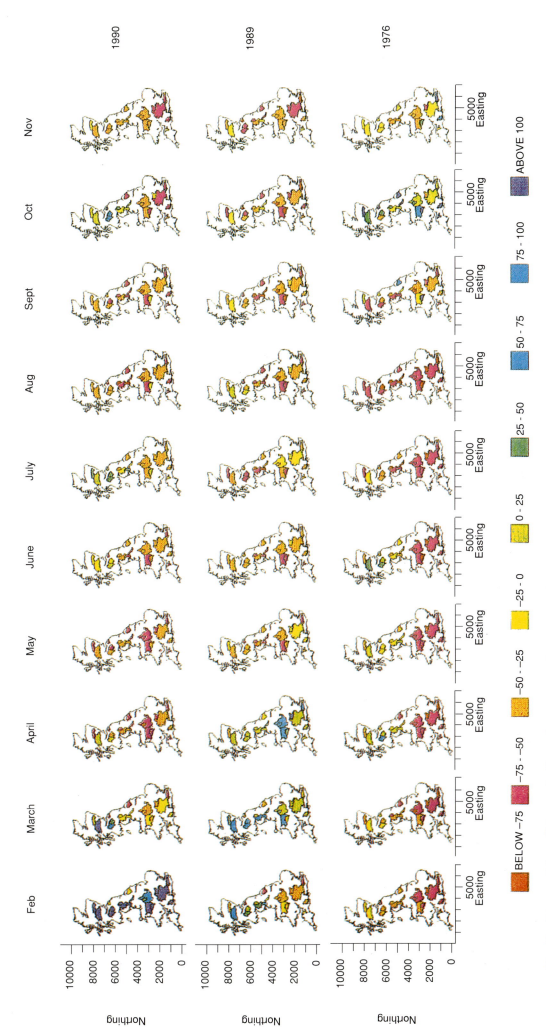

19 Monthly runoff from February to November expressed as a percentage departure from the long-term monthly mean, for 1990, 1989 and 1976.

Britain. In groundwater-dominated catchments this reflects not only the lower rainfall during spring and summer 1990 but also, and most strongly, the low base upon which recharge built at the end of 1989. Not only were total monthly flows lower in 1990 than 1989, but the duration that flows spent below critical thresholds were longer too. Flows on the Dove at Marston-on-Dove in Derbyshire, for example, were below the flow exceeded, in the long term, 95% of the time for 34 days in 1990, compared with only 19 in 1989. (The flow exceeded 95% of the time is frequently used to set limits on abstractions and effluent returns.)

Generally, flows during the summer of 1990 were considerably higher than minimum flows recorded in 1976. Summer flows in 1976 were over 70% below average across much of lowland Britain. A number of streams dried up completely and discharge across Teddington weir on the Thames ceased during August. During summer 1990, flows were generally 1.5 to 2 times larger than in 1976. River flows during August 1990 were lower than in 1976 in a small part of East Anglia (in the Welland catchment).

However, low flow conditions in 1989 and 1990 persisted for rather longer into winter than in 1976. In 1976, flows returned to near-average values during the autumn whereas in 1989 the recovery was delayed until December (with no substantial recovery even by then in eastern regions). In 1990, although heavy rainfall in October gave some relief, very low flows were recorded across much of lowland Britain in November. November flows in central southern England were among the lowest on record. Recovery in lowland Britain only really began in late December, although it had begun rather earlier in western and northern regions. The rise in flows during December in many lowland rivers – including the Thames – was rapid, but less so than in 1989. River flows in groundwater-fed catchments in central southern England – including the Kennet, Avon (Hampshire) and Stour (Dorset) - and in eastern England remained low into 1991 heralding a further sustained period of depressed runoff rates.

1.2.6 Water management responses during the summers on 1989 and 1990

Water supply problems in the UK fall into two categories. "Resource" problems arise when the amount of water held in reservoirs, rivers or groundwater storage is insufficient to meet demand. "Distribution" problems arise when local parts of the water supply system, such as feeder reservoirs and water towers, have insufficient capacity to deal with peak demands. Such problems tend to be localised and short-lived, but have direct impacts on consumers. Higher than usual demands for garden watering often trigger distribution problems in early summer.

The UK water industry adopts a hierarchical approach to coping with water shortages, with activities ranging from the implementation of pre-planned alterations to usual practice and appeals for restraint by users, through hosepipe bans, emergency changes in operation and restrictions on public use to, as a last resort, rationing. The higher stages in this hierarchy can be implemented only with the permission of the Department of the Environment through the imposition of a Drought Order. A Drought Order might allow a water supply undertaking to extract a greater amount from a river, for example (leaving a lower "compensation flow"), or might allow the undertaking to impose restrictions on the direct consumption of water by commercial and public organisations. Hosepipe bans do not need the prior approval of the Department of the Environment.

In 1989, the drought began in south east England during a very dry winter. Water management schemes were implemented and some consumer restraint was urged in late winter, but hosepipe bans are of course largely irrelevant at this time of year. The first Drought Order to increase abstractions was applied for in February 1989 by Southern Water in Kent, before a hosepipe ban was applied: the East Surrey Water Company followed soon after. The rainfall during early spring eased fears of a serious summer water shortage for a time, but large increases in demand during the very warm and dry May led to hosepipe bans being applied in many areas in southern England. Water companies reported peak demands between 30 and 50% higher than expected in some areas, due largely to the use of garden sprinklers. By the end of August 1989 around 12.5 million domestic consumers in five water service company regions (Southern, South West, Thames, Welsh and Severn-Trent, plus several of the smaller water supply companies) were affected by a hosepipe ban, and bans were imposed in parts of Yorkshire in October (note that the bans in parts of the Thames region reflected water quality problems at a treatment works rather than a water shortage or distribution problems per se). Throughout the summer 1989, water companies encouraged restraint amongst consumer through advertising campaigns of varying degrees of intensity: South West Water hired an aeroplane towing a "Save it" banner.

A further batch of Drought Orders was applied for as the dry, warm summer progressed, and resource problems appeared possible towards the end of the year if autumn were to turn out dry. By the end of July, Drought Orders were in force in the Southern, South West and North West Water areas (some implemented by the water supply companies), and Yorkshire Water applied for its first Drought Order in mid-September,

The next stage in drought response was entered on 1 August 1989, when Southern Water was empowered under the terms of a Drought Order to restrict non-essential commercial uses in some areas. Further applications for similar Drought Orders were made between August and October by several water companies in central and southern England. In late August, South West Water

20 Area with hosepipe bans as of August 21 1990. (Redrawn from Water Bulletin, August 24).

prepared to enter the last stage in drought response by installing standpipes in north Cornwall, but rainfall in mid September meant that they were not needed. (In north Devon in 1976, standpipes were actually brought into use.) Restrictions in all but the most southeastern districts were relaxed during November, but many of the Drought orders remained (albeit not applied).

Resource problems remained likely through the early part of the winter of 1989/90, and the Colne Valley and Rickmansworth Water Company appealed to their customers to conserve water in late January 1990: at the same time, additional Drought Orders were applied for by the Mid Kent and Mid Sussex Water Companies. By the beginning of March 1990, restrictions on public water use were lifted by all water companies (although Drought Orders remained in place).

Water supply companies in southern and eastern England began again to appeal for restraint by customers in May 1990 – often in response to heavy water demand – and the first new hosepipe ban of 1990 was introduced in the Medway catchment in Kent. By the end of June hosepipe bans and restrictions on garden sprinklers were in force across much of southern England, in the groundwater-fed parts of east Yorkshire, and in a small part of Devon. By the end of August 1990, 18 million consumers in England and Wales (Figure 20) were affected by restrictions which aimed to cut consumption by 10%. (In August 1989 hosepipe bans affected around 12.5 million consumers.) Anglian Region of the National Rivers Authority went so far as to ban abstractions for spray

irrigation in some Fenland catchments in late July. The bans were introduced both to safeguard downstream public supply abstractions and to ensure that low river flows did not lead to water quality problems and increased fish kills. Drought Orders to restrict non-essential commercial and public uses were applied for by the Eastbourne Water Company in mid-September, and by the Bristol Water Company in early November. Hosepipe bans in most areas were lifted by January 1991, although limitations were still in force in spring 1991 in parts of East Anglia and the South.

Alongside hosepipe bans and Drought Orders, the water industry during 1990 implemented a number of pre-planned and emergency activities (as in 1989). Southern Water, for example, began drilling exploratory boreholes to find new sources and rejuvenating old wells in May, and Severn-Trent Water bought water from North West Water to supply Buxton.

1.2.7 Discussion

Both 1989 and 1990 were years of extremes. In 1990, rainfall for England and Wales as a whole was not very different from average, but it was far more highly concentrated in winter than is usual and regional variations in annual totals was accentuated relative to the long-term average; the English lowlands being notably dry. The third wettest winter since 1766 was followed by the driest spring for more than 100 years. The dry spring 1990, together with higher than average evapotranspiration losses, meant that groundwater levels, river flows and reservoir contents fell rapidly, and the water resources situation at the beginning of summer 1990 was more fragile than at the same time in 1989. In the event, although river flows and groundwater levels were lower than in 1989, the drought in 1990 was rather less severe than that in 1976 and the water industry was better able to respond to water shortages.

There are several important aspects of the hydrological characteristics of the summers of 1989 and 1990. First, there were a number of similarities between the two years. Rainfall in both summers was close to (and frequently well above) average in the north and west of the UK, particularly in north west Scotland whereas rainfall deficits increased towards the south and east. Also, in both years river flows and groundwater levels remained lower than average until well into winter. By contrast, in 1976 river flows in most catchments in southern England returned to average by the late autumn.

Secondly, there is one important difference between the hydrological characteristics of the two summers. The summer 1989 followed a period with rather wetter than average conditions (with the dry conditions generally beginning in late summer 1988), whilst 1990 followed the dry weather of 1989. Groundwater levels in particular in 1989 had been sustained by higher than average recharge until 1987/88. The limited recharge in eastern England over the winter of 1989/90 had to build upon a much lower base than the recharge during 1988/89. Groundwater-fed rivers during 1990 therefore had to cope with a long term shortfall in rainfall. To have one dry year is unfortunate: to have two in succession is much more worrying.

A third important aspect of the rainfall patterns in 1989 and 1990 was that the areas with the greatest long-term deficiency were also those which rely on groundwater for sustaining river flows and providing public supplies, and where even in an average year, rainfall and run-off are meagre. Since such regions also coincide with areas of high population density, industrial activity and intensive farming where demand is high and accelerating, the potential impact of the drought is considerable. The impact of the meteorological drought on water resources was exaggerated by this unfortunate geographical coincidence.

The demand for water in 1989 and 1990 was considerably higher than in 1976. Although industrial demand in many areas has declined, peak domestic demands have increased with implications for the reliability of distribution systems. However, during the droughts of 1989 and 1990, water managers had the benefit both of a wider range of water management schemes and a more flexible legislative framework than were available during the 1976 drought. Many of the new water management schemes – involving inter-basin transfers and groundwater augmentation of river flows, for example – were a response to the 1976 drought and were implemented for the first time during 1989. Kielder Water and its associated water transfer scheme enabled Northumbrian Water to operate through the dry summer with no distribution or resource problems. Legislation introduced during the course of the 1976 drought (in particular the 1976 Drought Act) enabled water managers to introduce restrictions on supply at an early stage of the 1989 drought, although the detailed effect of the improved legislation awaits further study.

The drought in 1989 provided the first test of many of the drought management schemes implemented following the 1976 drought. It also highlighted the demands that may result from garden watering in early summer, and the additional disruption caused by mechanical failures in the distribution system. Water managers will be looking closely at the lessons of 1989 and 1990, and considering ways of alleviating impacts in the future. Close attention will be paid to the results of the metering trials currently being undertaken in several areas (what effect does metering and unit-based pricing have on use of water during a dry summer?), and plans for new resources will be prepared: as early as January 1990, a consortium of water companies in drought-stricken Kent announced the revival of the long-dormant Broad Oak reservoir project.

1.2.8 Conclusions

1. The summer of 1989 had less rainfall than average across most of the UK, with the exception of a wet period in October, particularly in the west. Both May and September were generally dry, unlike in 1976. Overall, the period May–September 1989 was the second driest in England and Wales since records began in 1766.

2. Potential evapotranspiration rates during the summer of 1989 were among the highest on record, and actual evapotranspiration over the entire country was higher than during the summer of 1976 (because of the greater availability of water in 1989). Soil moisture deficits in excess of 100–125 mm occurred in many parts of eastern Britain during the summer of 1989, and, in many places, deficits were maintained throughout the winter of 1989/90.

3. Both groundwater levels and river flows were higher during the summer of 1989 than in 1976, but the lack of widespread autumn rainfall meant that levels and flows in many areas continued to decline until December.

4. Rainfall in the summer of 1990 (June, July, August) was not exceptional; it was 68% of average in England and Wales, and 97% of average in Scotland. In fact, rainfall in June was greater than normal.

5. The unusual feature of the rainfall in England in 1990 was the contrast between winter and spring; 1989/90 was the third wettest winter since 1766, and the 1990 spring was the driest in 100 years. The ratio of winter (October–March) to summer (April-September) rainfall in the UK is normally about 1.0, but in 1989/90 it was 2.2, more like a Mediterranean climate.

6. Despite the rainfall in June, there was an exceptionally long period with high soil moisture deficits in the summer 1990 in most of England; deficits greater than 100 mm persisted for more than 20 weeks in large areas in the south and east. This severe and persistent drought was due to low rainfall in spring and the highest potential evaporation rates on record (since 1961) in summer (June–August), so that actual evaporation rates in summer exceeded rainfall.

7. The high rainfall in January and February 1990 led to rapid rises in groundwater levels (and considerable flooding) with the notable exception of wells in the chalk in eastern England. However, the dry spring meant that both groundwater levels and river flows fell rapidly, and by early summer were below 1989 values. Levels and flows continued to decline during the summer, but remained above those recorded

during the 1976 drought until August 1990. As in 1989 autumn was dry, and the seasonal recovery in river flows and groundwater levels was delayed. Levels and flows in November were lower than the values recorded at the end of the 1976 drought across large parts of southern and eastern England. Groundwater-fed catchments were particularly affected, especially in the east. River flows in some groundwater-fed catchments fell below average in summer 1988 and had not risen above average by January 1991. In contrast, river flows remained close to average (and in some months well above average) in catchments in the north west.

Chapter B2
Impacts on the Terrestrial Environment

B2.1 IMPACTS ON PLANTS

2.1.1 Introduction

Impacts of the 1989 and 1990 hot, dry summers on herbaceous plants and forest and amenity trees are described in this section. The sources of information are varied ranging from detailed long term monitoring data on individual species at specific sites to nationwide anecdotal observations made during the "Countryside Survey 1990".

B2.1.2 Herbaceous flora

FACTORS WHICH INFLUENCE THE RESPONSE OF HERBACEOUS SPECIES TO HOT DRY SUMMERS

It is neither possible, nor sensible, to attempt to generalise about the effect of two hot, dry summers on individual species throughout their range. The intensity and length of the droughts varied from region to region (Chapter B1.2) and the impact of the drought on any species will have depended on soil type, aspect, slope and vegetation management. If a grassland site is unmanaged, competition from tall growing species with deep root systems may result in the death of lower growing species, which would have survived if the site had been managed.

Species which began growth early in the season and flowered in early to mid-summer were not affected by the summer's climate, whereas some of those species which normally flower in mid to late summer either failed to produce functional flowers or failed to produce any aboveground reproductive structures.

In view of the difficulties of separating the many factors which influence the response of individuals to drought and high temperatures experienced in the summers of 1989 and 1990, most comments will be restricted to plant responses observed at particular sites.

SPECIES OF MOIST HABITATS

Species restricted to moist habitats suffered greatest shoot damage, and, for some species, significant levels of mortality occurred. Among the species most affected were nationally rare species with a western or northern British distribution.

Ferns, amongst the higher plant groupings, are most vulnerable to summer drought. Many exploit rocky habitats with little soil, and the juvenile stage of their life cycle (the prothallus) is vulnerable to desiccation. An early casualty of summer drought in lowland central England in 1989 was hart's-tongue fern (*Phyllitis scolopendrium*) – mature fronds died early and plants growing on cliffs did not recover. This species can be found in a range of habitats in the UK, such as clayey ditch banks in woods, hedge banks and shaded cliffs. However in Eastern England it survives only in moist to wet habitats.

EFFECTS OF 1989 DROUGHT ON SHALLOWLY-ROOTED SPECIES

During 1989, the shoots of most grasses in agricultural pastures became brown and withered, while the foliage of adjacent herbs with long tap-roots (e.g. ribwort plantain (*Plantago lanceolata*) and cat's-ear (*Hypochoeris radicata*)) remained green. Similarly, in lowland calcareous grassland, species with a deep tap-root (e.g. greater knapweed (*Centaurea scabiosa*)) remained green (if in some instances wilted) while the shoots of grasses such as quaking-grass (*Briza media*) were totally killed. In lowland woods, woodland herbs wilted, particularly dog's mercury (*Mercurialis perennis*), before any signs of foliar damage were evident on the trees.

Thus, deeply-rooted species that were able to exploit subsoil moisture were less adversely affected by drought than shallow-rooted species, including most pasture grasses.

EFFECT OF THE 1990 SUMMER ON GRASSLANDS AND LAWNS

Pastures on the Boulder Clay soils of Huntingdonshire had turned brown by early July and by mid August the vegetation appeared almost white from a distance, with only the green leaves of deep-rooted species such as tall fescue (*Festuca arundinaceae*) remaining green. Soil moisture deficits at Monks Wood reached 113 cm on 1 August and were 100cm on 8 October (see also Chapter B1.2.3).

At Upwood Meadows – low lying permanent grassland situated on ancient ridge and furrow appeared brown and dead, and vegetation on prominent ant-hills looked particularly droughted. Measurements of the water table (made in a series of dip wells since 1985), showed that the water table was 56 cm below the surface on 15 May and by mid-June was more than a meter below the surface. By the end of December 1990 the water table was still 58 cm below the surface. In "normal" years, the water table is 5–10 cm below the surface in summer and in some years there has been standing water in the furrow in July. Observations of these sites during the winter

1990/91 showed that the vegetation has returned to its normal colour, the apparently "dead" grass producing new tillers from underground stems. Many of the forbs species in Upwood Meadows, such as primrose (*Primula veris*), knapweed (*Centaurea nigra*), hoary plantain (*Plantago media*) and dropwort (*Filipendula vulgaris*) had already produced new leaves by early March 1991 and it seemed unlikely that the summer of 1990 would have any long-term effect on the floristic composition of this site.

Green-winged orchid (*Orchis morio*), one of the many rare species which occur at Upwood Meadows, did not seem to have been affected by the drought. Leaf emergence began at the end of September, and by 14 October the basal rosette had on average about 3 leaves, which is at about the same as in the previous 11 years. This suggests that the underground tubers of the orchid, situated in the top 5 cm of soil, were not desiccated during the summer period when this species had no above ground parts.

Lawns which were not watered through the summer of 1990 turned brown and looked dead, but as with pastures, recovery was good during the winter and by March 1991 they were green and growing rapidly.

EFFECTS ON BRECKLAND HEATHS IN 1990

Poor shoot growth and premature shrivelling of flowers of heather (*Calluna vulgaris*) was reported from many sites in Breckland. At Dersingham in Norfolk, the warden reported that die-back occurred on heather shoots growing on the higher ground over an area of about 40 ha, but that no damage was observed to other species. Similar observations were made at Roydon Common. Nature reserve wardens who could remember the drought of 1976, commented that similar damage had been noted then, but was of little consequence as few of the heather plants had been killed and that most recovered in the following spring. At Cavenham Heath NNR, heather flowered poorly in comparison with "normal" years and in July and August plants were attacked by the heather beetle.

At Weeting Heath, 400 flowering spikes of spiked speedwell (*Veronica spicata*) were counted in 1988. In 1990, the plants looked desiccated and produced only 4 spikes. However, in December, new, green basal leaves appeared and the plants appeared to have recovered. *Hieracium pilosella* behaved similarly, plants appearing desiccated and flowerless in August, but recovering during the winter. Maiden pink (*Dianthus deltiodes*), another Breckland rarity growing on Weeting heath, appeared unaffected by the drought, 149 flowering plants being counted in late July, which is about the same as noted in previous years.

OBSERVATIONS ON SPECIES IN ESSEX

a) **Least lettuce (*Lactuca saligna*)**: Almost the whole British population of this species occurs on the Thames

Table 1: Numbers of flowering spikes of *Orchis morio* and *Spiranthes spiralis* at Toothill, Danebury, 1987–1990 (G. Pyman, *pers. comm.*).

Year	O. morio	Spiranthes spiralis
1987	2000	160
1988	1600	20
1989	400	20
1990	500	26

estuary and was intensively studied in the early 1980s (A. Hare). Since then, it has been routinely monitored by former NCC staff. In 1987 and 1988, concern was expressed that the number of plants was decreasing, but in both 1989 and 1990 a major recovery appeared to take place. This was largely attributed to the droughts, which forced cattle from adjacent fields to forage on the sea walls where the plant grows. This foraging caused slumping and erosion, with in many places more than 50% bare ground. These conditions appeared to be ideal for *Lactuca*, which flourished despite heavy grazing.

b) ***Halimone pedunculata***: This salt-marsh species was thought to be extinct in Britain when it was discovered at a new site in south Essex in 1987. Since then it has been monitored annually by former NCC staff. Population counts were as follows: 1987 – 1714 plants; 1988 – 1667 plants; 1989 – 685 plants; 1990 – 4121 plants. The slump in numbers in 1989 was attributed to the drought, resulting in the failure of late cohorts. In 1990, after a summer with even less rain, it was expected that the population would again decline, but instead numbers increased to 4121. The 1990 increase could reflect increased moisture at a critical time for seedling establishment; on the other hand it could be a natural fluctuation in an annual species. Populations on the western coast of France are known to fluctuate considerably from year to year.

c) **Sea bindweed (*Calystegia soldanella*), sea kale (*Crambe maritima*), samphire (*Crithmum maritimum*), sea pea (*Lathyrus japonicus*), *Polygonum oxyspermum* and scentless chamomile (*Tripleurospermum maritimum*)** all increased in dune systems in north east Essex in 1990, whereas **sea spurge (*Euphorbia paralias*)** declined. These changes may be related to climatic fluctuations; alternatively, they may be the result of independent coastal processes.

d) **Teazel-headed clover (*Trifolium squamosum*), grass vetchling (*Lathyrus nissolia*) and sea hard-grass (*Parapholis strigosa*)** which grow on sea walls in Essex, did well in 1990, possibly as a result of reduced competition from coarse grasses.

e) **Bog pimpernel (*Anagallis tenella*)**: At its only site in Essex, the Bog Pimpernel flowered profusely in 1990, possibly as a result of stress induced by the dry condition of the fen in which it grows.

f) **Green-winged orchid (*Orchis morio*) *and* autumn lady's tresses (*Spiranthes spiralis*)**: At Toothill,

Danebury, these two orchids grow on glacial gravels overlying London Clay. Counts made since 1987 (G. Pyman, *pers. comm.*) indicate that the number of flowering spikes was greatly reduced in 1989 and 1990 probably as a result of dry conditions, although the number of spikes of *Spiranthes* was also low in the previous year (Table 1).

EFFECTS ON AMERICAN DUCKWEED (*Lemna minuscula*) IN CAMBRIDGE

This American duckweed was first recorded in the British Isles in a ditch on Coe Fen, Cambridge in 1977. Since then, it has been found in small quantity elsewhere in the county and at numerous other localities in the UK. In 1990, in a survey of the many ditches and other water bodies around the Cambridge colleges (C. Preston, *pers. comm.*) it was found growing in great abundance, often forming continuous and usually dense stands. At many sites it appeared to be replacing the native lesser and ivy duckweeds, (*Lemna minor* and *L. trisulca*). It is interesting to speculate why American duckweed was so abundant in Cambridge in 1990. It may have been re-introduced to the area and spread explosively. Another possibility is that it was favoured by the hot summer, either because it benefitted directly from the high temperatures, or because the reduced water flow in ditches provided

conditions under which the populations could build up, possibly related to water chemistry. It may be significant that Surrey botanists noted a population explosion in this species in the hot summer of 1989.

LONG-TERM OBSERVATIONS ON ORCHID POPULATIONS

Long-term studies have been conducted on the population dynamics and biology of five orchid species in Bedfordshire and Cambridgeshire. The background to these studies is given in Appendix I. The percentage of plants of three species that flowered over a 25-year period are given in Table 2. These species flower in summer and autumn.

The musk orchid (*Herminium monorchis*) was particularly sensitive to drought, as shown in Figure 1, which gives the absolute numbers of plants that flowered in a 444 m^2 area at Totternhoe, Bedfordshire. The adverse effect of the 1976 drought was carried over to 1977, and the population did not fully recover for 4 years. The dry summer of 1984 also adversely affected flowering and in 1989, only 19% of the plants flowered. In 1990, only 4 out of 331 plants flowered, and those plants did not produce viable seed. It seems likely that no flowers will be produced in 1991, and if future summers are hot and dry, the musk orchid could face extinction at this locality.

Autumn lady's tresses (*Spiranthes spiralis*) was adversely affected by the 1976 drought, but it recovered quickly in 1977. In 1989 and 1990, 26% and 14% of plants flowered, respectively. This species is obviously less affected by drought, and the soil water deficit at Knocking Hoe was probably not as great in 1989 or 1990 as in 1976. The hot, dry summer resulted in both shorter flowering spikes and few flowers per inflorescence (Appendix 2, Table 1). Thus, the mean inflorescence heights of *Spiranthes* in 1976, 1989 and 1990 were 5.8, 8.1 and 8.2 cm, respectively, compared with 9.4–12.7 cm in other years: similarly, the numbers of flowers per spike were 10.0, 9.8 and 9.4 in 1976, 1989 and 1990, respectively, compared with 10.0–12.4 in other years.

The man orchid (*Aceras anthropophorum*), a member of the Continental Southern element of the British flora, reaches its northern limit in Europe in England. It would be reasonable to expect this species to benefit from the hot dry summers of 1989 and 1990. At Totternhoe Knolls this was not the case. From 106 plants in 1966, the population grew steadily to 339 plants in 1980, but since then the number of plants have fallen steadily reaching 203 in 1986. The population fell by half the following year, recovered slightly to 135 plants in 1988 but fell to 100 plants in 1989 and to an all-time low of 51 plants in 1990. The percentage of plants which flowered was also unusually low in 1989 and 1990 (4.3 and 4.0% respectively, compared to 10.7 to 72.7% in previous years). It seems likely that grazing from rabbits during the winter months, which has been unusually severe since about 1986, had a deleterious effect on the population which could lead to its extinction at this site. Observations made

Table 2: Percentage of plants of three orchid species that flowered each year from 1966 to 1990. Man orchid and musk orchid flower in mid-summer; autumn lady's tresses flowers in autumn.

Year	Man orchid (*Aceras anthropophorum*)*	Musk orchid (*Herminium monorchis*)*	Autumn lady's tresses (*Spiranthes spiralis*)**
1966	67	38	74
1967	73	13	57
1968	51	16	45
1969	31	16	45
1970	18	8	19
1971	31	7	23
1972	31	37	37
1973	53	19	42
1974	37	28	23
1975	33	11	35
1976	45	0	1
1977	39	0	31
1978	33	11	20
1979	36	32	21
1980	33	24	33
1981	17	35	18
1982	27	20	32
1983	10	13	13
1984	25	6	6
1985	10	7	18
1986	13	20	22
1987	11	14	25
1988	4	31	16
1989	3	19	26
1990	4	1	14
Mean	**29**	**18**	**27**

* At Totternhoe, Bedfordshire
** At Knocking Hoe, Bedfordshire

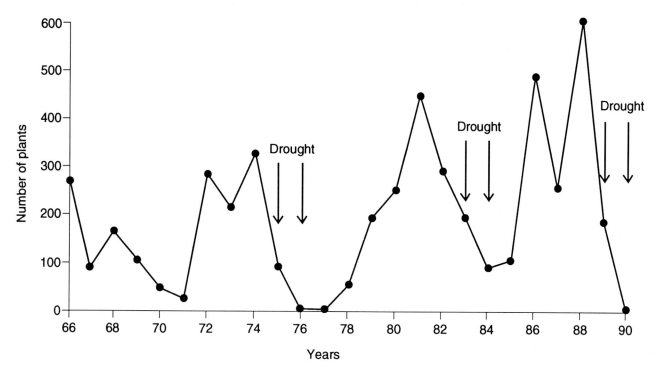

1   The musk orchid (*Herminium monorchis*) – number of plants flowering in a 444 m^{-2} area at Totternhoe, Bedfordshire, 1966–90.

at Barnack Hills and Holes, Cambridgeshire, in 1990, demonstrated that flowering was "normal" at a site where rabbits were controlled, a mean spike height of 19.6 cm being recorded on 10 June, from a random sample of 50 plants. The important point demonstrated by this comparative study of the same species growing at 2 sites situated in the same climatic zone, is the complexity of the flowering process and the difficulties associated with isolating individual causal factors.

The bee orchid (*Ophrys apifera*) and green-winged orchid (*Orchis morio*) produce new leaves in autumn and have leafy rosettes which persist through the winter months. It might be expected that a long, hot, dry summer could delay leaf emergence in the autumn, but there was no evidence of this occurring in 1990. A few leaves of green-winged orchid were seen with their tips emerging on 13 September, and by 14 October most plants had between 2 and 7 leaves, which was comparable to the previous 11 years. Leaves of the bee orchid were first seen on 2 October, which is about the time they appear every year. Mean flower spike height and mean number of flowers per inflorescence in bee orchid were significantly lower (p < 0.05) than in previous years (Appendix 2, Table 2), almost certainly as a result of the drought. However, despite the dry conditions, some plants were successful in producing seed, although the number of capsules was reduced. In contrast, green-winged orchid, which flowers about two months earlier than bee orchid, produced flower spikes which did not differ significantly in size or in number of flowers from mean values recorded in the previous 8 years (Appendix 2, Table 3).

The bee orchid belongs to the Southern Eurasian element

of the British flora and has a widespread distribution in the Mediterranean and Asia Minor. It has been suggested (Wells and Cox, 1989) that it is growing under sub-optimal conditions on the clay soils at Monks Wood, Bedfordshire, and it might be expected to increase its propensity to flower if the climate became warmer. However, there was no evidence of a significant increase in flowering in either 1989 or 1990.

LONG-TERM OBSERVATIONS ON THE MARSH GENTIAN (*Gentiana pneumonanthe*)

The marsh gentian, a long-lived perennial plant, occurs on wet, acid lowland heaths in England, and on Anglesey. Its growth habit is to produce one or more shoots each summer which die back in winter. In southern England, growth starts in early April and flowering occurs in August and September. In most natural populations a high proportion of plants do not flower and it is rare for a plant to produce more than five flowers. Observations on populations of the marsh gentian have been made since 1977 as four sites, two in south east Dorset and two in the New Forest (Chapman *et al.* 1989). A computer model, MGEN, highlights two key factors in the maintenance of gentian populations: (i) the frequency of vegetation burning, and (ii) year-to-year differences in flowering due to climatic variation.

A Spearman Rank correlation was used to examine the relationship between number of flowers per plant and both the current year and the previous year's summer temperatures. Summer air temperature was calculated as the average of the daily maximum and minimum temperature for the period April to September. There

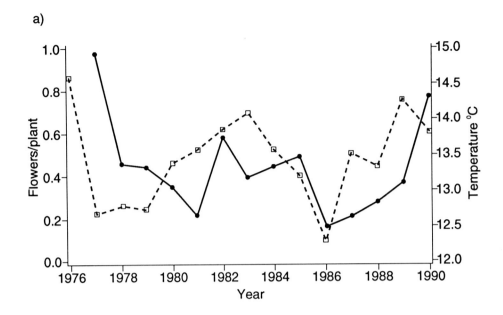

a)

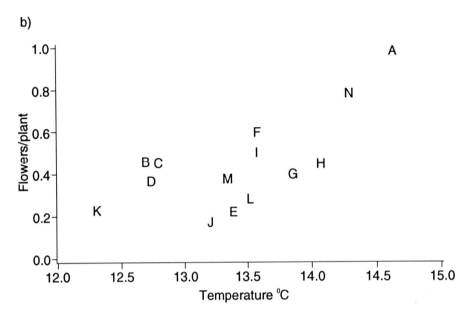

b)

2 (a) Numbers of flowers per plant of marsh gentian (*Gentiana pneumonanthe*) (——) shown in relation to mean summer temperature (– – – –). Data are means for sites in east Dorset and the New Forest.

(b) Relationship between mean summer temperature in the previous year and the numbers of flowers per plant on marsh gentian (*Gentiana pneumonanthe*). Letters refer to flowering years, A=1977, B=1978 . . ., N=1990.

was no significant correlation (Figure 2a) between flowering performance and the current year's summer temperature (r = 0.02); on the other hand there was a significant correlation between flowering performance in the current year and the summer temperature of the previous year (r = 0.60, p < 0.05). The effect of high summer temperatures in 1976 and 1989 on flowering in 1977 and 1990 is shown in Figure 2b. It is likely that plants are able to accumulate larger quantities of storage products in root systems in hot summers enabling greater growth and flowering in the following year. It is possible, but not proven, that more flower initials are formed in hot summers than in cooler years. Whichever explanation is correct, it is clear that the enhanced flowering seen in 1990 reflects the warm summer of 1989 and that the effect

of the hot summer in 1990 should result in exceptionally good flowering of the marsh gentian in 1991.

LONG-TERM OBSERVATIONS ON THE BEARDED FESCUE (*Vulpia ciliata spp. ambigua*)

Bearded fescue is a winter-annual grass confined to the UK and a few sites in northern France. Within the UK, the distribution of this sub-species is centred around Breckland in East Anglia. Typically it is found on disturbed, sandy soils with a low cover of perennial grasses. It has been studied since 1987 at its most northerly point in Britain, at Holme-next-the-sea, Norfolk. Seeds germinate in July-October. Growth remains fairly static until the spring when plants produce more leaves.

Table 3: Pooled data collected from two groups of four quadrats (A and B) from four generations of bearded fescue at the most northerly population of the sub-species in Norfolk. Row 1 gives the number of seedlings observed in the Autumn (− = not recorded). Row 2 gives the number of flowering individuals the following spring. Row 3 is the mean number of seeds produced per plant.

| | 1987–1988 | | 1988–1989 | | 1989–1990 | | 1990–1991 | |
	A	B	A	B	A	B	A	B
Seedlings	82	52	0	10	−	−	117	37
Flowering	8	7	0	1	26	10		
No. of seeds per plant	3.75	4.28	0	7	7.71	10.0		

Inflorescences are produced between April and the end of May. The plant senesces as seeds are set and is dead by the time the seeds are dispersed in June–August. There is no seed bank. Generations are discrete and the population size in any one year is dependent on the number of seeds produced in the previous year. A consequence of this life-history strategy is that seed production and thus population size is likely to be strongly affected by extreme climatic conditions with one disastrous year causing local extinction. Seed production of individual plants is strongly influenced by the number of their perennial grass neighbours. In hot dry summers larger gaps will appear in the vegetation as the perennial grasses die and thus more suitable sites for bearded fescue become available. Climatic conditions could, therefore, have both a direct and an indirect effect on performance.

Data collected from eight 20 × 20 cm quadrats, set up in October 1987 and recorded annually since then, are presented in Table 3. Quadrats were separated into two groups of four at different points in the population (groups A and B). The total number of plants recorded in the two groups varied considerably between 1987 and 1990. The drop in numbers from 1987/88 to 1988/89 was probably a consequence of the very wet period in June and July 1988 which caused seeds to germinate earlier than normal. Many seedlings died during August and September which were dry. The hot dry summer in 1989 had both a direct and an indirect influence on the population. The warm dry spring followed by the hot summer resulted in individuals producing more seeds than in previous years. The drought conditions caused many perennial plants to die back leading to gaps which provided germination sites for bearded fescue seedlings in the autumn. This process was repeated during the hot dry summer of 1990. As a result, the population of bearded fescue, which was on the verge of extinction in 1988, has increased substantially.

Extreme weather conditions cause fluctuations in population size in this annual grass. It is worth noting that a *series* of hot, dry years or cool, wet years will have a much greater effect on population size than events in a single year.

2.1.3 Phenology of flowering plants

Observations were made by Professor F T Last of the presence or absence of flowers of over 200 species or

hybrids in his garden at Longniddry, East Lothian (55°58′N, 2°57′W) almost every week for 12 years. Observations made in 1989 and 1990 were compared with the average for 1978–88.

Overall, the 1990 season was later than that of 1989 but still significantly earlier than 1978/88 average except for January. Many species that usually come into flower between May and September started to flower appreciably earlier, sometimes significantly earlier in 1990 than in 1989.

When considering the phenology of plants in any year, it is obviously difficult to distinguish between the effects of a previous hot summer, and a previous mild winter. Observations of first flowering at Longniddry in 1989 and 1990 have already been discussed in Section A. In this section, evidence of a cumulative effect of successive warm years is described.

EARLY FLOWERING OF WOODY PERENNIALS

Table 4: Some woody perennial garden species that flowered significantly earlier in 1990 than in 1989 at Longniddry, East Lothian. Units are weeks after 1st January when first flowering occurred.

	1978/88	1989	1990
Forsythia x intermedia	15.0	11	9
Lonicera x tellmanniana (a form of honeysuckle)	17.8	16	12
Prunus avium	18.1	17	14
Azalea spp.	18.5	14	11
Escallonia garden var.	25.2	26	20
Cornus sp.	22.6	23	16
Sumach (*Ahus glabra*)	36.0	33	32

(* Mean first flowering dates for the period 1978–1988).

Most, but not all, of the species that flowered earlier in 1990 than in 1989 were woody perennials. Some examples are given in Table 4. These observations suggested that there may have been a cumulative effect of successive warm years. Such a suggestion is supported by observations related to 11 species/hybrids of *Rosa*. Table 5 shows that all 11 species flowered in the same week or earlier in 1990 than in 1989.

Table 5: Week of the year (after 1 January) when eleven rose (*Rosa*) species/hybrids first flowered at Longniddry, East Lothian.

	Dates of first flowering		
	1978/88	**1989**	**1990**
R. hugonis	20.8	19	18*
R. rugosa	21.6	21	18*
R. sericea	22.4	23	18*
Glory of Edzell	23.0	22	19*
Fruhlinsgold	23.2	19*	19*
Nevada	23.3	23	19*
R. californica	23.6	25	22
R. rubrifolia	24.4	25	23
Hybrids	24.7	21	18*
R. moyessii	24.8	25	23
Scarlet fire	25.6	23	23
Mean	**23.4**	**22.4**	**20.0**

* Date of first flowering in 1989 or 1990 differed from that of the mean (1978/88) by more than 2 × SD of the mean

Table 6: Number of plant species (or hybrids) in flower in a garden at Longniddry in autumn months of 1989 and 1990 compared with the mean of 1978/88. Units are weeks after 1 January.

	1978/88	**1989**	**1990**
August	69	76	79
September	54	68	62
October	35	42	42
November	17	19	25
December	12	21*	21*

* more than 2 × SD larger than 1978/88 mean.

AUTUMN FLOWERING

In late autumn 1990, there were some parallels with the exceptional events that started in autumn 1988 and continued in 1989. Some plants started to flower exceedingly early: in December 1990 as in December 1989 there were significantly more plants flowering than in December 1978/88 (Table 6).

Whereas winter jasmine (*Jasminum nudiflorum*) started to flower in week 49 in 1989 compared with week 50 for 1978/88, it commenced in week 46 in 1990. The differences were even larger in *Viburnum fragrans*, its flowering starting in week 33 in 1990, week 41 in 1989 and week 44 in 1978/88.

As in autumn 1988, some spring flowering plants began flowering in autumn 1990. Thus trumpet gentian (*Gentiana acaulis*) which usually starts flowering in week 17 recommenced flowering in 1991 during week 5 as did bear berry (*Arctostaphylos uva-ursi*) which normally starts in week 25 – these events were recorded in Dundee in addition to Longniddry.

CONCLUSION

As expected, plants leafed out and flowered early in 1990 following the mild winter and warm spring. A more unexpected observation was the early flowering in 1990 of summer-flowering woody perennials, including roses. These species flowered earlier than in 1989, when it was similarly warm. It seems possible that there was some cumulative effect of continued warmer-than-usual temperatures, which had persisted since the winter of 1988/89.

2.1.4 Forest and amenity trees

1989 SUMMER

Drought symptoms occurred widely in southern Britain. The most common were a general reversible wilting of many deciduous broadleaves and the yellowing, browning and premature shedding of the older leaves on many deciduous and evergreen broadleaves and conifers, e.g. birch (*Betula* spp.), beech (*Fagus sylvatica*), poplar (*Populus* spp.), hornbeam (*Carpinus betulus*), yew (*Taxus baccata*) and some clones of Leyland (*Cupressocyparis leylandii*) and Lawson cypress (*Chamaecyparis lawsoniana*) (Innes *et al.*, 1989; Strouts *et al.*, 1991). Widespread and conspicuous browning of oak (*Quercus* spp.) foliage was due to attack by the aphid *Phyloxera glabra* while a similar browning of lime (*Tilia* spp.) was due to the lime mite *Eotetranychus tiliarium*.

1990 SUMMER

FRUITING

There were numerous reports of very heavy production of fruits in beech and hornbeam in 1990. For the former species it was the second successive mast year on some trees – a most unusual event. Hornbeam, normally an inconspicuous tree, was rendered very noticeable by its long clusters of fruits, particularly after the bracts had turned yellow in late summer. Maples and many berry-bearing trees (notably hawthorn (*Crataegus*), apple (*Malus*) and white beam (*Sorbus* spp.)) also cropped heavily. Since the 1990 flowers were formed from buds initiated in 1989, heavy fruiting cannot be considered to be an effect of the 1990 summer *per se*. However, in some cases, the demands on the trees placed by the developing crops must have exacerbated the stress posed by the extreme weather conditions.

It may be noted, *en passant*, that acorn production was quite low. This may have been due, at least in part, to the damage to developing flowers caused by the sharp frosts of early April 1990.

FOLIAGE SYMPTOMS

Not surprisingly, given the heavy winter rainfall and the cool, grey weather in June 1990, there was little evidence of drought-determined foliage symptoms in trees until the onset of the very hot weather of early August. When symptoms did show up they were largely restricted to central and southern England. Thus, the foliage yellowing of larch (*Larix* spp.) that was recorded in Scotland in 1989 did not recur there in 1990.

With its shallow rooting system, birch is noted for its drought susceptibility, and leaf discoloration and defoliation were conspicuous on a wide range of sites. Frequently only a scattering of green leaves remained at the tips of the twigs on affected trees.

Many observers reported that much of the beech in southern England began the season with unusually small leaves, and supporting evidence for this comes from the Forestry Commission's main monitoring programme (Innes, 1991). Following the extremely hot weather in early August 1990 (see Chapter B1.1.5), it was observed that many trees showed severe foliage browning, normally at the periphery of the crown. These brown leaves soon fell, so that by early September the trees were characterised by only a thin sprinkling of green leaves on the older parts of the twigs. Most of the observations of this phenomenon related to roadside or parkland trees. Evidence for the same kind of process operating in woodland beech comes from the work of Innes (1991) on the change in condition of beech at 7 sites in the monitoring programme. Two assessments were made during the summer: initially between the second and fourth weeks in July and subsequently in the last week of August. Increases in leaf discoloration were recorded commonly, as were changes in the frequency of leaf rolling (a probable drought response) and in crown density.

Other trees on which leaf discoloration was common included cherry, field maple (*Acer campestre*), hawthorn, rowan (*Sorbus aucuparia*) and sweet chestnut (*Castanea sativa*). Ash (*Fraxinus excelsior*) was reported as showing wilting at several locations, but relatively little leaf death and leaf fall occurred – the principal impression created being one of a general shabbiness.

In general, oak provided a marked contrast to other species. In most areas its dark green leaves provided welcome relief in the bleached landscapes. However, dramatic foliage browning associated with branch dieback did occur at a few sites (see below).

Among the conifers, leaf symptoms were most conspicuous on larch and Norway spruce (*Picea abies*). Flagging of fronds on western red cedar (*Thuja plicata*) was also noted.

As usual, trees on chalk fared notably better than those on other subsoils. This is because chalk has a high water storage capacity and because water can move upwards through the fine pores.

DIEBACK AND DEATH

Dieback and death of birch on free-draining soils occurred much more commonly in 1990 than in 1989. It did not approach the scale of damage recorded in 1976, but seems likely to have been appreciably more severe than that which occurred in 1983 and 1984.

On oak, conspicuous drought-related branch dieback occurred at several sites south of Reading in Berkshire. The damage first appeared in 1989 and additional trees were affected in 1990. The trees were sited on seasonally waterlogged or ground water gley soils where the normal deep rooting system may not have been able to develop.

Beech suffered little dieback during 1990, but some trees that had been severely stressed died during the 1991 growing season under the influence of weakly pathogenic fungi such as *Nectria coccinea* and *Hypoxylon* species (see Lonsdale 1980, 1983). However, losses were nothing like as severe as those experienced after 1976 (Aldhous 1981). Shoot growth was very poor in 1991 as an invariable consequence of a dry summer in the preceding year (Lonsdale *et al.*, 1989).

In broadleaves, the most striking example of dieback and death linked to the 1990 summer was caused by sooty bark disease of sycamore (*Acer pseudoplatanus*). This disease, caused by the fungus *Cryptostroma corticale*, killed a considerable number of trees in south east England. *C. corticale* was first recorded as a pathogen in north east London after the hot dry summer of 1947, and during the next few years gave rise to much concern. Thereafter it went into "eclipse" until the hot summer of 1959 (Pawsey, 1962). In 1975, it was again recorded in London, and in 1976 it was very widespread, with serious mortality being recorded as far north as Chester and as far west as Plymouth (Young, 1978). The fungus has a relatively high temperature optimum for growth (25°C) and has been shown by experiments to develop more rapidly in water-stressed trees than unstressed ones (Dickenson and Wheeler, 1981). Interestingly, it was not reported in 1983, 1984 or 1989.

It may be noted that there was no indication of an upsurge in Dutch elm disease during 1990 in the new populations of English elm (*Ulmus procera*) that have developed from root suckers in many parts of southern England. Although the activity of the bark beetle vectors would have been promoted by the hot weather, their population levels were still extremely low. In addition there is some evidence from experiments conducted in 1976 that high temperatures and drought stress are not conducive to the rapid development of the causal fungus, *Ophiostoma ulmi*, in infected branches (Gibbs and Greig, 1977).

Among the conifers, drought was implicated in the death of Norway spruce in Gloucestershire and Lincolnshire. Here the cumulative effect of the two successive droughts seemed likely to be important. There was also some damage to larch but this was less serious than in 1976. Young Western hemlock (*Tsuga heterophylla*) and various *Abies* spp. were also killed at some locations.

AUTUMN LEAF FALL

Although many trees showed premature leaf fall, good autumn colour was by no means absent in 1990. It was noted as being spectacular and extended in some localities, and indeed many oaks were still in full leaf at the end of the first week of December.

2.1.5 "Countryside survey 1990" observations

During the summer and early autumn of 1990, ITE completed a field survey of land cover, habitats and plant species in Great Britain. The survey was part of a wider project, "Countryside Survey 1990", which was funded by the Natural Environment Research Council (NERC), Department of the Environment (DoE) and Department of Trade and Industry (DTI), with additional support from the then NCC.

This section reports anecdotal observations made by some surveyors during February and March 1991 before field records were fully analysed.

SOUTH ENGLAND

The major area of drought extended eastwards from Dorset. Kent and parts of Sussex were most affected. Surveyors found some difficulty in plant species identification and in making ground cover estimates in roadside vegetation plots, which were badly scorched and, in places, resembled "coconut matting". Watercourses, and ditches in particular, were usually dry in the east of the region, and in some parts of the south-west. There was a suggestion that aquatic marginal vegetation was being replaced by a "developing dry flora". Many farmers were having problems providing fodder for their cattle. Some were proposing to plant maize instead of grass while others were concentrating on winter crops because summer growth was failing. Farmers expressed uncertainty about future cropping patterns, as a direct result of perceived changes in climate.

EAST ANGLIA AND THE EAST MIDLANDS

Unusual, or extreme, conditions were not noted before early August 1990. From then, vegetation in roadside and hedge-bottom habitats appeared to die off and many vegetation quadrats contained non-green vegetation. However, by the second week in September, there was a general greening of the verges as coarse grasses such as couch (*Agropyron repens*) and tall oat-grass (*Arrhenatherum elatius*) produced fresh growth. Lawns which turned brown during late summer were reported to have fully recovered by mid-November. Some hedgerow plants were thought to have flowered for a second time late in the seasons (*e.g.* cow parsley (*Anthriscus sylvestris*) and campion (*Silene* spp.)). Many recently planted trees died (as many as 75–90% in places) especially where planted on higher or well drained ground. Birch trees were seen to turn brown and shed their leaves in July. At Colne in Lincolnshire, a plum crop was abandoned but damsons, pears and apples produced near-normal yields (see Chapter B4). Most ditches were dry from late June onwards. At Weston-by-Welland (Northants) a stream was said to have dried up for the first time in living memory. Conversely, at a farm in Nottinghamshire, where cattle had been fed hay since May, springs and streams remained flowing throughout the summer, against all expectation. In Warwickshire, artificial pools dried up for the first time and fish had to be rescued. Soil erosion by wind in large arable fields was reported to be greater than normal due to dry conditions, and soil compaction and settling exposed tree roots. Farmers were experiencing difficulty in preparing the land for drilling because of hard ground.

WALES AND THE WEST MIDLANDS

In north Wales, there were no reports of unusual weather conditions. However, in east Wales, and in Pembrokeshire, grass was described as tinder dry and farmers were starting to use winter feed in July. In the west Midlands, conditions were drier than normal and fruit crops were described as poor (especially plums).

NORTHERN ENGLAND AND SOUTH-WEST SCOTLAND

In general, areas east of the Pennines were described as very dry (even in September and October) with considerable wind erosion of dry soils in agricultural areas and high risks of fire on heather moorlands especially the North Yorks moors. In these areas, streams had dried up, at least in the upper parts of river catchments.

SCOTLAND

There were few reports of unusual weather patterns in mid-Scotland. Also in north Scotland, there were no obvious effects of the dry summer on individual plant species, although some boggy habitats were easier to access than usual. One report suggested that midge populations were reduced compared to a normal summer.

2.1.6 Conclusions

1. It is difficult to separate the effect of hot summers (or mild winters) from the effects of other factors which determine growth and distribution of plants. Comparison must be made with past years and long term monitoring data are very important. Thus the systematic records of orchids and other species, and the long term garden observations described, were especially valuable. However, these data provide a local rather than national picture. The broader, more anecdotal, information demonstrated the spatial variability in the impact of hot summers (or mild winter) in the UK. Clearly, one must be cautious about generalizing from observations on individual species/communities at one location.

2. Some species, particularly those occurring in warmer southern regions of the country appeared to respond directly to increased temperatures and sunshine duration. For example:

i) The American duckweed (*Lemna minuscula*), first recorded in the UK in 1977, flourished in water bodies in Cambridge in 1990, replacing native duckweeds. A similar population explosion was recorded in Surrey in 1989. High temperatures, low river flows and/or changes in water chemistry were probably responsible.

ii) The marsh gentian (*Gentiana pneumonanthe*), which occurs on wet, acid heaths in lowland England, flowered profusely in 1990, apparently owing to high temperatures in the summer of 1989 which may have favoured floral initiation and/or the accumulation of root storage materials.

iii) Populations of bearded fescue (*Vulpia ciliata* spp. *ambigua*), which was on the verge of extinction in its UK distribution in the Breckland in 1988, increased substantially following the two hot, dry summers of 1989 and 1990. Warm spring and summer temperatures favoured seed production in this winter annual, and summer droughts created gaps for seed germination and colonization in the autumn.

iv) In Essex, a number of species increased in 1989 and 1990. While some increases were clearly drought related if only indirectly, (e.g. increases of *Lactuca saligna* on the Thames estuary) others may have been the result of independant coastal processes or natural fluctuations in species numbers.

3. The advantages of high summer temperatures were outweighed in many cases by adverse effects of drought:

i) Species with deep tap-roots, like ribwort plantain and greater knapweed, which occur in agricultural pastures or in calcareous grasslands remained green during the 1989 drought, whereas shallowly-rooting grasses went brown, and, in some instances, died.

ii) Plant species of moist habitats suffered shoot death during the summer of 1989, especially ferns, such as the hart's tongue fern growing in rocky cliffs with little soil.

4. Although many species and communities showed severe symptoms of drought stress, most recovered without any apparent lasting affects:

i) Grasslands and lawns in southern and eastern England were brown (almost white) by August 1990, but all species observed at sites near Monks Wood recovered from underground organs by March 1991.

ii) On some English heathlands, *Calluna* dieback occurred, as in 1976, but all recovered in the spring of 1991.

iii) Most trees that showed summer wilting, dieback and/or premature leaf fall survived and recovered in 1991.

5. The phenology of species is an important factor in the response to drought. Species which flowered in early to mid summer were generally little affected by the two hot summers, whereas some of those which normally flower later either failed to produce functional flowers or to produce above-ground reproductive structures.

i) Long-term observations on orchid species showed that populations of musk orchid (*Herminium monorchis*) declined as a result of the 1976 drought, and took four years to recover. In 1990 only 4 out of 331 plants in a samples plot in Cambridgeshire flowered, and none produced viable seed. If future summers are hot and dry the musk orchid may die out at many sites.

ii) *Orchis morio* also declined in 1989 and 1990, the number of flowering spikes being greatly reduced in both years at an Essex site. However, in Cambridgeshire, flower numbers in 1989 and 1990 did not differ significantly from the mean value recorded in the previous 8 years. Site differences were found for other species and emphasised the complexity of many flowering processes and the difficulties in isolating causal factors.

6. In East Lothian, garden plants flowered earlier in 1989 and 1990 than the 1978–88 average. Although overall flowering was later in 1990 than in 1989, most woody perennials flowered earlier in 1990 than in 1989, suggesting a possible cumulative carry-over effect of the 1989 summer.

7. Drought symptoms also occurred widely in forest and amenity trees in 1989 and 1990. The most common were a general reversible wilting of many deciduous broadleaves and leaf discoloration and premature defoliation of deciduous and evergreen species.

i) Beech in southern England was particularly badly affected; many trees produced small leaves in 1990 (following the 1989 drought) and by September 1990 many crowns had only a thin sprinkling of green leaves; parkland, roadside and woodland beech were all affected. Cherry, field maple, hawthorn, rowan and sweet chestnut were also adversely affected.

ii) Birch, which has a shallow root system, suffered conspicuous leaf discoloration and defoliation at a wide range of sites.

iii) Oak generally retained more green leaves than other tree species, but drought-related branch dieback occurred at several sites in Berkshire where normal deep rooting had been prevented by seasonal waterlogging.

iv) Sooty bark disease of sycamore killed many trees in the London area, Berkshire and Bedfordshire in 1990, and was a problem in previous hot, dry summers (1947, 1959, 1976). The fungus (*Cryptostroma corticale*) has a high temperature optimum (25°C) and develops rapidly in water-stressed trees.

v) Many tree species flowered and seeded heavily in

1990. It was a second consecutive "mast" year for beech. Hornbeam bore conspicuous clusters of fruits. Many berry-bearing trees were spectacular (hawthorn, apple, *Sorbus*). (However acorn production was low, possible owing to frosts in April.) The demands of the developing fruit crops may have exacerbated stresses imposed on the trees by extreme weather.

8. During 1990, observers were surveying vegetation throughout the UK. Their anecdotal observations support more quantitative evidence and indicate the extent of drought effects.

    i) In southern England, some natural vegetation resembled coconut matting; previously aquatic vegetation was said to be being replaced by dryland vegetation following two dry summers; farms were short of cattle fodder, and were intending to grow more maize and winter cereals.

    ii) In East Anglia and the Midlands much natural vegetation was brown by August, but it recovered soon after November rain. Some hedge plants flowered for a second time in the autumn. Many recently planted trees died. Soil erosion by wind was worse than normal. Farmers had difficulty preparing the land for drilling because of hard ground.

The uncertainty of farmers about future cropping patterns is an indication of the severity of the impact of the two hot dry summers on agriculture (see Chapters B4).

9. Most of the changes described in this chapter concern the responses of individual species. While the increase or decrease of individual species particularly those that are rare will affect the overall value of a particular community, the effects of the hot dry summers on whole communities have not been addressed. Community changes are very difficult to evaluate and require detailed long term observations. Several more years of observations may be necessary before the impact of the hot, dry summers of 1989 and 1990 on plant communities can be evaluated.

B2.2 IMPACTS ON ANIMALS

2.2.1 Introduction

In this section impacts of the hot summers of 1989 and 1990 on invertebrates and birds are described. Insect groups such as butterflies, moths, grasshoppers and crickets tend to be favoured by hot summers and would be expected to respond to the hot summers. A major effect of the hot dry summers on birds is expected to be on their breeding success. Fire numbers for 1989 and 1990 in the UK and Dorset are also included in this section and the impact of the fires on nature reserves is discussed.

2.2.2 Invertebrates

BUTTERFLIES

Hot summers generally favour butterflies (Beirne 1955, Pollard 1988) and 1989 was especially favourable. Several species were more numerous in the second generation than in the first, while some, such as wall (*Lasiommata megera*) and small copper (*Lycaena phlaeas*), had substantial third generations. Butterfly numbers decreased slightly in 1990, as shown by the results of the ITE Butterfly Monitoring Scheme (BMS) where numbers of butterflies have been recorded on fixed walks on a series of sites since 1976 (Pollard & Yates 1991). The total number of sightings of the commonest ten butterflies in the BMS was 95,861 in 1989, and 91,758 in 1990. However, numbers were still high in 1990, e.g. at Kingley Vale NNR, where there have been weekly counts of sightings on a five mile butterfly recording walk since 1976, total numbers were the second highest after 1984 – also a warm year (Williamson *pers. comm.*) (Figure 3a).

The main cause of declines in single generation species in 1990 was the drought in the previous year (1989), while for those with two or more generations, the cause was the more widespread and severe drought in 1990. The weather can cause changes in butterfly populations over wide areas by influencing oviposition success and the rate of larval development and survival (Pollard 1991a). However, the indirect effects of weather on the condition of food-plants is very important to butterflies. Where drought occurs during summer, species feeding as larvae are worst affected. The brown argus (*Aricia agestis*) has fluctuated in abundance due to drought induced changes in its food plant, rock rose (*Helianthemum nummularium*) on certain sites (Bourn, 1989; Bourn and Thomas, 1992). Rock-rose was more severely affected by drought on the thinner soils of the Purbeck Hills in south Dorset compared with most of northern Dorset, accounting for a drop in numbers of brown argus in south Dorset compared to the north. Other affected species were the green veined white (*Pieris napi*), feeding on Crucifers, the white admiral (*Ladoga camilla*) feeding on honeysuckle, speckled wood (*Pararge aegeria*) and ringlet (*Aphantopis hyperantus*) feeding on grasses. South and south-eastern England were most affected by these declines, especially on dry south-facing slopes. The hot dry summer of 1976 produced similar effects, and Thomas and Merrett (1980) classified butterflies on the Purbeck Hills into three groups, (a) those feeding during the time that their food-plants were destroyed; (b) those not feeding when their food-plants were destoryed; and (c) those whose food-plants were little damaged. The first group included common blue (*Polyommatus icarus*), adonis blue (*Lysandra bellargus*) and brown argus. After the hot dry summer of 1976, populations of adonis blue crashed (Thomes & Merrett, 1980).

Spring-feeding species, whose food-plants were not affected, increased in numbers – the hedge brown or

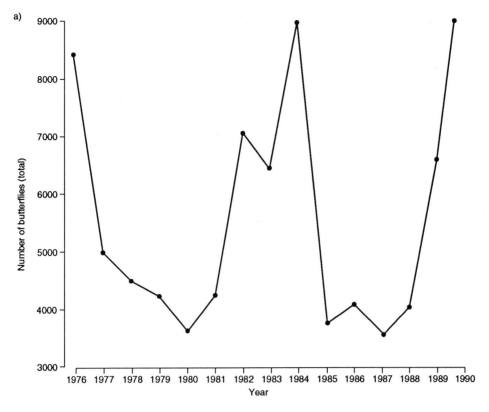

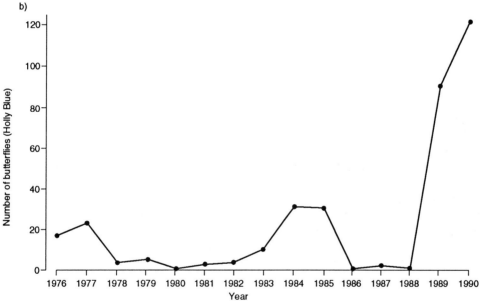

3 (a) Total numbers of butterflies of all species counted each year at Kingley Vale NNR in the ITE Butterfly Monitoring Scheme (Williamson, pers. comm.).

   (b) Total numbers of holly blue (*Celastrina argiolus*) butterflies counted each year at Kingley Vale NNR in the ITE Butterfly Monitoring Scheme (Williamson, pers. comm.).

gatekeeper (*Pyronia tithonus*) showing a remarkable increase. Other examples were the orange tip (*Anthocharis cardomines*), marbled white (*Melanargla galathea*), grayling (*Hipparchia semele*) and less common species like wood white (*Leptidea sinapis*), Duke of Burgundy (*Hamearis lucina*), small pearl bordered and pearl bordered fritillaries (*Argynnis selene* and *A. euphrosyne*).

The greatest increases were shown by the holly-blue (*Celastrina argiolus*) in 1990 for the second year running (Baker, 1990). This species feeds on various shrubs, like holly, ivy, spindle and snowberry, which are presumably more drought resistant than herbs. It normally has two generations, but some third generation individuals were seen in the south in October 1990 (BMS). At Kingley Vale NNR, 95 holly blue butterflies were recorded in 1989 and 121 in 1990, easily the highest numbers since records began (Figure 3b). This species has also expanded

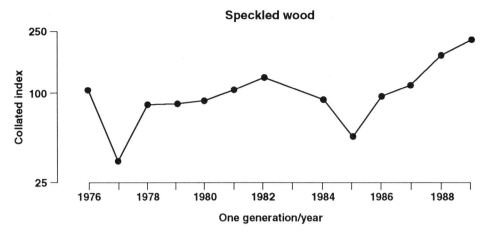

Speckled wood

4   Mean UK trend in the abundance of the speckled wood (*Pararge aegeria*) butterfly since 1976, taken from the ITE Butterfly Monitoring Scheme. Collated indexes are shown numerically with numbers plotted on a logarithmic scale (the 1976 index was arbitrarily set at 100 and subsequent years are related to this (Pollard and Yates, 1989)).

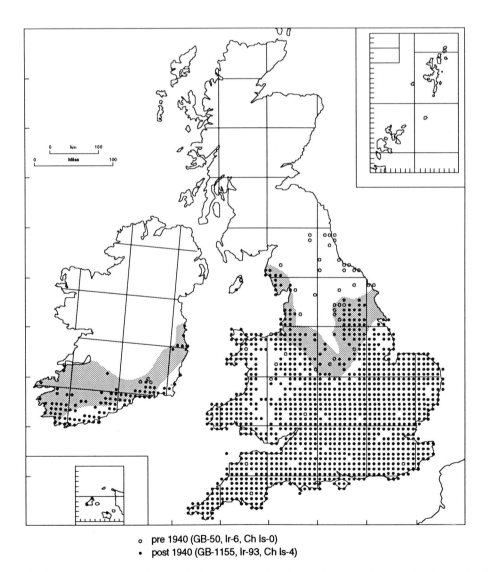

o   pre 1940 (GB-50, Ir-6, Ch Is-0)
•   post 1940 (GB-1155, Ir-93, Ch Is-4)

5   Distribution of the hedgebrown (or gatekeeper) butterfly (*Pyronia tithonus*) in the UK and Ireland. The hatched areas mark the northward expansion of the species range since 1970 as determined by the ITE Biological Records Centre. The closed circles mark the distribution of the species since 1940. The open circles mark sighting of the species north of its present range before 1940.

in range, reaching Tynmouth for the first time (Dunn 1990b). Factors other than climate may be involved in these population changes.

Scotch argus (*Erebia aethiops*) declined on all BMS sites in 1989 and on two in 1990. This species, which is restricted to Scotland and northern England, would be expected to decline under warmer climatic conditions in Britain on the southern boundary of its range.

During 1989 and 1990 there was a further expansion in the range of several species, including the speckled wood, small skipper (*Thymelicus sylvestris*) and comma (*Polygonia c-album*) (BMS). The speckled wood increased steadily over the period of mild winters and hot summers (Figure 4) reaching the highest recorded level in 1989. It became numerous near the northern edge of its range and expanded in the east where it occurred at Woodwalton and Holme Fens (Pollard and Yates, 1989). Changes in the range of the hedge brown, which reached the Derbyshire Dales (Lathhill Dale) in 1989 (Pollard and Yates, 1989) were correlated with an increase in flight period (Pollard, 1991b). This species had been expanding its range northwards in the UK and Ireland since 1970 (Figure 5).

The summer 1990 was a good but not exceptional year for the three commonest migrants, painted lady (*Vanessa cardui*), red admiral (*Vanessa atalanta*) and clouded yellow (*Colias croceus*). However migration is related to large scale air movements as much as to temperature. Neither 1989 nor 1990 matched 1976 when unusually high numbers of migrants were recorded, presumably because of differing patterns of winds.

The timing of butterfly flights was affected. Butterflies were on the wing early in 1989 after the mild winter, and larvae finished feeding early. The meadow brown (*Maniola jurtina*) at Monks Wood was first sighted in late May 1990 (Figure 6), two weeks earlier than at any site over the 15 years of observations, the mean flight time being similar for 1976, 1989 and 1990 (Pollard & Yates 1991). Flight periods of many species seemed particularly short in 1990, and life spans may have been shortened because of the continuous activity.

Dennis and Shreeve (1989) considered that wing size, colour and pattern gradients for UK butterflies can be related to basking (thermoregulatory) behaviour. Some are plastic in relation to temperature. In 1976, many specimens of both butterflies and moths were smaller. In 1989, there were fewer wild aberrations than expected (British Entomological and Natural History Society *pers. comm.*).

MOTHS

Data from the Rothamsted light traps indicated that 1990 was not particularly unusual for numbers of moths – not comparable to the large numbers in 1976 (Woiwodd *pers.*

comm.). Analysis of records for 1965–87 at Brooms Barn in Suffolk showed that, in the hot summers of 1976 and 1968, there were higher numbers but diversity was little affected; however there were long-term diversity trends due to environmental change locally (Riley 1990).

Many species, e.g. muslin moth (*Diaphora mendica*), were flying earlier than usual at the start of the 1990 season in spring and summer (Woiwodd *et al.* 1990). A few species, normally migrant, e.g. silver Y (*Autographa gamma*) survived as larvae overwinter and were flying early in spring. The advance in phenological timing of the first generation often persisted through the summer e.g. wave moths (*Idaea* spp.) (Townsend and Riley, 1990). Many species of moths produced unusual second broods late in 1989, because their development was faster at the high temperatures. In southern England, species of macromoths which are known to produce second broods occasionally, did so readily in 1989 and in Devon and northern England (Chester and Tyne, *pers. comm.*) second broods were produced by some species which were not previously known to produce second broods. Large yellow underwing (*Noctua pronuba*) was particularly notable in 1990, being very numerous in some areas (Dunn 1990) and flying very late, probably due to prolonged aestivation because of the hot dry summer (Woiwodd *pers. comm.*). Aestivation could also have been a contributory factor in the late appearance of some other species. Similarly, some species which normally have a single brood and overwinter in the larval stages, apparently had delayed emergence (Owen *pers. comm.*).

Humming bird hawk moth (*Macroglossum stellatarum*), which is normally a summer migrant, was recorded by several people to have overwintered in the UK in 1989/90 (Kennard, 1990; Philp, 1990). 1990 was not particularly noteworthy for migrant species, although bedstraw hawk (*Hyles gallii*) was noted as far north as Durham (Dunn, 1990a).

APHIDS

There is a good statistical relationship between winter temperatures, the time of the earliest detectable flight of a wide range of aphid species, and aphid numbers in early summer (Harrington *pers. comm.*; Morrison and Spence 1989). This is especially true for "anholocyclic" species, i.e. those that pass the winter in all stages of development and which are parthenogenetic (reproduce asexually). These species usually increase in numbers during mild winters and migrate early (Bale 1989). This process may then result in outbreaks and damage to plants later in the season, and there is also an increased spread of plant viruses. However, the statistical relationships between aphid numbers and winter and spring temperatures become increasingly poor the further into the season that aphid numbers are predicted, because of the buffering effects of natural enemies as well as unpredictable changing weather.

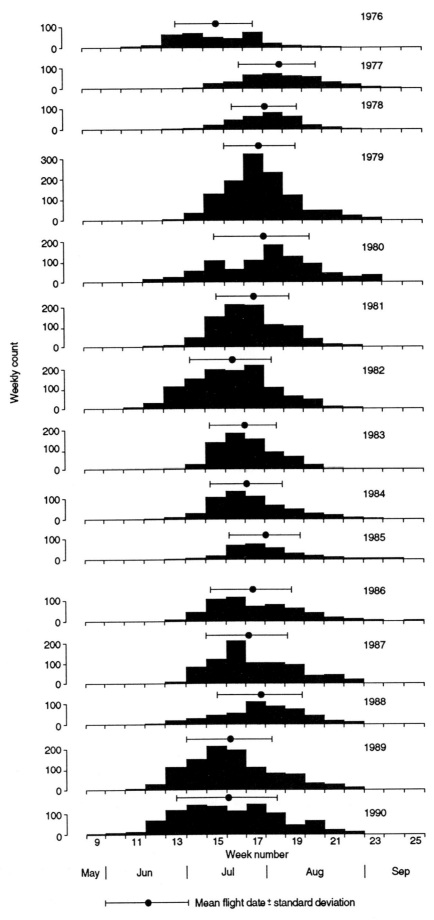

6 The flight period of the meadow brown (*Maniola jurtina*) 1976–1990, showing the mean flight date for each year.

Table 7: Numbers of aphids caught in the Rothamsted suction trap 1990 up to 1st July (Harrington 1990 unpublished report).

Species	Number	Rank out of 23 (1968–1990)
Acyrthosiphon pisum	73	3
Aphis fabae	22	6
Brachycaudus helichrysi	502	14
Brachycaudus brasicae	202 (27)	2 (4)
Cavariella aegopodii	130	16
Drepanosiphum platanoidis	1160	4
Elatobium abietinum	12	17
Euceraphis punctipennis	115	7
Hyperomyzus lactucae	33	3
Metopolophium dirhodum	580	2
Macrosiphum euphorbiae	70 (115)	3 (2)
Myzus ascalonicus	33 (416)	17 (1)
Myzus persicae	283	3 (2)
Periphyllus testudinaceus	38	13
Phorodon humuli	141	8
Rhopalosiphum padi	464	4
Sitobion avenae	217	11

(Figures in brackets were forecast by February).

In 1989 and 1990, the first migrations of agriculturally important aphids were early, as shown by results in suction traps at Rothamsted Experimental station) (see Chapter A2.2.2). By the 1 July 1989, the numbers of aphids (per species) were very high, e.g. the numbers of the peach-potato aphid (*Myzus persicae*) were the second highest in 23 years. However, numbers trapped to 1 July were generally not exceptional. None were ranked more than second highest in the 23 year record (Table 7). Data from 21 years of suction trap results for peach-potato aphid, showed that although mean temperatures from December to June 1990 were the highest recorded, the numbers of aphids in July were only the third highest, and less than in 1989 (Harrington 1990 unpublished report) – probably because of poor host plant condition during the drought, and to large numbers of predators (see section on beetles for ladybird predators). Predator numbers built up during the hot summer of 1989, and winter survival was good. Thus early aphids were scarcely able to reproduce before being eaten. Predators are thought to account for outbreaks of the black aphid (*Aphis fabae*) occurring in alternate years (Dixon, 1985). The outcome in 1990 was considerable virus spread as a result of early flights, but little direct feeding damage as populations did not become very large.

On horticultural plants and fruit trees, aphids also appear to have been numerous earlier in the summer of 1990 rather than later on, with the pear-bedstraw aphid, (*Dysaphis pyri*), being especially troublesome (Halstead *pers. comm.*).

HYMENOPTERA (WASPS, BEES AND ANTS)

a) Wasps
There was a marked increase in social wasp populations in 1989 and 1990, and 1990 in particular must be regarded as a "wasp year". Statistics on wasps are recorded by Environmental Health officers. In Bath there were 472 complaints in 1989 and 842 in 1990. In Barnet, there were over 100 complaints per week in late summer 1990, and contract workers had to be employed for much of the work.

Rentokil also recorded increased numbers of calls for control of wasps' nests in 1990.

Good long-term monitoring records are available for two sites. In Surrey, at the Royal Horticultural Society's Gardens in Wisley, the numbers of wasp nests destroyed was recorded from 1921–49 (Fox-Wilson, 1946; Archer, 1985) while a more accurate record with specific identification of the species of wasps involved has been made since 1986 (Archer *pers. comm.*). Nest numbers of all species tend to vary in the same direction, indicating the likely importance of weather factors. In 1990, 43 nests of *Paravespula vulgaris* were found – a marked increase on the previous five years, when between 10 and 20 nests were found.

The second set of data comes from a Malaise trap in a Leicester garden operated by D. Owen for a number of years. In 1990 this trap produced 170 workers of *P. vulgaris* and 23 workers of *P. germanica*. During the previous five years the number of workers of *P. vulgaris* varied between 60 and 199 and *P. germanica* between three and 29 (Archer *pers. comm.*). There is no evidence in these data for increased abundance in 1990, probably due to regional variation in social wasp abundance, which certainly occurs.

The factors controlling abundance of wasps are very complicated and still not clearly understood – numbers of nests, size of nests and numbers of queens are involved. Archer (1985) found that there was a tendency for years of abundance and scarcity to occur in pairs, and that there was also a possible seven year cycle. He believed that this was due to the occurrence of endogenous mechanisms for damping colony counts to equilibrium. Superimposed on these mechanisms were exogenous factors, particularly good summer weather, when successful colonies were more frequent. Queen production also increased in good autumns. Spradbery (1973) tabled 21 factors influencing wasp abundance and included three weather factors. One factor was the beneficial effects of good summer weather on foraging and consequently the maturing colony. Another was good weather during colony establishment. A third was deleterious effects of warm late spring weather on nest foundation, because premature awakening depleted fat stores.

Solitary wasps and bees also increase during good weather. Using data from the Malaise trap in Leicester and the Davis Index of Summer Weather (Davis 1968), Archer (1990) showed that numbers of solitary wasps were more closely correlated than solitary bees to summer weather conditions.

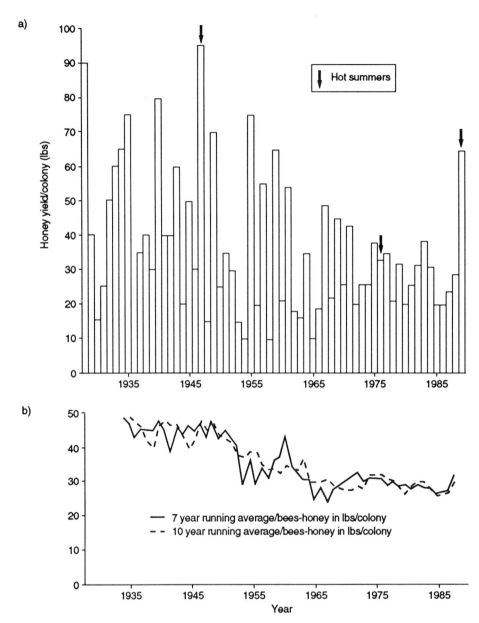

7 Long term records (1934–1989) for honey yields from the Bee Farmers Association (Ellis, pers. comm.) (a) mean yield in lbs/colony of bees, (b) 7 and 10 year running mean yield in lbs/colony of bees.

b) Bees

There were reports in 1989 and 1990 of early foraging of bees in spring, and increases in the abundance of bumble bees (e.g. in the Pennine moorlands). Honey yields (kg/colony) in Britain are positively related to the number of days in July-August with temperatures above 20–25°C (Hurst, 1970). Records of the Bee Farmers' Association showed high yields in the hot summers of 1947 and 1989 (Figure 7), and yields in 1990 were said to be high (Ellis *pers. comm.*). However, yields in 1976 were considered to be limited by adverse effects of severe drought in flower development and nectar production. Since 1955, there has been a steady decline in mean honey yields per colony thought to be related to intensification of agriculture and a reduction in the numbers of wild flowers.

c) Ants

In one species of red ant, *Myrmica rubra*, production of queens is reduced in warm, dry springs, which do not favour the production of young winged queens, and in hot, dry, late summers which delay the nuptial flight and reduce the recruitment of new queens into existing colonies (Elmes, 1990). The usual number of queens per colony is about 8 but in the hot summers of 1975, 1976 and 1989, there were 3.3, 5.6 and 0.9 per colony, respectively.

Although sexual production in *Myrmica* ants was poor in 1989, heat-tolerant species in the genus *Formica* were not adversely affected. If hot, dry summers continue, *Myrmica* colonies may move into habitats with cooler

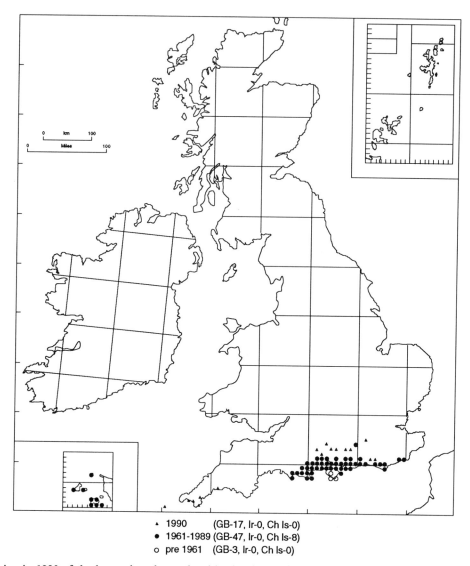

▲ 1990   (GB-17, Ir-0, Ch Is-0)

● 1961-1989 (GB-47, Ir-0, Ch Is-8)

○ pre 1961 (GB-3, Ir-0, Ch Is-0)

8   Range expansion in 1990 of the long-winged cone head bush cricket (*Conocephalus discolor*) (from Haes, 1990 and Biological Records Centre, Monks Wood).

conditions such as dark woodlands and the *Myrmica* free habitat may eventually be filled by more xerophilous species, which are presently either rare or absent from Britain (Elmes *pers. comm.*).

GRASSHOPPERS AND CRICKETS (*ORTHOPTERA*)

Grasshoppers and crickets occur mainly in the south of Britain and depend on warm conditions. Most species are not adversely affected by drought. The two mild winters and hot summers have resulted, therefore, in an increase in the abundance of many grasshoppers and crickets and many new field records were made for the new Atlas of Orthoptera (Haes 1990).

Some species in Britain normally have only very small proportions of long-winged forms (macropters), which are capable of flight, e.g. Roesel's bush cricket (*Metrioptera roeselii*). As in locusts, these changes in morphology are related to crowding and high temperatures and result in dispersive phases in the life cycle. In 1976, Roesel's

bush cricket appeared on waste land around London with high proportions of long-winged individuals (M. Skelton, *pers. comm.*). In 1989, this species was reported as spreading further north and inland and in 1990 was also recorded from several new localities with the first records for Bedfordshire. Macropters of the long-winged cone head (*Conocephalus discolor*) were much commoner than usual (at 10–20%) in a population at Rainham Marshes, and in Ireland 4 long-winged specimens were noted out of 55 adults (Eversham, *pers. comm.*). In 1990, the species was found for the first time in mainland Cornwall and North Hampshire and Surrey (Figure 8) and has also been reported as spreading in long grass alongside motorways (Hayes 1990 and *pers. comm.*). The meadow grasshopper (*Chorthippus parallelus*), which is usually short-winged, also produced macropters in various areas (Eversham, *pers. comm.*) and the lesser marsh grasshopper (*Chorthippus albomarginatus*) also spread extensively in southern and eastern countries.

In 1989 and 1990, many species of grasshopper matured

early (Haes 1990), with May sightings of the common green grasshopper (*Omecestus viridulus*), meadow grasshopper, common field grasshopper (*C. brunneus*) and stripe-winged grasshopper (*Stenobothrus lineatus*). Bush crickets also matured early with records for long-winged cone head, bog bush cricket (*Metrioptera brachyptera*) and grey bush cricket (*Platycleis albopunctata*) by the first week of June, and great green bush cricket (*Tettigonia viridissima*) in the first week of July. The rare wart-biter, (*Decticus verrucivorus*) on the edge of its range in southern England reached maturity four to five weeks early in 1989 (Cherril & Brown 1991).

BEETLES, ESPECIALLY LADYBIRDS (COCCINELLIDAE)

Large numbers of ladybirds overwintered, following the mild winter of 1989–90. Numbers of aphid prey were also high and a population explosion of ladybirds was expected (Majerus, 1990). However, although a few early summer swarms were reported (mainly seven spot, *Coccinella septempunctata*) in the south, and one plague at Weston-super-Mare in July was mentioned in the Daily Mail, large numbers were not widespread. In 1976, a plague of ladybirds was one of the most conspicuous phenomena of the year (Hearn & Gilbert, 1977).

On nettles at Box Hill, Surrey in early summer 1990, there were several dozen ladybirds on the leaves of each stem; most being seven spot and two spot (*Adalia bipunctata*), with a few ten spot, (*A. decempunctata*) and fourteen spot, (*Propylea quattuordecimpunctata*) (Majerus 1990). On one nettle stem as many as 126 larvae, pre-pupae or newly emerged adults were counted and it was estimated that on approximately 550 m² of nettle-bed there were very large numbers, with 70,000 seven spot and 15,000 two spot in various stages of development. However, by mid-July, aphid populations on drought-stricken plants declined and at the same time other aphid predators and parasites were very active. As a result, the aphid food source for late developing larvae and newly emerged ladybirds appeared inadequate and cannibalism was recorded.

Additionally, there was a dramatic increase in numbers of ladybird parasites of the genus *Phalacrotophora* (Diptera, Phoridae). At Box Hill, over 60% of two spot and 75% of seven spot ladybird pupae were affected. Several parasites may develop in a single pupa; exceptionally, as many as 22 specimens were recorded in the larger seven spot ladybird (Majerus 1990). Species with this facility for gregarious parasitism can obviously respond quickly to an increase in the number of prey. Another parasitic wasp, *Perilitus coccinellae* (Hymenoptera Braconidae) was only present in small numbers.

The response of populations of predatory and parasitic species to increases in prey populations can be seen as a secondary effect of weather which had affected the prey species originally.

There were reports in 1990 (e.g. from the Royal Horticultural Society's gardens at Wisley) of large numbers of damaging vine weevils, (*Otiorhynchus* spp.), whose larvae are thought to be able to continue feeding overwinter on roots in mild weather, with resulting large populations of adults in spring and early summer.

INSECTS AND MITES LIVING IN DOMESTIC AND OTHER HEATED BUILDINGS

Infestations by insects and mites in houses, prisons, hospitals etc. rose during the hot summers and mild winters. This was related to faster life cycles at higher temperatures, better survival in mild winters, and increased chance of success in dispersal.

Cockroach numbers also rose in several areas. In Westminster, for example, cases of infestation reported by environmental health officers have virtually doubled over the period 1985–1990, rising to nearly 6,000, while in Tower Hamlets reports rose from 5463 in 1989 to 7170 in 1990. Four cockroach species have been reported, the small brown German, the large black Oriental, the Australian and the American. High rise flats and closely grouped housing estates in urban areas have been at greatest risk, as this is combined with other factors, like difficulty of eradication with so many suitable places for survival. Oriental Cockroaches can survive out of doors on rubbish tips if the weather is not too cold.

The minute Pharaoh's ant (*Monomorium pharaonis*) is similar to the cockroach in habit, being dependent on centrally heated buildings. It is reported to have spread in urban areas and high rise blocks of flats and to have increased its range further in Britain. Unlike many other species of ants, Pharaoh's ant has multiple queens (polygynous), so that small fragments of a colony are likely to contain fertile queens. Reproductive rate can be fast in hot weather, and the minute ants are easily dispersed and established, provided temperatures remain high enough for survival throughout the year.

Fleas, especially the cat flea which lives as larvae in carpets, also increased in number. The Medical Entomology Centre in Cambridge (Hamer, 1990) received more than ten times as many complaints in 1990 than in a normal year. Bird fleas also increased. These enter houses from vacated nests of wild birds such as pigeons and starlings. Similarly, there were higher numbers of parasitic mites from birds nests (Medical Research Centre).

Increased incidence of high levels of pests in food, particularly mites and sub-tropical moths, were reported to the Medical Entomology Centre. Sub-tropical moths usually have a slow life cycle in the UK, but in sustained summer temperatures of 24°C as in 1990, there may be several generations in a short time and infestations become very noticeable, e.g. in imported dates.

GLASSHOUSE SPECIES

These species are very similar to pests of domestic premises, relying on warm winters for survival, and being able to reproduce fast and spread out of doors and into un-infested glasshouses during hot summers. In 1990, the Royal Horticultural Society's Gardens at Wisley (Halstead *pers. comm.*) noted outdoor infestations of the glasshouse leaf hopper, (*Hauptidia maroccana*), glasshouse red spider mites, (*Tetranychus* spp.) and the glasshouse white fly, (*Trialeurodes vaporariorum*). The polyphagous leaf-mining *Liriomyza* species of the fly family Agromyzidae, which are serious pests, may have also spread outside glasshouses.

MOSQUITOS, FLIES AND MIDGES

The tropical mosquito (*Aedes aegypti*), which could be a health hazard in vectoring certain diseases, was said to be breeding in parts of Britain (Hamer, 1990). Bracken and biting flies increased in northern England (Dunn, 1989).

Midges, which live in damp habitats, were said to be less numerous in 1989 and 1990. Crane flies (*Tipula* spp.), which live in damp moorland, were severely reduced in numbers, e.g. on Thorne Moors in Yorkshire (Eversham, *pers. comm.*). *Tipula subnodicornis* declined to about 1% of its former population at several sites in the Pennines (Coulson, *pers. comm.*).

SLUGS AND SNAILS

Hot dry summers are very damaging to many species of slugs and snails, which are not very successful in controlling water loss through the body surface, and consequently live in damp habitats and are often nocturnal in habit. In dry weather, most species aestivate – many snails secreting a protective mucous membrane to seal the shell, while slugs move into shelter or down in the soil. Even in autumn 1989, fewer slugs and snails were recorded because of the lack of large fungi on which they feed (Evesham *pers. comm.*).

Slugs were adversely affected during 1990; the long drought prevented them from feeding, and curtailed their reproductive output. A study of two large slug species, *Limas flavus* and *L. maculatus*, on walls in Huntingdon suggested that there was no juvenile recruitment into the population (Eversham 1990). As these slugs live three or more years, one unsuccessful year may not have any long-term effects on large populations, but isolated populations may become locally extinct.

In a study of slug activity in relation to their pest status on autumn sown cereals in Northumberland, Young and Port (1989 and *pers. comm.*) found that autumn soil temperature remained relatively constant from 1988 to 90, but soil moisture rose relatively late in 1989 and 1990

Influence of weather on slug activity

Slug activity is measured using time lapse video recording apparatus and represents the distance covered by slugs over an area of 60 by 40 cm in a single night.

Data are means for the period 1.9 to 1.11 in each year. Bars are 1 standard deviation.

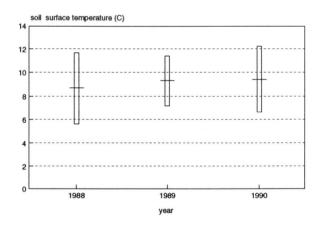

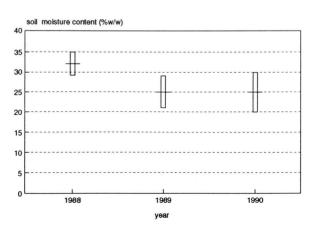

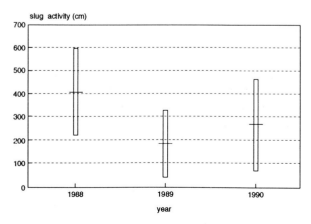

9 Influence of weather on slug activity in 1988, 1989 and 1990 (Young and Port, pers. comm.).

in comparison to 1988. Slug activity was much lower in those years (Figure 9), reducing the risk of crop damage.

In semi-aquatic and aquatic habitats, populations of Molluscs were reduced by drying out of the habitat. One nationally rare species *Lymnaea glabra* (Red data book category 2) which seems to be especially vulnerable to droughts that start early and dry out the habitat, was badly affected in 1976 and again in 1990 (Evesham *pers. comm.*).

SPIDERS

Spiders are less well recorded than some of the popular insect groups, nevertheless they have been affected by the hot dry summer. The wasp spider (*Argiope bruennichi*), a conspicuous yellow-banded species first recorded in Rye in 1922, expanded its range, and in 1990 many specimens were noted in several coastal areas in the south and as far inland as Wimborne in Dorset (Snazell *pers. comm.*).

Steatoda nobilis has a toehold in Britain on the south coast and became established more successfully during the hot summers. This spider has an unpleasant bite and was recorded several times in the past on bananas, (Jones 1979). Populations in Swanage have expanded and the species has now been recorded in Essex and Worthing (Snazell *pers. comm.*).

AQUATIC AND SEMI-AQUATIC COMMUNITIES

In 1990, species dependent on wetlands and water-bodies were affected by the drying out of their aquatic habitat. At Ainsdale Sand Dunes NNR, for example, measurements of water depth in 6 excavated ponds showed (Table 8) that more ponds dried out in 1989 and 1990 than in the previous 2 years and in September 1990, the water table was at its lowest level ever recorded. At the Suffolk Nationalist Trust Reserve of Lopham and Redgrove Fens all 40 ponds dried up in 1990. This endangered the rare

Table 8: Monthly records 1987–90 of mean water table in six excavated ponds at Ainsdale Sand Dunes NNR (cms measured to pond datum marker) (Simpson NNC, *pers. comm.*).

	1987	1988	1989	1990
No. of ponds dried out	0	1	5	5
January	67.5	58.9	52.3	55.8
February	F	67.8	52.3	64.6
March	66.4	53.9	61.9	66.9
April	74.3	63.7	66.6	65.8
May	69.5	63.6	57.6	52.6
June	54.1	59.8	49.3	30.2
July	65.1	42.0	50.3	26.0
August	60.1	42.0	24.0	0.8
September	53.3	36.5	16.0	−13.8
October	46.5	28.9	−4.7	−7.4
November	54.8	39.6	29.9	19.9
December	51.8	45.6	27.7	28.7

F = excavations frozen

great raft spider, (*Dolomedes plantarius*), which is only recorded in Lopham and Redgrave Fens NNR, and which may be vulnerable to climatic change (Barkham and Macquire, 1990). The population crashed and only six individuals were seen in 1990. However, populations did recover from a similar disaster in 1976 when no spiders were seen.

Many aquatic insects are affected by drying out of water bodies. The scarce emerald dragonfly (*Lestes dryas*), which occurs in eastern England in ditches almost filled with reeds or rushes, was reduced in numbers (Barkham and Macquire, 1990). The southern hawker, (*Aeshna cyanea*), which has a larval phase extending over two seasons was also affected (Smith & Smith 1991).

A survey of Diptera on Thorne Moors NNR in Yorkshire in 1990 (Skidmore 1991), showed that the effects of the dry summer were exacerbating the problems caused by drainage operations on the peat bog. Far more Muscid flies occurred in 1990 than in 1987 (435:332), but there were fewer species (15:21). Over the entire reserve the internationally rare *Phaonia jaroschewskii*, which breeds in wet active *Sphagnum*, was replaced by *Helina evecta*, a ubiquitous humicolous fly intolerant of waterlogged conditions. *P. atriceps*, which breeds in stems of aquatic plants in standing water, was not recorded in 1990. Also on Thorne Moor, one nationally rare species *Lymnaea glabra* (Red data book category 2), which seems to be especially vulnerable to droughts, was badly affected in 1990, as in 1976.

However, many species which live in ephemeral or small water bodies must be adapted to survive, either by aestivation and dormant cocoons or eggs (e.g. freshwater snails), or by frequent dispersal to new habitats. In two breckland meres, 70 aquatic species were found to be capable of hatching from resting stages in mud (Hearn and Gilbert, 1977). Dragonflies emerged early in 1990 and were apparently on the wing for longer e.g. the common blue damselfly (*Enallagma cyathigerum*) was on the wing for over six months (Smith & Smith 1991). The migrant hawker (*Aeshna mixta*) seems to have been particularly favoured by the weather – the number of records in the Odonata recording scheme was over 60% higher than in 1989.

It may even by surmised that occasional drying out of ponds is beneficial to invertebrates, because fish are more likely to die at such times, allowing subsequent insect populations to increase unchecked.

2.2.3 Birds

INTRODUCTION

It was anticipated that a major effect of hot dry summers on British bird populations would be on their breeding success though more complicated relationships apparently occurred (see A2.2.4).

The Nest Record Scheme (organised by the British Trust for Ornithology) monitors breeding success from nests found throughout Britain. Preliminary results (Glue, 1989d; Crick and Glue, 1990) reported high breeding success for some resident species including robin, nuthatch, goldcrest, tree creeper, pied wagtail and long-tailed tit, but less good success for hole-nesting titmice. Summer migrants apparently did well, including pied flycatcher, redstart, sand martin, sedge warbler, yellow wagtail, nightjar, whinchat and swallow. Tawny owls and long-eared owls had very poor breeding success, but barn owl and kestrel faired well. Curlew, redshank, lapwing and kingfisher bred poorly. According to the authors of these reviews, the hot dry summer could have contributed to the success of the summer migrants through "a wealth of insect life" and to the failure of waders and kingfisher through "parched meadows, marsh and moorland" and "reduced river levels".

The results of catching passerine birds using standard procedures ("Constant Effect Sites" organised by the British Trust for Ornithology) give some support to the nest record results. Comparing the numbers of juvenile birds caught in 1989 with numbers in 1988, there were significant changes in 7 of the 23 species monitored (Peach and Baillie, 1990). Sedge warbler and reed warbler juveniles were more abundant in 1989. In contrast, juveniles of blackcap, chiffchaff, willow warbler and great tit were less abundant, suggesting they bred poorly.

On a more local basis, a summary of the 1989 breeding season in Scotland (da Prato, 1989) endorsed much of what had been noted nationally. Few data were given, except to note very poor breeding success for barn owls in one study in south-west Scotland, and an average year for kestrels in Ayrshire. Birds of prey are monitored closely on an annual basis and data from the Scottish Raptor Study Groups (Benn, 1990) suggested good breeding for golden eagles and peregrines, less good for kestrels and poor for buzzards. The poor success for buzzards, as for owls nationally, was attributed to low populations of field voles, a major prey. Both red kite and Montagu's harrier bred very well (Glue, 1989d). In general there are well established positive relationships between dry summers and high breeding success for several bird-of-prey species (Newton, 1986 for sparrow-hawks; Mearns and Newton, 1988 for peregrines; Newton *et al.*, 1989 for red kites) so it was not surprising that they did well. Both sparrowhawk and red kite had the highest breeding success that had been recorded in these respective studies in the last two decades (I Newton, *pers. comm.*).

Game "bags" are used as annual indices of the populations of some game species, despite some problems of interpretation (Tapper and Cook, 1990). The numbers of grey and red-legged partridges and woodpigeons shot in 1989 were little different to numbers shot in 1988. More

pheasants were shot in 1989, but this was attributed to more pheasant poults released in that year. Red grouse numbers are not supplemented by released birds; the numbers shot were lower in 1989 than in 1988, particularly in England, and this was attributed by the authors to high parasitic worm burdens, not the hot summer. More woodcocks were shot in 1989 than in 1988 and this may have reflected an increased autumn population as night counts at that time were much higher than similar counts in two previous years (Potts, 1990). A study of black grouse was newly started in 1989 and so had little comparative data, but nevertheless reported high breeding success (Baines, 1990). Capercaillies have been studied for much longer and, as was predicted from earlier work (Moss, 1986), the hot dry summer (1989) was accompanied by very high breeding success (R Moss, *pers. comm.*).

Studies of a population of red-breasted merganser and goosander breeding on rivers have spanned only 4 years, but 1989 was the best for duckling production of both species (Marquiss, unpublished) on the river North Esk (Angus).

The results of the Seabird Monitoring Programme (co-ordinated by the Nature Conservancy Council, Walsh, 1990) suggest that for at least 4 species of seabirds, breeding success varied on a national scale in 1989. Data given for kittiwake showed better breeding success in 1989 than in 1988. Poor breeding success for seabirds in the northern North Sea has been linked to the poor availability of small fish and could be associated with long term changes in sea conditions (Harris and Wanless, 1990) but there is no evidence for a direct effect of the 1989 hot summer weather.

To summarise, preliminary reports on the breeding success of birds in 1989 listed 72 species. Although 31 were reported to have done well and 23 poorly, data was available on only 42 species. Of these, differences between success in 1989 and other years were statistically significant for 13 species. For 5 of these species the breeding success could plausibly be attributed to the hot dry summer enhancing their foraging behaviour (sparrow-hawk and red kite) or their invertebrate prey (sedge warbler, reed warbler and capercaillie).

THE 1990 BREEDING SEASON

The Nest Record Scheme's preliminary results (Glue 1990) suggested large variation in breeding success between species, and between the regions of Britain. The information however was largely anecdotal at that stage and few figures were given. Nevertheless, some trends were attributed to the hot summer weather and its associated drought. Early nesting resident insectivores such as wren, goldcrest, long-tailed tit, tree creeper and grey wagtail had "another very productive year", whereas rooks (which feed on soil invertebrates) did poorly. Receding water levels along many rivers and lake margins

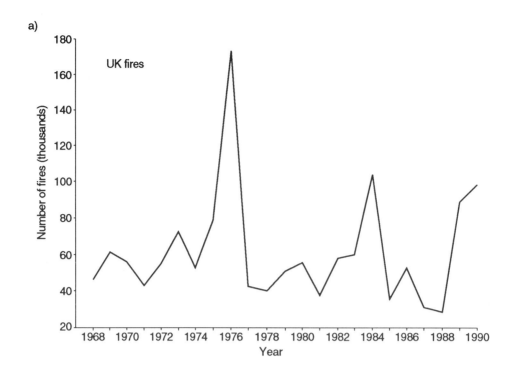

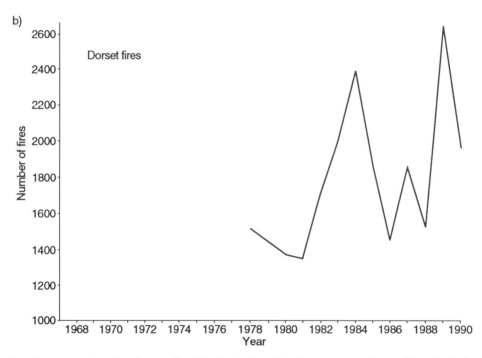

10 Number of outdoor secondary fires in grassland (includes heathland), crops, woods *etc*. (Fire Statistics UK, 1987, 1988; Home Office Statistical Bulletin, 38/90).
(a) In the UK 1968–90.
(b) In the Dorset Fire Brigade area 1978–90.

were blamed for exposing the nests of ducks, rails and dippers to predation (see Chapter A3.4.4). Nesting waders such as lapwing and golden plover may have done poorly whereas little ringed plovers and ringed plovers apparently did well. The continuing "warmth and dryness encouraged many species to make extra nesting attempts" including ringed plover, stone curlew, nightjar, wheatear, starling and chaffinch. Late nesting was also recorded for little grebe, moorhen, bullfinch, linnet and song thrush.

Anecdotal reports of variable breeding performance also came from Scotland (Gordon 1990) with some supporting data for the varied fortunes of raptors (Benn 1991). Such varying success was attributed to several factors including poor food supply (owls, seabirds, peregrines and ospreys), good food supply (siskin and crossbill), human persecution (hen harrier and peregrine), and egg-collecting (osprey). "Good weather" was mentioned as being responsible for the good breeding success of kestrels in

Ayrshire, whereas "bad" or wet weather was blamed for the loss of several osprey chicks, the loss of pied flycatcher broods, and the flooding of wood warbler nests.

The most rigorously quantitative data so far published is from the BTO's Constant Effort Site scheme, which records changes in the proportions of juvenile birds caught by bird ringers – a figure which could reflect well the breeding success of British passerine birds. Of the 23 common bird species for which data were given, 1 showed no change, 9 increased and 13 decreased (Peach and Baillie 1991). Overall, there were no obvious patterns associated with bird size, diet or habitat. Most of the changes were small and only one was statistically significant – garden warblers had fewer juveniles caught in 1990 than in 1989. If there were significant effects of the 1990 hot summer, they must have been localised or not particularly obvious.

It should be noted that it is difficult to detect anything other than large, dramatic effects of weather anomalies on birds. This is because, in the absence of experimentation, the most than can be done is to associate weather and population parameters. The best evidence comes from pre-existing quantified associations which would allow prediction. Provided such prediction is fulfilled, "cause and effect" could be implied if explanations of the mechanisms involved were plausible. In practise, this situation is rare because it requires long-term intensive studies allied to broad scale, national, annual monitoring.

2.2.4 Fires and the hot dry summers 1989 and 1990

FIRE RECORDS FOR THE UK AND DORSET

Statistics on numbers of fires are published for the UK by the Home Office and for some individual areas; records for Dorset are kept by the Fire Research Station at Boreham Wood. The category of fires reported here is outdoor fires in grasslands, heaths, woods and straw and stubble burning.

Figure 10a shows the total numbers of outdoor fires recorded in the UK from 1968 to 1989. The peak in 1976 is very obvious, while 1984 followed by 1990 and 1989 are the next highest. (Home Office statistical Bulletin 28/91). For all fires in the UK of all types, 1990 followed 1976 with 467,000 fires and 496,000 fires, respectively.

County records for the numbers of grass fires in Dorset are shown in Figure 10b from 1978–1990. Again, the 1984 and 1989 figures were high. Some of the fires recorded will not have affected wildlife, but nevertheless the relationship between hot summers and fires in the countryside is clear.

Fire brigade statistics must be used with care: in Dorset large fires needing five engines or more are counted under a property category! The size of fires may also be changing; it appears that there were more large heath fires in Dorset in previous years – now more fires are

reported at an early stage and brigades attend quicker. Additionally, there are more people in the countryside with increased likelihood of fires starting.

IMPACTS OF FIRES ON NATURE RESERVES

Hearn and Gilbert (1977) thought that, in 1976, fires had more important effects than drought, with longer lasting repercussions. In Nature Reserves, 110 fires were recorded in 1976, including some unusually hot fires and affecting several large areas. There were also more fires in the late summer than usual. Fires in 1990 were less serious.

FIRES IN THE PEAK DISTRICT NATIONAL PARK

In the Peak District National Park in Derbyshire, records of severe fires go back to 1762, and most seem to be associated with hot, dry summers (Radley 1965). The numbers of fires has increased with larger numbers of people on the moors this century. Records for the years 1970–1990 showed that 1976 was easily the worst year with 80 fires, followed by 1984 with 32 fires and 1989 and 1990 with 24 fires each (Table 9). Anderson (1986) analysed the occurrence and numbers of these fires up to 1982 in relation to meteorological factors, and showed that the best correlations were with cumulative rainfall and high temperatures.

SEASONAL CHANGES IN FIRE OCCURRENCE

The monthly occurrence of fires throughout the year tends to show two peaks. Figure 11 shows total grass fires in

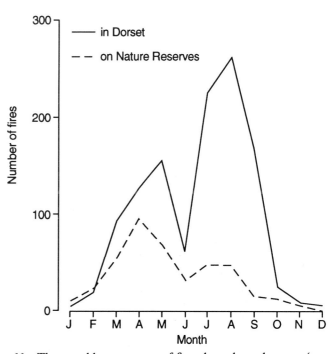

11 The monthly occurrence of fires throughout the year. (———) total outdoor fires in Dorset in each month in 1990 (Greet, pers. comm.); (– – – –) total numbers of fires on National Nature Reserves in each month since 1968 (using all available records from the NCC).

Table 9: Numbers of fires in the Peak District National Park in Derbyshire [1970–82 from Anderson (1984); 1983–90 from Jackson (Peak Park Ranger Service, pers. comm.)].

1970	71	72	73	74	75	76	77	78	79	80	81	82	83	84	85	86	87	88	89	90
18	0	3	1	3	4	80	20	0	0	25	2	9	8	32	2	2	2	12	24	24

Table 10: The numbers of fires recorded on National Nature Reserves in England and Wales 1968 (using all available records from the former NCC).

National Nature Reserves	No of fires	Habitat
Ainsdale Sand Dunes	67*	sand dunes, slacks and wood
Studland Heath	29	sand dunes, heath and wood
Oxwich	25	sand dunes and wood
Saltfleetby-Theddlethorpe Dunes	23	sand dunes
Dyfi	22	sand dunes and bog
Hartlebury Common	19	heath
Holkham	12	sand dunes
Cors Erddreiniog	11	birchwood and heath
Thursley Common	10	bog, heath and wood
Lindisfarne	8	sand dunes
Walberswick	8	reedbeds, heath and wood
Castle Eden Dene	7	woodland and limestone grass
Castle Hill	7	chalk grass
Winterton Dunes	6	sand dunes
Wye	6	chalk grass, scrub and wood
Yarner Wood	6	oak-birch wood and moor

* records more closely investigated

each month of 1990 in Dorset, and the total numbers of fires on National Nature Reserves in each month since 1968 (the latter using all available records from the NCC). Fires in the spring appear to be more frequent on nature reserves than in the summer, unlike the broader countryside where July and August are more important. These peaks in numbers are related to the amount of vegetation that can burn easily after dying off in winter or drying out, as well as to the number of people starting fires. The latter are usually related to the school holidays. Anderson (1986) showed that, in the Peak National Park, 44% of fires started at weekends.

VULNERABILITY OF DIFFERENT VEGETATION TYPES

Coastal dunes are the most vulnerable nature reserves in the figures summed over all the years of records obtained from the former Nature Conservancy Council (Table 10). However in 1976, Hearn and Gilbert (1977) recorded more fires on heathland/moorland than on any other habitat. Some reserves have a greater frequency of fires than might be expected and this is usually due to vandalism. e.g. Castle Eden Dene, Hartlebury Common.

Although the numbers of fires are correlated with damage, the actual size and temperature of fires are the more important figures in relation to ecological impact. At Ainsdale Sand Dunes NNR there were ten fires in both 1989 and 1990, but a much larger area was burnt in 1990 (Table 11). Where burning is severe, leaching and later erosion can occur, especially on peat moors like those of Derbyshire (Anderson, 1986). Recovery time in vegetation succession can be very prolonged indeed when fires

Table 11: The total area (m²) burnt annually and numbers of fires at Ainsdale Sand Dunes NNR, Simpson *pers. comm.*)

Year	Square metres	Number of fires
1986	30,000	3
1987	15,250	5
1988	1,600	1
1989	18,466	10
1990	92,900	10

have damaged the soil seed bank (Hearn and Gilbert, 1977). However, fires can be beneficial on overgrown areas, and when controlled can be used as a management tool on heaths, moors and grasslands.

Numbers of most invertebrates are depressed immediately after fires and recovery and recolonisation can be slow in severely burnt areas (e.g. 7–10 years in the Peak Park) (Anderson, 1986). Changes in habitat structure also affect breeding birds, e.g. the Dartford warbler in Dorset is reduced in numbers when gorse bushes are burned (Dorset Naturalist's Trust & RSBP 1977), while areas of burnt heather are avoided by all bird species except the golden plover. Loss of cover may affect small mammal numbers.

2.2.5 Conclusions

1. It is clearly difficult to dissociate the effects of warm summers from those of warm preceding winters where they occur together. For a wide range of aphid species there is a good statistical relationship between winter

temperatures and numbers in early summer. Further into the summer the relationship tends to break down due to changing weather and the buffering effect of natural enemies. Thus, in the summer of 1990, although extremely large numbers of aphids were anticipated following the warm winter temperatures, numbers were not exceptional largely owing to a build up of aphid predators and parasites.

2. Following the mild winter of 88/89, the emergence and flight periods of many insects were earlier and generation times were shorter. This resulted in additional generations of some species, particularly as the summer and autumn continued to be warmer than average. Butterflies, for example, were very active in England during the sunny summer of 1989, and the numbers recorded in the ITE monitoring scheme approached the record numbers seen during the hot, dry summers of 1976 and 1984.

   In 1990, numbers of butterflies were high, but not as high as in 1989. (Holly blue butterflies were especially numerous in 1990.) The drought in 1989 adversely affected single-generation species, while the more prolonged drought in 1990 adversely affected two-generation species. The indirect effects of weather on the condition of food plants is very important to butterflies. Species feeding as larvae on plants vulnerable to drought were especially vulnerable, e.g. green-veined white feeding on crucifers and the brown argus on rock-rose.

3. With increasing populations, crowding and higher temperatures, invertebrate dispersal may be increased. There was evidence of increased geographical spread in a number of butterfly species, e.g. hedge brown, speckled wood, small skipper and comma. Conversely, the Scottish argus butterfly which occurs in northern Britain became less numerous. Grasshoppers and crickets (which are not adversely affected by drought) became more numerous and produced more long-winged forms which can fly (in response to high temperatures). Two species of bush cricket spread further north.

4. High summer temperatures increased the rate of development of moths, and many species produced unusual second broods late in 1989 and 1990.

5. The yields of honey per bee colony in 1989 and 1990 were the highest for 32 years (according to the Bee Farmers' Association records), owing to the warm sunny weather and the absence of a drought as severe as that of 1976.

6. There was a marked increase in social wasp populations in 1989, and 1990 was regarded as a "wasp year". Weather is considered to be only one of many factors affecting wasp population ecology. However, it is likely that mild winters and hot summers were beneficial particularly in increasing overwinter survival and in prolonging summer foraging time.

7. Other pests such as cockroaches, fleas and mites in buildings continued to increase and disperse further owing to high temperatures and mild winters. Pests in food reproduced faster and some glasshouse species were able to spread out-of-doors (e.g. leaf hopper and red spider mites).

8. The hot, dry summers had a marked effect on the habitats of animals.
   i) Aquatic communities were damaged by drying out of their habitats, with rare species at the greatest risk. However, many species living in small water bodies were able to survive or disperse.
   ii) Soil dryness also adversely affected some species such as moorland crane flies, snails and slugs.
   iii) Grassland and heathland dried out leading to increased risk of fire. Fire records for the UK (Home Office) and for Dorset showed large numbers of countryside fires in the hot, dry summers of 1976, 1984, 1989 and 1990. In the Peak District National Park there were 80 fires in 1976, and 24 in both 1989 and 1990. Populations of smooth snake, sand lizard and Dartford Warbler were damaged on some heaths.

9. In the summer of 1989, there was some evidence that the hot dry weather improved the breeding success of some bird species, probably by enhancing their foraging success (sparrowhawk and red kite) or the abundance of their invertebrate prey (sedge warbler, reed warbler and capercaillie). Anecdotal information suggested the breeding performance of birds in 1990 was variable, but there was no good evidence to attribute any of this to summer weather.

   There is a need for long term intensive studies, and for experimentation, to establish relationships between bird populations and climate or weather variables.

APPENDIX 1 Background to studies on 5 orchid species in Bedfordshire and Cambridgeshire

Studies of the population dynamics and general biology of *Spiranthes spiralis*, *Aceras anthropophorum*, *Herminium monorchis*, *Orchis morio* and *Ophrys apifera* have been in progress for 28, 25, 25, 12 and 12 years respectively at sites in Bedfordshire and Cambridgeshire. The data derived from these long-term studies provide a baseline from which changes in orchid performance and behaviour may be assessed in relation to a range of environmental factors.

SITE DETAILS

All of the 5 species studied occurr in calcareous grasslands. The sites of *Spiranthes*, *Aceras* and *Herminium*

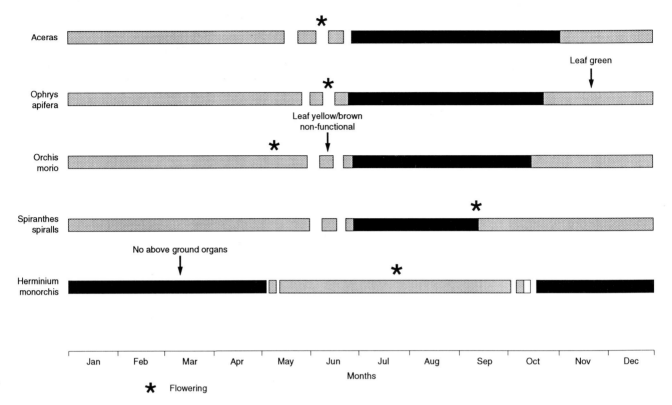

A1 Generalised phenology of 5 species of orchids growing in Bedfordshire (*Aceras*, *Herminium* and *Spiranthes*) and Cambridgeshire (*Ophrys apifera* and *Orchis morio*).

were on soils derived from the Lower Chalk, whereas *Ophrys apifera* and *Orchis morio* grew on heavy clay soils. The sites on chalk soils, at Knocking Hoe NNR and Totternhoe Knolls LNR in Bedfordshire, have been managed over the past 20 years with a mixture of cattle and sheep grazing, interspersed with years in which no grazing has taken place. For the past 2 years, Knocking Hoe has been sheep grazed during the spring and early summer with the result that competition from the dominant grass, *Bromus erectus*, has been less than in previous years. At Totternhoe, there has been no grazing by sheep since 1988, but the vegetation has been kept short by heavy rabbit grazing.

At Monks Wood, where a population of *Ophrys apifera* has been studied since 1979, the grass has been cut annually for hay in late July each year. At Upwood Meadows, the site of the *Orchis morio* study, the species-rich grassland has been grazed annually from late June until early December by 10–12 cattle. The management at each site has been described in some detail because the effects of management and climate are confounded. Broadly speaking, management at Monks Wood and Upwood has been consistent over the study period, and any changes in the performance of the population are likely to be related to climatic factors. At Knocking Hoe and Totternhoe, management has been more variable and it is much more difficult to ascribe changes in the

performance of individuals in the populations with any degree of certainty to climatic factors.

GENERAL BIOLOGY AND PHENOLOGY OF THE 5 ORCHID SPECIES

Figure A1 shows the generalised phenology of the 5 species based on field observations of individual plants made over at least 5 seasons. The species differ in the time when leaves appear above ground and in the time spent above ground. *Herminium* differs from the other species studied in that its leaves appear in late May at the earliest, with leaf expansion not usually occurring until mid-June. Leaves are present above ground until about early September, after which they die down. This species remains below ground for about 8 months of the year. In contrast, the leaves of the other 4 species appear above ground from early September onwards (*Spiranthes* is first, followed by *Ophrys*, *Orchis* and *Aceras*) the exact timing varying considerably from year to year. The leaves remain green throughout the winter, presumably photosynthesising when the temperature rises above a critical minimum, although this threshold is unknown at present.

Leaves of *Spiranthes* were covered by snow for 62 consecutive days in the winter of 1962–63 without either any apparent damage to the plants and without affecting flowering the following year.

Damage to leaves from cold and frost is not common, although drying winds in Spring, associated with low temperatures, can cause premature blackening of leaves in *O. apifera* and *O. morio*, which severely curtails their ability to function normally and in some circumstances leads to leaves dying.

Current photoperiod research suggests that the cue or stimulus for flowering is received through the green leaf or shoot and is transmitted chemically to the shoot tip, thereby initiating flower primordia (Vince-Prue *et al.*,

1984). Based on a detailed study of inflorescence initiation in *O. apifera*, it has been suggested (Wells and Cox, 1989) that inflorescences in tuberous orchids are initiated a year before the plant actually flowers, and that whether the plant produces an inflorescence is dependent on the food manufactured via the leaves in the current year or from resources stored in the previous years tubers. The important point to stress is that there may be a time lag of a year or more in the plants response to climatic events which may influence flowering.

APPENDIX 2

Table 1: Mean height (cm) and number of flowers per spike in undamaged inflorescences of *Spiranthes spiralis* at Knocking Hoe, Bedfordshire in 1976 and in the period 1980–90.

Year	Height (cm ± SE)	Number of flowers ± SE	N=
1976	5.79 ± 0.08	10.00 ± 0.90	11
1980	10.78 ± 0.17	12.41 ± 0.24	193
1981	10.58 ± 0.30	10.81 ± 0.44	57
1982	12.71 ± 0.23	12.03 ± 0.25	143
1983	12.01 ± 0.39	10.57 ± 0.44	54
1984	10.71 ± 0.73	10.14 ± 0.66	14
1985	10.14 ± 0.32	11.98 ± 0.38	60
1986	9.37 ± 0.24	11.19 ± 0.37	53
1987	10.09 ± 0.32	10.00 ± 0.36	71
1988	9.58 ± 0.34	10.50 ± 0.58	24
1989	8.14 ± 0.28	9.79 ± 0.43	39
1990	8.24 ± 0.33	9.39 ± 0.47	33

Table 2: Mean height of inflorescences and number of flowers per spike of a population of *Ophrys apifera* at Monks Wood, 1979–90.

Year	n=	Height (cm) ± SE	No of Flowers ± SE
1979	56	26.08[bcd] ± 0.69	2.42[bc] ± 0.09
1980	92	27.94[ab] ± 0.54	2.63[bc] ± 0.09
1981	77	29.05[ab] ± 0.50	2.93[abc] ± 0.09
1982	149	32.30[a] ± 0.46	3.24[a] ± 0.09
1983	129	29.34[ab] ± 0.46	3.19[ab] ± 0.09
1984	75	22.80[cd] ± 0.54	2.28[c] ± 0.11
1985	45	31.57[a] ± 0.73	3.22[ab] ± 0.11
1986	10	29.00[ab] ± 2.01	2.82[bc] ± 0.25
1987	21	27.50[abc] ± 1.45	2.60[bc] ± 0.12
1988	62	27.40[abc] ± 0.56	2.54[bc] ± 0.11
1989	47	21.63[d] ± 0.54	2.20[c] ± 0.10
1990	18	14.36[e] ± 0.68	2.05[e] ± 0.09

Means with the same letter are not significantly different at p < 0.05 (Scheffe's Test).

Table 3: Mean height of inflorescences and number of flowers per spike of a population of *Orchis morio* at Upwood Meadows, Cambs. 1978–90.

Year	n=	Mean height (cm) ± SE	Mean No flowers (cm) ± SE
1978	24	7.54 ± 1.64	ND
1979	21	8.95 ± 2.03	ND
1980	38	10.86 ± 0.53	5.13 ± 0.31
1981	3	7.73 ± 4.23	4.67 ± 2.75
1982	58	11.75 ± 1.60	5.67 ± 0.82
1983	67	12.03 ± 1.54	5.65 ± 0.69
1984	26	10.44 ± 0.75	4.33 ± 0.31
1985	15	10.27 ± 0.71	3.93 ± 0.32
1986	46	16.63 ± 0.44	5.50 ± 0.32
1987	58	14.06 ± 0.49	4.77 ± 0.24
1988	43	18.31 ± 0.65	5.51 ± 0.34
1989	12	15.37 ± 0.83	3.83 ± 0.29
1990	27	13.00 ± 0.82	4.41 ± 0.36

Chapter B3
Impacts on Freshwater Ecosystems

B3.1 INTRODUCTION

In this chapter, the effects of the dry summers of 1989 and 1990 on freshwater ecosystems in the UK are considered. The chapter has largely been compiled from published and unpublished sources within the Institute of Freshwater Ecology and the Institute of Terrestrial Ecology. Long-term data sets have been analysed wherever possible, so that comparisons can be drawn with the exceptionally warm summer of 1976. The chapter is divided into three sections covering physical, chemical and biological aspects of the dry summers.

B3.2 PHYSICAL ASPECTS

3.2.1 Stream and river temperatures

River and stream temperatures tend to be closely correlated with the average air temperature (Crisp & Howson, 1982). Figure 1 shows the average summer

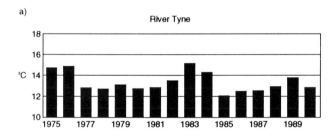

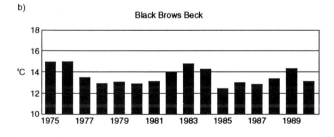

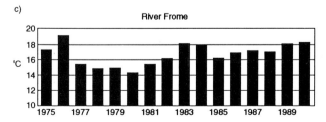

1 Sixteen year records of the average summer (June, July, August) water temperature in (a) the River Tyne (Northumberland), (b) Black Brows Beck (Cumbria) and (c) the River Frome (Dorset).

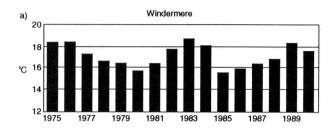

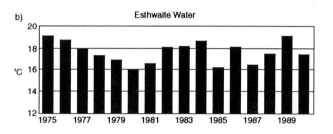

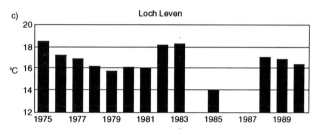

2 Sixteen year records of the summer surface temperatures in (a) Windermere (Cumbria), (b) Esthwaite Water (Cumbria) and (c) Loch Leven (Fife). The plotted temperatures are the average of weekly readings in June, July and August.

(June, July, August) temperatures for three rivers in England between 1980 and 1990. The values from the river Tyne have been estimated using the regression equations given in Crisp (1988a). Those for Black Brows in Cumbria and the Frome in Dorset are calculated directly from field measurements. The average temperatures in the Tyne and Black Brows (Figure 1a and b) in 1989 and 1990 were by no means exceptional, but the average temperatures in the Frome (Figure 1c) were very close to the record temperature in 1976.

3.2.2 Lake temperatures

Lake temperatures are influenced by seasonal changes in wind speed and intensity of solar radiation as well as air temperature (George, 1989). The average summer temperatures recorded in three U.K. lakes over the last sixteen years are compared in Figure 2. The North Basin of Windermere (Figure 2a) and Esthwaite Water (Figure 2b) are two thermally stratified lakes in Cumbria but Loch

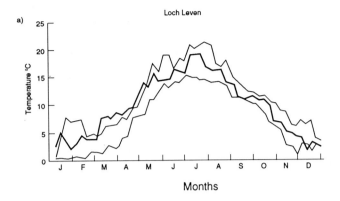

a)

Loch Leven

Months

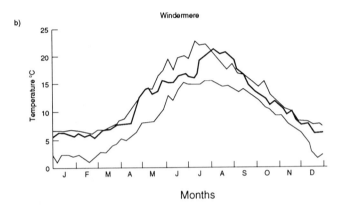

b)

Windermere

Months

3   The seasonal variation of surface water temperatures in (a) Loch Leven (Fife) and (b) Windermere (Cumbria). The temperatures recorded during 1990 (thick line) are compared with the maxima and minima recorded between 1979 and 1989 (thin line).

Leven (Figure 2c) is a shallow isothermal lake near Kinross (Fife). The three time series demonstrate that the water temperatures recorded during the summer of 1989 were no higher than those recorded in the mid 1970's and early 1980's. Indeed at Loch Leven, the most northern site, the average summer water temperature in 1989 was almost 2°C lower than that recorded in 1976. More recent trends in the annual temperature cycle of Loch Leven and Windermere are shown in Figure 3. Actual temperatures recorded in 1990 are presented

together with the range of temperatures recorded in the same weeks between 1980 and 1989. At Loch Leven, (Figure 3a) the summer temperatures in 1990 fell within the 1980–89 range. In Windermere, (Figure 3b) the early summer temperatures also fell within this range but the temperatures in August were consistently higher.

B3.3 CHEMICAL ASPECTS

3.3.1 The concentrations of nitrate in a lowland river

In recent years, many of our southern rivers have become enriched with nitrate from agricultural and domestic drainage. Nitrate concentrations are always much lower in summer than in winter, but summer droughts and winter spates can accentuate this seasonal difference. Casey & Clarke (1979) developed a simple sine wave model to describe the seasonal variations in the concentration of nitrate in a southern chalk stream. This model reliably predicted the weekly concentrations of nitrate in the River Frome between 1965 and 1975, but produced a very poor fit for 1976 which was an exceptionally dry year.

In Figure 4 the predicted and observed concentrations of nitrate in 1976 are compared with those predicted and observed in 1989. In both years, a summer deficit was followed by a winter surplus. However, nitrate levels during the summer of 1989 were higher than those in the summer 1976 and proportionately less nitrate appears to have been leached from the catchment during the mild winter of 1989/90 than during the cold winter of 1976/77.

3.3.2 The effects on streamwater chemistry flowing from an upland wetland in mid-Wales

INTRODUCTION

In many upland catchments in the UK, the valley bottom contains an area of wetland or flushed peat. This zone acts as the riparian margin between the stream and steeper valley sides dominated by mineral soils. The location of riparian ecosystems makes them potentially important for

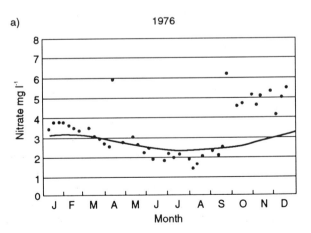

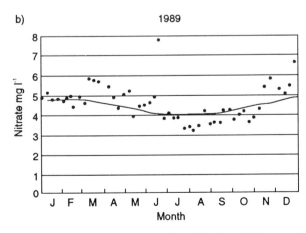

4   Observed (●) and predicted (—) concentrations of nitrate in the River Frome in (a) 1976 and (b) 1989. The 1989 curve has been adjusted to account for recent general increases in the concentration of nitrate (estimated as *ca.* 0.11 mg/year).

Table 1: Mean and maximum streamwater pH and selected solute concentrations from water flowing into and out of wetland at Llanbrynmair Moor, mid-Wales during the summer of 1989 and 1990 (May to September).

	Year	pH	Al[1] ug l^{-1}	colour[2]	Fe	Ca	DOC mg l^{-1}	NO$_3$–N	RedN[3]
Wetland inflow	89	5.9	45.1 (181.0)	149 (700)	2.1 (4.5)	2.1 (2.8)	5.1 (16.0)	0.02 (0.03)	0.34 (0.75)
	90	(5.9)	80.5 (260.0)	66 (150)	1.2 (5.9)	2.0 (2.6)	7.6 (15.0)	0.02 (0.06)	0.21 (0.62)
Wetland outflow	89	5.6	36.5 (160.0)	91 (250)	1.5 (5.1)	2.3 (4.5)	7.8 (21.0)	0.04 (0.74)	0.47 (0.74)
	90	5.0	58.0 (136.0)	34 (130)	0.6 (2.5)	1.7 (2.5)	5.6 (13.0)	0.01 (0.06)	0.21 (0.40)

[1] Total monomeric aluminium
[2] Hazen colour
[3] organic-N + ammonium-N

regulating element fluxes between hillslope water and the stream.

Recent research has indicated that riparian ecosystems can act as nutrient filters (Lowrance *et al.*, 1985, Petersen *et al.*, 1987). The ability of a riparian ecosystem to retain nutrients will depend on its hydrology (Hynes, 1983). In particular, drying and drainage of such an area may cause it to become a source of nutrients (Heathwaite, 1990) and other elements, rather than a sink controlled by the degree of aeration and water logging. Depression of the water table in summer will result in aeration, oxidation and enhanced rates of decomposition, leading to a release of solutes.

SITE LOCATION

As part of a large-scale monitoring programme investigating streamwater quality in a forested catchment in mid-Wales, streamwater samples were taken from February 1989 at fortnightly intervals from water flowing into and out of a wetland located in a base rich subcatchment of Llanbrynmair Moor. A comparison of the effects of extended dry periods on streamwater chemistry during the summers of 1989 and 1990 were made using these data.

The wetland input had no effect on the annual mean concentrations of most major anions and cations in the streamwater (Emmett and Reynolds, 1991). Within a year, however, the wetland had a significant effect on the fluctuations in streamwater attributes of particular interest to water quality managers, *e.g.* colour, aluminium, dissolved organic carbon (DOC) and iron.

A COMPARISON OF THE EFFECT OF THE SUMMER DROUGHT IN 1989 AND 1990

During the summer drought of 1989, elevated concentrations of a range of solutes including aluminium, iron and DOC were recorded (Table 1). For many solutes, the maximum concentrations of 1989 during this period were

recorded in the water flowing from the wetland. For example, the maximum concentration of total monomeric aluminium was 160 µg/1, of iron, 5 mg/1 and of DOC, 21 mg/1 (Figure 5). This compares to means over the two year period of 49 µg/1, 0.9 mg/1 and 5.4 mg/1, respectively. The increased decomposition of organic matter in the surface peat horizons with the lowering of the water table, and subsequent increase in DOC concentrations in water flowing from the wetland, increased the mobility of both iron and aluminium (Figure 5).

Concentrations of total reduced nitrogen (ammonia + organic nitrogen), nitrate, sulphate, calcium and magnesium in the water flowing from the wetland also increased above the concentrations in the inflowing water during this period (*e.g.* Figure 5). Increased concentrations of reduced nitrogen (ammonium + organic-N) were probably a consequence of stimulated nitrogen mineralization, which is known to occur with increased fluctuations of the water table. The lowering of the water table would also stimulate the transformation of ammonium to nitrate due to the increase in the ammonium substrate and the presence of aerobic conditions in the upper peat horizons. This microbial transformation is particularly sensitive to reduced oxygen availability.

At this site mean fortnightly rainfall during the summer of 1990 was higher than for 1989 (45 mm and 36 mm respectively). The effects of the dry period in the summer of 1990 were therefore less severe than those observed in 1989. The pH of the streamwater flowing from the wetland increased to a maximum of 7.0 in the summer of 1989 during baseflow conditions, compared to only 5.6 in 1990. Mean solute concentrations were generally lower during the summer period May – September 1990, and maximum concentrations were lower for total monomeric aluminium, iron, DOC, nitrate-N, reduced-N, calcium, magnesium and Hazen colour (Table 1). The time series plots in Figure 5 illustrate this point, with few high concentration events when streamwater flowing from the wetland contained higher concentrations of solutes relative to the inflowing water.

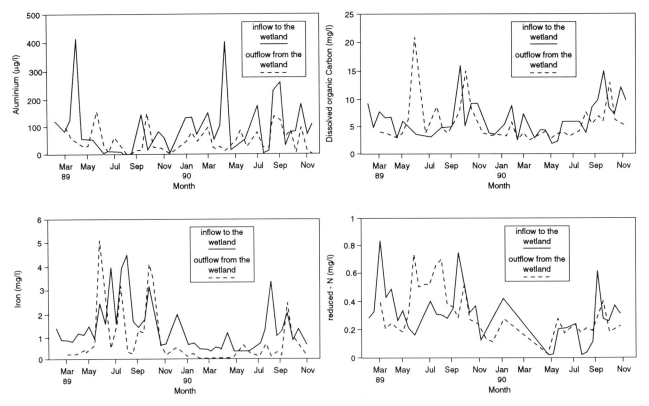

5 Concentrations of aluminium, iron, dissolved organic carbon and reduced nitrogen in water flowing into and out of a wetland area at Llanbrynmair Moor, mid-Wales in 1989/90.

B3.4 BIOLOGICAL ASPECTS

3.4.1 Lake phytoplankton

THE DEVELOPMENT OF DEEP WATER ANOXIA IN STRATIFIED LAKES

When a lake becomes thermally stratified, very little oxygen moves across the thermocline from the upper to the lower layers of water. The concentration of oxygen in the lower layer is then controlled by the reducing properties of the sediment and the rate at which organic particles decompose in the water column. The deep waters of most oligotrophic lakes remain well oxygenated throughout the summer, but more productive lakes show some degree of deep water anoxia.

Most lakes develop a pattern of deep water anoxia that remains relatively constant from year to year. In some lakes, however, the concentration of oxygen in the deeper water changes from year to year as different weather conditions promote different algal successions. In the South Basin of Windermere, the deep water becomes anoxic only when weather conditions favour the growth of the alga *Oscillatoria bourellyi*, (Heaney, 1986). This alga is denser than water and requires turbulence to keep it in suspension. In relatively windy years, dense crops of *O. bourellyi* appear near the surface and give rise to very low oxygen tensions in the deep water after they have ultimately sunk and decayed. In calmer years, the *O. bourellyi* crop is typically replaced by species that tend to remain in suspension and be remineralised in the upper

rather than lower layers of water. The contrast between "*Oscillatoria*" and "non-*Oscillatoria*" years in Windermere can be graphically illustrated by comparing conditions in the lake during the warm summers of 1976 and 1989. In 1976 (Figure 6a) episodic calm periods restricted the growth of *Oscillatoria* and there was no serious depletion of oxygen in deep water. In 1989 (Figure 6b) early summer conditions favoured the growth of *O. bourellyi* and the subsequent rain of decaying cells into the lower layers consumed most of the deep oxygen.

3.4.2 Algal blooms

Most species of blue-green algae grow rather slowly but many possess gas vacuoles that allow them to float to the surface and then accumulate downwind. Such local accumulations are aesthetically unsightly and can also be a danger to humans and animals if the cells produce toxins. About 25 species of blue-green algae are known to produce chemicals that are toxic to humans and it is wise to assume that any bloom is potentially toxic. In the summers of 1989 and 1990, problem blooms of blue-green algae were reported from a number of lakes and reservoirs in the UK. In 1989, a survey commissioned by the National Rivers Authority (1990) revealed that bloom problems were encountered in 25% of the water bodies sampled in England and Wales. Five NRA regions also organised toxicity tests on a total of 78 waters and reported that nearly 70% of these blooms were toxic.

Since this was the first bloom survey commissioned in the UK, these results cannot be placed in any historic

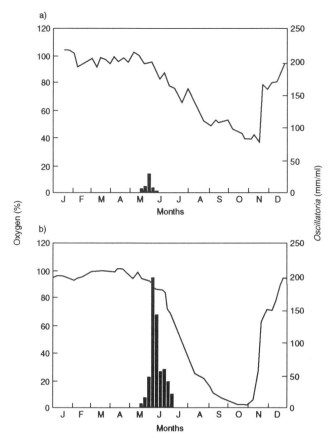

6 The effect of sinking *Oscillatoria bowellyi* on the deoxygenation of deep water in the South Basin of Windermere. (a) 1976 a warm year with a poor growth of *Oscillatoria*. (b) 1989 a warm year with a strong growth of *Oscillatoria*. The *Oscillatoria* numbers are plotted as histograms and the points show the concentration of oxygen at a depth of 30 m.

perspective. More blue-green incidents were, however, reported in the media than in any previous year. The most serious was the hospitalisation of two soldiers in Staffordshire (Turner *et al*, 1990) and the deaths of sheep and dogs after allegedly drinking from Rutland Water also caused great concern.

At one time, blue-green blooms were regarded as an almost inevitable consequence of lake enrichment. However, although very dense crops form only where nutrients are plentiful, relatively modest concentrations of phosphorus can still support nuisance blooms. It has become clear in recent years that dense blooms appear in certain lakes only if the weather conditions are favourable (Steinberg & Hartman, 1988, George *et al*, 1990). Most genera of blue-green algae grow very slowly but their growth rate can be accelerated by high temperatures and prolonged periods of relative calm.

The mild winters of 1988/89 and 1989/90 enabled large numbers of blue-green cells to overwinter in open water, forming heavy inoculum that was quick to respond to the warm spring weather. In 1989, the early summer growths of blue-green algae were, to a large extent, checked by windy weather, but the return of high pressure systems in late August promoted a further cycle of growth and

accumulation. The effect of wind mixing on the growth and decline of a blue-green bloom can be illustrated by contrasting the development of *Aphanizomenon* in Esthwaite Water in 1985 and 1989. The summer of 1985 (Figure 7a) was cold and windy. The *Aphanizomenon* crop appeared late in the year and its growth rate was soon checked by intense mixing in late August. In 1989 (Figure 7b) the early summer was not only warm but unusually calm so dense blooms of *Aphanizomenon* appeared in late May and persisted for much of the summer.

Oscillatoria agardhi is another species that only grows well when the lake is poorly mixed and very calm. Figure 8 shows the effect of increased winter and summer temperatures on the average summer crops of *O. agardhi* in the south basin of Windermere. Although the input of phosphate into the south basin has changed little in the last decade (Figure 8a), appreciable growth of *O. agardhi* (Figure 8b) has been recorded only in the late 1980's. The average temperatures in Figure 8c show that growths of *O. agardhi* are most likely to occur when warm summers are combined with mild winters.

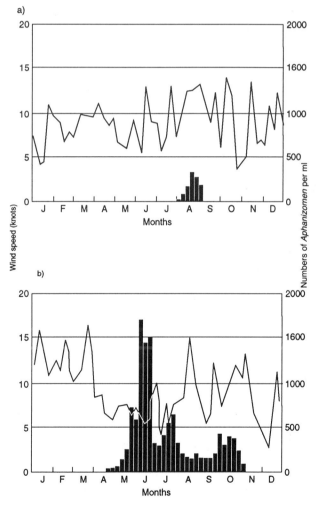

7 The growth of the blue-green alga *Aphanizomen* in Esthwaite Water in 1985 and 1989. (a) 1985 a cold windy summer. (b) 1989 a warm relatively calm summer. The *Aphanizomenon* numbers are plotted as histograms and the points show the average weekly wind speeds.

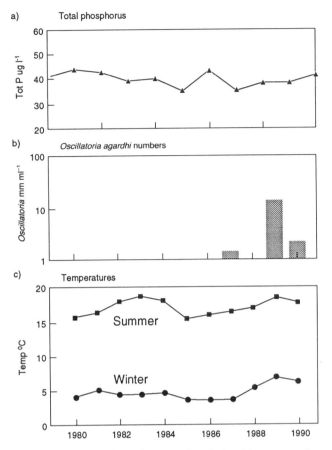

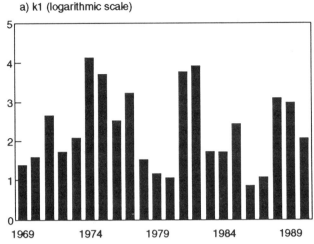

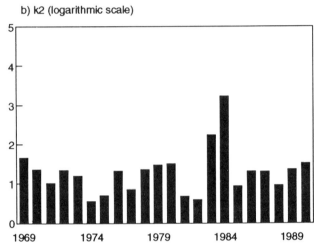

8 Factors influencing the growth of the blue-green alga *Oscillatoria agardhi* in the South Basin of Windermere between 1980 and 1990. (a) Winter concentrations of total phosphorus. (b) Year to year changes in the average summer crop of *O. agardhi*. (c) Year to year variations in the average winter (●) and summer (■) temperatures.

3.4.3 *Freshwater fish*

Many salmonid populations in the UK were adversely affected by the high temperatures and low flows recorded in 1989 and 1990. The effects of the dry summers were felt most acutely in southern Britain. In the north, many streams were replenished by late summer rains, so catastrophic mortalities were generally avoided.

THE SURVIVAL OF TROUT IN A CUMBRIAN STREAM

Elliott (1984) showed that population density of eggs and alevins at the start of each year had an important effect on the subsequent survival of young trout, *Salmo trutta* L. In Black Brows Beck Cumbria, the number of recruits to each year class can be related to the initial egg density by dome shaped stock recruitment curves of the type described by Ricker (1954). Year to year variations in water temperature appear to have little effect on survival, but high mortalities are invariably recorded in exceptionally dry years. Figure 9 summarises the yearly losses recorded from two early stages of trout in Black Brows between 1969 and 1990. The method used to compare the loss rates is "key factor analysis" (Varley *et al.* 1973).

9 The year to year variation in (a) the number of trout lost between the alevin stage and the parr stage in May/June (k1) and (b) the parr stages in August/September (k2). The loss rates have been calculated by key factor analysis.

In this method, population density is expressed on a logarithmic scale and loss rates (k values) are calculated between successive stages in the life cycle. The k values in Figure 9 are those calculated for fish at the beginning (k1) and end (k2) of their first summer. The two time series show little relationship between fish losses and the warm summers of 1975, 1976, 1989 and 1990. The critical factor appears to be the duration rather than the intensity of the warm, dry period. In 1990, the early summer was exceptionally dry in the Lake District but the streams were then recharged by the heavy August rains.

THE PRODUCTION OF TROUT IN A CUMBRIAN STREAM

The annual production of young trout depends on their growth rate as well as their survival. The mathematical models developed by Elliott (1975) demonstrate that warm summers can check the growth rate of trout but they also show that warm winters can enhance growth rates early in the season. Elliott (1984, 1985) has produced a detailed analysis of the factors influencing the biomass

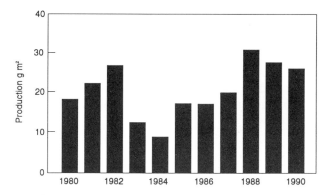

10　The year to year variation in the production of trout under three years old in Black Brows Beck (Cumbria).

and production of young trout in Black Brows Beck, Cumbria. Figure 10 shows year to year changes in the production of fish up to 3 years old between 1980 and 1990. The lowest production figures were recorded during the droughts of 1983 and 1984. In 1989 and 1990, more one and two year old fish survived and the young fish also emerged earlier and grew faster in spring and early summer. Thus, again, it cannot be said that the warm summers of 1989 and 1990 had any notably adverse effects.

THE GROWTH OF TROUT IN WELSH UPLAND STREAMS

The mathematical models developed by Elliott (1975) have also been used to study the effect of temperature on the growth of trout in a number of upland streams, (Weatherly & Ormerod, 1990). Table 2 compares the simulated growth of young brown trout in a moorland and forest stream in mid-Wales during the summers of 1986, 1987, 1988 and 1989.

The temperatures in the moorland stream exceeded the optimum for trout growth for 11 consecutive weeks in 1989, whereas the temperatures in the forest stream seldom exceeded the notional optimum of 13.3°C. The simulations suggest that, whilst the fish in the forest

Table 2:　Simulated growth of O-group brown trout in a moorland and upland stream in Wales. Emergence date was fixed at 15 April for each year and the weight on emergence set at 0.1 g. Growth was calculated from measured temperatures using Elliot's method (1975).

	Weight on 31 October (g)	
Emergence date	Moorland stream	Forest stream
15.4.86	3.9	3.3
15.4.87	6.5	4.5
15.4.88	5.7	4.4
15.4.89	5.7	6.1

stream generally grow rather slowly, their growth rate can exceed that of the moorland fish in an abnormally warm summer.

SALMON MIGRATION IN THE RIVER FROME

In 1973, a salmon counter was installed on the River Frome in Dorset. Welton *et al*, (1989) analysed seasonal variation in the numbers of salmon ascending the counting weir, and they still maintain an annual record of fish movements. In most years, there are two distinct periods of migration with one run in the summer and another in the autumn. The number of fish moving upstream in summer is not closely related to the mean flow but the autumn runs generally coincide with periods of high flow. Very low flows at any time of year can, however, restrict fish movement and may even prevent the fish from reaching the spawning grounds.

Figure 11 shows the effects of the dry summers of 1976 and 1989 on the movement of fish in the Frome. In 1976, very few fish moved upstream but the number of potential migrants may also have been rather low. The stock of salmon in the Frome has increased considerably in recent years, but the number of fish moving upstream in summer was unusually low in 1989. In the autumn, very few fish moved upstream in 1976, whereas in 1989 most of the fish trapped downstream in the summer finally completed their migration in the autumn. In 1990, the number of autumn migrants was also low but it is not yet clear what effect this will have on the long-term development of the fishery.

B3.5 CONCLUSIONS

1. During the summers of 1989 and 1990, river and lake surface water temperatures were above average, but not exceptionally so, mostly falling within the range recorded in recent decades, and below the high temperatures recorded in 1976.

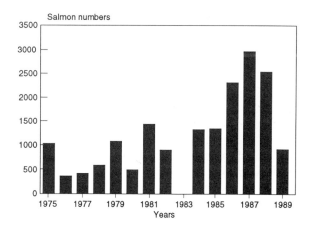

11　The year to year variation in the number of salmon moving up the River Frome in summer. The numbers are the numbers logged on a resistivity counter positioned in a gauging weir. The counter was not operating in 1983.

2. A detailed study of water flowing from a wetland in mid-Wales found high concentrations of dissolved organic matter, reduced-N and iron in the outflow water when it rained after dry spells. These peaks were most pronounced in 1989.

3. Blooms of blue-green algae occurred on 25% of lakes and reservoirs surveyed by the National Rivers Authority and many blooms were toxic. The calm, warm early summer of 1989 following a mild winter, was observed to favour a build-up in populations of the blue-green algae *Oscillatoria* in Windermere and *Aphanizomenon* in Esthwaite Water.

4. The hot summers, like the mild winters, had no major effects on freshwater fish numbers, although drought restricted salmon migration in some streams, and warm temperatures may have increased trout weight in otherwise cool forest streams.

Chapter B4
Impacts on Agriculture and Horticulture

B4.1 INTRODUCTION

This chapter provides an overview of the effects of two hot summers on agriculture and horticulture in the United Kingdom although it is obvious in many cases that it is not possible to separate these effects from those caused by the two preceeding mild winters.

The chapter follows the same format as chapter A4 with sections on individual crops, livestock, pests and disease. In order to avoid repetition, the section on pests and diseases is fairly brief.

B4.2 SOIL CONDITIONS

The summers of 1989 and 1990 (encompassing the period May to October) both began by inheriting the problems of the previous mild winters. However, the summer of 1990 also inherited the problems of the dry 1989 summer and by May 1990 soil moisture deficits were large (see Chapter B1.2).

With lower-than-average rainfall and high soil moisture deficits, many farmers relied more heavily than normal on irrigation. With the increased demand upon water supplies, reservoirs began to dwindle, and water courses ran dry. In 1990, in the east and south east, first restrictions on river abstraction were imposed by mid May. By mid June, ADAS were warning farmers in eastern coastal areas about chloride levels in water used for irrigation. In August, Southern Water suspended 200 irrigation licences to abstract water from the River Stour, Kent, when soil moisture deficits reached 177 mm. Other abstraction bans are shown in Table 1.

B4.3 PESTS AND DISEASES

Generally, the pattern of diseases was that expected from the weather conditions. There was a lower incidence than normal of leaf diseases which rely on rainsplash for dispersal, and on wet or humid environments and cool

Table 1: Number of farms experiencing National River Authority abstraction bans, summer 1990.

AREA	NO. FARMS
Anglian	600
Lincs Cambs Essex	400
Severn Trent	200
Welsh	170
Yorkshire	100
Wessex	40
Thames	6

temperatures (10–15°C). Examples of such diseases are *Septoria tritici*, downy mildew and leaf spot. In many cases these diseases were less evident in 1990 than in 1989 due to the prolonged drought conditions.

Powdery mildew appeared early in 1989 but was not as damaging as in previous wetter years. In 1990, it proved to be the biggest foliar disease problem. It occurred on sugar beet much earlier than previously, and was found north of York for the first time. It was also found in many linseed crops for the first time in 1990.

Of the cereal diseases, brown rust was much more of a problem than yellow rust in 1989 and 1990 due to their differing optimum temperatures. Yellow rust is active at 10–15°C and kept in check when temperatures rise above 25°C, whereas brown rust which is aerially dispersed on dry windy days, prefers 15–22°C.

As in 1976, there was little evidence of blight in potatoes in 1989 or 1990 as there were few "Smiths" periods (two days of temperatures greater than 10°C and humidity over 90%). Blight tended to be found only in irrigated crops grown under plastic. The amounts of *Alternaria* and *Botrytis*, which are the main threats to sunflowers, linseed and brassicas (especially at flowering), were also low or non existent.

Only five cases of *Rhizomania* were reported from 2000 inspected crops of sugar beet. This is a soil-borne fungal disease which has an optimum temperature of 25°C. It does however require soil moisture for zoospore movement and hence transmission (4/5 of the cases were from irrigated crops).

The root disease take-all became increasingly evident towards harvest. This is an infection from root- and stem-base debris which may persist in the soil for at least two years. It is favoured by a combination of a mild winter, moist cool spring and early dry summer and is particularly damaging to winter-sown crops. All these conditions were experienced by the 1989/90 crop.

Viral diseases (virus yellows, beet western yellow virus, barley yellow dwarf virus (BYDV) and potato mild mosaic virus) were a severe problem in 1990 due to the high numbers of aphids. The degree of infection was sometimes confused with drought stress symptoms. At Brooms Barn, the yield of sugar beet lost due to viral infection in 1990 was estimated at 2 t/ha.

The main pests in 1989 and 1990 were aphids. As well as spreading viral disease, they caused direct feeding

Table 2: Cereal harvest yield for England and Wales 1984–1990. Source: MAFF statistics 208/90 (16.10.90).

| Year | Yield t/ha | | | | | | |
	1984	1985	1986	1987	1988	1989	1990
Crop							
Wheat	7.71	6.37	6.93	5.96	6.15	6.70	6.78
Total barley	5.68	5.18	5.33	5.12	4.66	4.87	5.06
Winter Barley	6.15	5.54	5.69	5.46	5.26	5.47	5.47
Spring barley	4.93	4.59	4.75	4.52	3.96	3.77	4.02
Oats	5.08	4.96	5.44	4.66	4.59	4.69	5.03

damage (see Chapter B2.2.2). In some areas the aphids were kept in check by a higher-than-usual number of aphid parasites and predators especially in 1990. Aphid numbers declined in the hottest weather due to the effect of drought on their host plants.

Other pests were not generally found at damaging levels, with the possible exception of pea and bean weevils. Pests such as slugs and leatherjackets were found in smaller numbers, as they tend to migrate down the soil profile in dry conditions. The hot dry conditions favoured the growth of populations of cut worms and carrot fly which were a problem to some vegetable growers.

B4.4 EFFECTS ON AGRICULTURAL CROPS

4.4.1 Cereals

The hot, dry summers had a profound effect upon cereal yields and quality as well as on growth and development. The effect varied in magnitude between regions, depending on local weather conditions and soil type. Winter cereals fared much better than their spring-sown counterparts. This was the result of good root system development over the mild winter which enabled crops to withstand the drought conditions better. Even so, by the end of May 1989 and 1990, many crops, especially in the southern and eastern counties, showed signs of severe drought stress. Depending on the degree of insolation received, cereals can withstand soil moisture deficits of around 100 mm. In 1984, a year of the bumper cereal harvests, soil moisture deficits at Rosemaund EHF, Herefordshire reached 95 mm at the end of July. In 1989 a 110 mm deficit had been already reached by the end of June, and in 1990 the deficit was 109 mm at the end of May.

In 1989 and 1990 cereal development was generally advanced. At Rosemaund, for example, crop growth in 1989 was several days earlier than average and in 1990 was up to two weeks ahead of 1989. Usually an advanced crop would be expected to benefit in grain growth provided that there was moisture available and indeed in 1989 rapid grainfilling and ripening did occur in most areas. However, in 1990 drought conditions were already in existence at the start of grain growth and in combination with high temperatures (which hastened senescence and reduced ripening time) decreased the period of grain fill.

Premature ripening meant that many crops in the south, especially on light soils, were beyond help from the rains which came in June 1990, and there was consequently a high proportion of shrivelled grains at harvest.

Yields in England and Wales were down on the long term average in both years, as in 1976, but in 1990, in spite of more severe conditions, the yields were greater than in 1989 (Table 2). This was partially due to the June rains, and to the early harvest in ideal conditions. Crops that were irrigated performed well; at Gleadthorpe, unirrigated winter barley produced 3.9 t/ha compared to 4.5 t/ha from an irrigated crop.

There were however regional differences as shown in Table 3 for 1990. Northern and Scottish crops performed exceptionally well. Winter wheat growing on heavy, well-structured soils in Humberside yielded up to 12.5 t/ha (equivalent to the 1984 yield) compared to 3.8 t/ha from drier lighter soils of Cornwall, Norfolk and Suffolk, although yields in parts of the East Midlands were as low as 1.3 t/ha.

The quality of wheat was also affected by the weather conditions. The majority of grain did not need to be dried prior to storage. In 1990, some farmers found that they were selling at a reduced price compared to normal, as price is based on 15% moisture and the 1990 crop was lighter. Some grain came off the field at over 30°C and had to be cooled to 10°C before long term storage, to prevent infestation or mould.

Table 3: Cereal harvest yield by region 1990. (MAFF statistics 208/90 (16.10.90) and * Scottish Agricultural College Edinburgh field trials.

| Crop | Yield | | | | |
	Wheat	Barley total	Winter barley	Spring barley	Oats
Region					
Scotland*	9.90	8.26	9.21	7.31	–
North	4.17	5.42	5.98	4.58	5.61
Yorkshire+ Humberside	7.44	5.69	5.92	4.72	5.60
North West	6.35	4.67	5.12	3.91	4.48
Wales	5.62	4.30	4.94	3.83	4.26
West midlands	6.25	4.73	5.07	3.56	4.73
East midlands	6.93	4.97	5.09	4.51	5.34
East Anglia	7.22	5.34	5.73	4.43	5.21
South east	6.41	4.94	5.53	3.43	5.27
South west	6.14	4.71	5.25	3.61	4.56

The 1989 harvest produced some of the highest quality breadmaking wheats for at least 16 years. Protein content was high, as expected in hot dry summers, with twice as much wheat over the 11% protein required for breadmaking compared to 1988. In Scotland the protein contents were lower (9.2%); this was a consequence of the longer growing season and dilution of protein by starch. In 1990, protein levels were very variable; in the south and south east, grain was coming off at 10.5–11% and 9–11% protein respectively, whilst in the east, proteins were around 11.3–13.4%. The reasons for the low protein values are not known.

4.4.2 Sugarbeet

In spring 1989, the majority of sugar beet crops were either sown early (March) or late (late April/May). The intervening period was not suitable for sowing because of wet weather. The early sown crops performed well as they developed a good early canopy able to utilise the above-average summer insolation. The later sown crops were more affected by the summer drought. They tended to form gappy stands which were more susceptible to aphid infestation and which provided only limited competition to late germinating weeds. In 1990 the whole sugarbeet crop was sown exceptionally early (80% by the end of March). Some patchy emergence occurred from crops sown into dry seedbeds. For example, in West Yorkshire some crops were redrilled, with peas and linseed.

High summer temperatures meant more rapid growth, and by mid-summers day at Brooms Barn (Suffolk), a leaf area cover of 52% and 75% was achieved in 1989 and 1990, respectively, compared with an average of 40%. The greater proportion of cover in 1990 compared to 1989 may well have been due to the early development of a good root system by the time high evaporation occurred.

Potentially, the 1990 crop was the biggest ever, but the drought later in the summer reduced this potential. Growth was uneven across the country, linked to soil type. The amount of irrigation needed in 1990 was higher than normal. In an average year, 50–100 mm is common but in 1990 150–200 mm was recommended, with the exception of the York area (90 mm). Only a small proportion of beet grown in Britain is normally irrigated (c. 13% in 1987, although this varies between 30% around Ipswich to less than 3% around York). Table 4 shows beet response to the amount of irrigation water used. In general, there was a 35% loss of potential yield due to drought. However, in a hot year the potential yield is greater than normal and the actual yield may not be affected to such a great extent.

Hot, sunny summers provide ideal conditions for the accumulation of sugar in beet and the five-year average sugar content was exceeded in 1989 and 1990 (Table 5).

Table 4: Results of irrigation trials at Brooms Barn in 1990.

Irrigation mm	Sugar yield t/ha	Root yield t/ha	% Sugar
0	8.8	67.9	18.0
92	11.2	84.0	18.6
118	10.2	81.5	17.6
150	12.3	95.3	18.1
163	12.1	94.0	18.1
260	13.4	104.1	18.2

Table 5: Sugarbeet quality in the UK. (Big Farm Weekly 23–8–90).

	5 yr average	1989	1990
Root weight (g/beet)	386	462	393
Sugar content (%)	13.9	15.9	18.7
Sugar/root (g)	54	74	73

Yields of early sown crops in 1989 were good, the high levels of disease induced by the previous mild winter (Appendix) tending to be offset by the favourable summer weather. Later sown crops were more affected by summer drought and did not yield so well. Although 1989 yields varied from near record to very poor, the national sugar yield was good at 7.2 t/ha sugar. In 1990, root size was small compared to 1989, although the crop potential was good on moisture-retentive soils and for irrigated crops. Yields in Suffolk were variable; greater than 49.4t/ha on irrigated light land and 24.7 t/ha on unirrigated soils.

4.4.3 Oilseed rape

In general, autumn-sown rape were well developed by summer 1989 and the effect of the drought was minimal. The hot weather further encouraged rapid ripening, and harvesting was early in near ideal conditions. Yields were generally above average. In contrast, spring-sown rape was rapidly affected by the dry weather and crops were slow to establish. This gave a longer "window of accessibility" to pests, especially birds. Yields of spring rape were usually below average. Table 6 shows some typical yields.

After the 1988/89 mild winter, there was a high incidence of disease on leaves, in particular *Altenaria*, leaf spot and downy mildew. However, the hot dry summer conditions were not conducive to the spread of disease. Figure 1 shows the amount of disease present on leaves and pods

Table 6: Yields of spring and winter rape at High Mowthorpe EHF in 1989 compared with 5 year average (data courtest of Mrs S. Ogilvy).

	1989 yield (t/ha)	5 year average yield (t/ha)
Winter rape	3.29	3.03
Spring rape	1.43	2.01

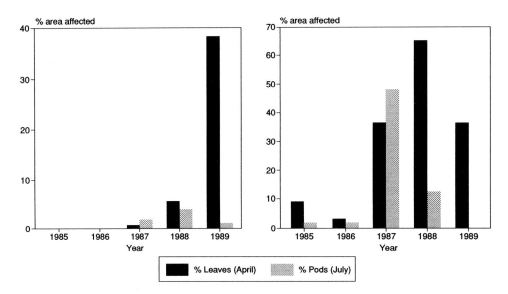

1 Incidence of the pathogens *Altenaria* (a) and *Pyrenopeziza* (b) on leaves (April) and pods (July) of winter oilseed rape (cv. Bienvenu) for January-March and June respectively, 1985–1989. (Courtesy of C J Rawlinson *et al.*, Rothamsted Experimental Station).

in 1989 after the mild winter in comparisons to that in previous years.

Although the incidence of disease was reduced over the hot summer, pests were frequent and active. Mealy aphid, pollen beetles, seed weevils and pod midge were especially problematic. High pest populations, together with the 1989/90 mild winter, meant that unusually large numbers of these pests overwintered to infest the 1990 crop.

The 1990 oilseed rape harvest was variable, due to differing drought severity and soil types (Table 7). Problems at harvest were found in some regions due to uneven ripening; many farmers needed to combine twice to harvest immature patches. In northern Britain 1990 yields were better than in 1989, but areas in the south reported one of the worst harvests ever, and the 8% price increase did not compensate for lost yield. Reduced yield was in part explained by small grain size, which was related to the lack of moisture at grain fill.

The 1990 crop was generally of good quality. The moisture content averaged 7.5%, and many growers were

able to take the small advantage of a premium for moisture contents between 6% and 9%. In Suffolk, parts of Scotland and Humberside, where crop moistures were below 6%, merchants refused to take delivery due to the difficulty of oil extraction. Oil contents were high, averaging 42% (38% – 45%).

4.4.4 Sunflowers

Table 8: Sunflower yields 1988–1990 at Sutton Bonington, Nottinghamshire. (School of Agriculture, Nottingham University).

| Year | Variety | Yield | |
		Seed (t/ha)	Oil (%)
1988	Sunbred-246	2.4–4.6	46–50
	S-47	2.2–3.2	39–41
1989	Sunbred-246	2.4–3.1	36–49
	S-47	1.3–2.9	38–42
1990	Sunbred-246	N/A	N/A
	S-47	1.5–2.0	30–35

N/A – Data not available

These crops are sown relatively late (April/May) and need a long growing season (± large thermal time). They are adapted to high temperatures and benefit from high insolation (97% of yield variation is explained by temperature and radiation). Both 1989 and 1990 proved to be good years for sunflowers; at Boxworth EHF, Cambridgeshire, the first commercial crop was harvested in 1990, yielding 2.5 t/ha at 8.5% moisture.

At Rothamsted Experimental Station, Hertfordshire, in 1990 early varieties yielded 2.5–3.0 t/ha at 30–40% oil content. Standard varieties, which require a longer

Table 7: Yield of oilseed rape (at 15% moisture) in Britain in 1990. Figures taken from ADAS Farm Bulletins published in Farmers Weekly (May – October 1990) and SAC Edinburgh.

Region	Yield range t/pa
South-west	2.3–2.9 disappointing to poor
South-east	1.8–3.5
East	2.0–5.4
Midlands + west	3.0–3.5 average
Wales	3.0–3.3
North	2.3–4.0 average to good
Scotland	4.1–5.0

growing season, yielded 4.0–5.0 t/ha with 40–50% oil content. Comparison of yields over the period 1988–1990, at Sutton Bonington, Nottinghamshire, can be seen in Table 9. It must be noted that these represent hand-harvested field trials (as does the Rothamstead yield), so the yields are above those that would be expected from a commercial crop. A commercial crop is considered to be successful if it yields 2.5 t/ha.

4.4.5 Linseed

As with sunflowers, linseed is sown late and requires a long growing season. Yields in 1989 and 1990 averaged 2.13 t/ha (1.25–3.0 t/ha), with water retentive soils giving the better yields. Crops generally ripened early in the dry weather and harvesting was easy, but some long stubble was left in the fields due to green stalks.

4.4.6 Potatoes

The summers of 1989 and 1990 had a variable effect on the potato crop. Unirrigated crops produced low yields of poor quality, whereas irrigated crops or those in areas without water shortage yielded well. For example, in 1990, in Pembrokeshire, where 80% of the 1616 ha of early potatoes were irrigated, lifting began ahead of schedule. By mid-May, 5% had been cleared, compared to 3.5% in 1989, and 60% were lifted by mid June. Crops in the east also grew well, although some needed irrigation, but in the Midlands and north west potato crops were under severe moisture stress.

The early potato harvest was good with more growers lifting early. In 1990, yields reached 35 t/ha in Suffolk and up to 43 t/ha elsewhere from irrigated crops. Second earlies did not achieve the same standards, being more affected by drought, and 1990 yields ranged between 29 t/ha and 60 t/ha, (Big Farm Weekly, 2-8-90) keeping the prices low.

The hardest hit were main-crop potatoes, as in 1976, the prolonged hot dry weather placing unirrigated potatoes under increasingly severe drought stress. Along with the lack of water came stresses due to lack of nutrients and *Rhizoctonia* (black scurf). These led to widespread early senescence especially on unirrigated crops. The difference in yield between irrigated and unirrigated main-crop potatoes at Gleadthorpe FHF, Nottinghamshire was 30–40 t/ha in 1989 and 1990 compared to 3–8 t/ha in 1986–1988.

In 1990, early senescence was also partially caused by physiologically older seed and earlier planting. As a result, crops matured 2–3 weeks earlier than 1989, with good skin set and less external damage. However, the late arrival of rain in the 1990 growing season (end of August-beginning of September) caused much damage to the crops. In Lincolnshire, there were signs of sprouting, secondary growth and occasional growth cracks on unirrigated crops. In Lancashire, early die-back and ridge

cracking gave increased tuber greening; this was also a problem in Humberside, especially for Pentland Dell grown on contract. The rain was not sufficient to change the soil conditions and hence many tubers were damaged on lifting. Some crops were as much as 70% bruised, making them virtually unsaleable.

Due to the depressed prices in 1990, many farmers decided to opt for long-term storage. Crops destined for storage were burnt off with acid to prevent further growth cracks. In East Anglia, cases of necrosis and rot were noted in October, and were thought to be due to the uptake of acid by burnt-off crops when soil moisture deficits were very high.

Tuber dry matter was high in both years, and in 1990 values of 1–8% above normal were not uncommon. For example, in Cambridgeshire and Northumberland, some crops were harvested at 27% dry matter as opposed to the normal 22%. Associated with high dry matter was a higher-than-normal incidence of internal bruising from lifting. The Potato Marketing Board reported up to 40% wastage from damage by greening, scab, cracking and bruising during lifting, especially where rain made the crop too wet to lift and secondary growth and cracking occurred.

Storage also produced other problems, not least of which was the temperature of the tubers at harvest; many were too hot for immediate storage. Sprouting due to the warm weather and the physiologically older state of the tubers at harvest was quite a common problem. In 1990, some main crop varieties had sprouts 2–3 cm long at the end of October. In both years, a few crops broke dormancy and sprouted before harvest.

4.4.7 Legumes

PEAS

Table 9: Yields of 2 pea varieties in 1990 with and without irrigation at Gleadthorpe EHF, Nottinghamshire.

Variety	Yield t/ha	
	Solara	Boatea
Irrigated	4.9	4.5
Unirrigated	1.9	2.6

In 1989, pea yields were lower than average but crop quality was good. In 1990, peas began the season well; many were flowering by the start of June. The effect of irrigation on yield at Gleadthorpe is shown in Table 9. Generally, peas held out well against the drought, partially due to a good response to the rain in June. The hot dry weather meant that combined peas ripened quickly, especially on light soils and in eastern counties. Short varieties, such as Solara, were worst affected by stunted growth, in some cases making harvesting difficult.

Table 10: Yields of 2 unirrigated pea varieties, 1987–1990 at Gleadthorpe EHF, Nottinghamshire.

Variety	Yield t/ha	
	Solara	Boatea
Year		
1990	1.9	2.6
1989	2.9	2.9
1988	4.1	3.5
1987	2.5	2.5

In eastern counties (Table 10), yields averaged 2–2.5 t/ha, although on heavier soils and/or in western regions they were higher than average (in the West Midlands, yields were reported over 3.75 t/ha).

BEANS

Generally winter beans having a more extensive root system were better able to tolerate the drought than spring beans, which were severely stressed unless irrigated. Table 11 illustrates the difference in yield between irrigated and non-irrigated spring beans in 1989.

As with peas, senescence was rapid, and harvest was up to one month early. The effect of the 1990 drought was seen, fortuitously, at Sutton Bonington, Nottinghamshire, when a water main burst in a field of winter beans. The accidentally irrigated areas yielded 1.32t/ha more than the rest of the field. Under normal conditions winter beans would be expected to yield 3.6–5.5t/ha, but in 1990 they gave 2–3t/ha. Spring beans were very badly affected, often struggling to make 1t/ha and some yields of less than 0.4t/ha were reported from Lincolnshire, compared to a normal 3–4t/ha.

The low yields were attributable to poor pod set, small beans and few beans per plant. In Nottinghamshire, one variety of winter bean (Borden) gave 543g/1000 seed compared to a normal 608g/1000 seed, and Troy (a spring variety) gave 318g/1000 seed compared to 448g/1000 seed normally.

Table 11: Yields of three varieties of spring bean (var. Gobo, Alfred, Tina) irrigated and non-irrigated at Nottingham University, School of Agriculture, Sutton Bonington (data courtesy of P Hebblethwaite, C Jones, C Pilbeam).

Sowing Date	Yield (t ha^{-1})	
	Irrigated	Non-irrigated
March	3.58	1.95
May	1.83	1.19

B4.5 EFFECTS ON HORTICULTURAL CROPS

4.5.1 Vegetables

Unlike cereals, and other determinate crops, most vegetables continue to accumulate dry matter until they are harvested and thus require a continuous supply of water throughout their growing season. Consequently they are the most likely crops to be adversely affected by a hot dry summer.

In 1989, crops grew and bulked well where soil moisture was sufficient. In 1990, the establishment of direct-drilled and transplanted crops was very difficult from April until September, giving either patchy germination or none at all where there was no water.

The majority of the growers in the north do not have irrigation schemes, as they usually receive plenty of rain; in the south, the use of irrigation schemes, was frequently limited either by low reserves or bans by the water authorities. Growers who managed to maintain an irrigation schedule still found it difficult to meet the high demands of the crop, as evaporation rates were high. As expected, where crops were not irrigated yields were lower than normal (Table 12).

Table 12: Yields of irrigated and unirrigated onion and carrots 1988–1990. Data courtesy of Gleadthorpe EHF, Nottinghamshire.

Crop	Yield t/ha			
	Onions		Carrots	
Year	Irrigated	Unirrigated	Irrigated	Unirrigated
1990	36	23	80	20
1989	40	21	112	48
1988	50	49	88	62

High temperatures caused early maturity and premature senescence, giving rise to stunted plants and smaller roots/bulbs/buttons/heads. This was due to an increased rate of accumulation of thermal time and hence a decrease in real time available to take up water.

The high temperatures affected the hearting in lettuce and led to premature flowering (bolting) of lettuce, cabbage and brussel sprouts. Having developed faster, crops became over-mature faster, making rapid harvesting imperative. Cauliflower and calabrese often lacked their protective and sustaining foliage at maturity, and curds were frequently deformed and multicoloured.

Yields varied depending upon irrigation and soil type. In 1990, some yields were saved by improved growth after August *e.g.* in Surrey leeks gave 70–80%, of the 1989 yield, whereas parsnips and salad onions gave only 60%.

Quality was variable. Cauliflowers suffered from curd rot

and hollow stems, whilst courgettes failed to set in the very hot temperatures. Root vegetables tended to be hard and tough and demand was low owing to warm weather. Quality deteriorated in areas where rains came just prior to harvest; new growth caused cabbages to crack and leeks to trim badly where the outside leaf split and turned back.

There was a high demand for seasonal salad produce over the summer. Exceptionally good light and temperatures in the early summer produced a heavy crop of cucumbers and tomatoes. There was some russeting and blotchy ripening in tomatoes owing to high light intensity and large diurnal variations in temperature.

Where crops were drought stressed to the extent that growth almost ceased, harvesting was earlier than planned. The telescoping of harvests affected both produce availability and national and local continuity programmes. There were also knock-on effects on labour availability and demand, which are often seasonal. Due to early and extended cropping of vegetables and fruit (coupled with the decline in numbers of the casual workforce), the demand and availability of labour were not synchronous. As a result, some crops remained partially harvested or unharvested.

In 1990, lower yields were not offset by an increase in market prices, as in 1989, and few growers made a profit. Despite the conditions, the markets seemed well supplied with almost every commodity. This was partially due to the large number of growers and to imported produce, whilst poor quality kept the prices low.

4.5.2 Fruit and flowers

APPLES AND PEARS

Warm sunny weather in May 1989 provided ideal pollination conditions for apples, which may have offset some of the earlier frost damage which occurred in April 1989. The warm weather gave fruit the potential to increase in size rapidly. However, in some orchards the lack of rain necessitated irrigation to expand cell size. High temperatures, particularly in the south, accelerated crop development. Cox trees in Hereford began to show signs of stress (leaf fall, slowing of fruit growth) from high temperature and drought in July. As a result of forward growth, most crops were harvested one to two weeks early. Some apples were small, mainly due to the dry conditions, especially when grown on thin soils and where they were not irrigated. Generally however, fruit yields were good (much better than initially expected), and the quality high. The Cox crop in several areas was one of the heaviest of recent years.

In some areas the harvesting window was narrower than usual, because rapid crop development and the seasonal stresses imposed on the trees caused fruit drop; this resulted in some losses. Despite this loss, the quantity of fruit meant that stores rapidly became filled with early

varieties, especially Cox leaving little room for mid/late season varieties. Growers had problems dealing with the volume of fruit and some remained unpicked. Much fruit had to be stored in barns. Poor storage conditions, and the continuing warm weather, meant that there was more wastage than usual in stores.

Pear trees, especially in Worcestershire and Warwickshire, were severely damaged by frost in spring 1989; crops from some orchards were reported to have been wiped out (MAFF). The remaining thin crops were not initially considered of high quality. However, possibly because of the light crop, fruit size and quality were good, especially of Comice. Harvesting was, on average, one week early. Because of the limited crop size, demand for pears was good, although some growers had too many small fruit. The high levels of sugar in Conference pears, resulting from the warm summer meant that there was less chance of freezing damage in store.

Despite the high yields in 1989, the quality of the fruit buds which formed for the 1990 crop was surprisingly good. This necessitated heavy pruning over the winter. The mild winter brought the buds forward. In Hereford, late dessert and Bramley apples were forward by an estimated 5 weeks, and the season was expected to be even earlier than that in 1989. In most areas, temperatures in February were considered too high for fruitbud quality to be good in both apple and pear crops. In the absence of more seasonal weather, cropping was expected to be modest. Buds which had developed quickly during the continuing mild weather of March, were retarded slightly by some cold nights towards the end of March. Flowering in pears was early by 3–4 weeks, and some flowering crops suffered considerable damage from cold in late March. Even more severe frost damage occurred in apple and pear crops during early April, especially in Worcestershire and Warwickshire. Despite this damage most apple orchards retained the potential for a heavy crop. This was partially attributable to subsequent fine weather which allowed the development of secondary blossom and encouraged an abundance of pollinators. The apple crop in 1990 was more advanced than in 1989 and reported to be the largest ever in some areas. As with the 1989 crop, pear blossom was early due to the mild winter and was badly affected by frost. Once again, pear yields in 1990 were light.

STONE FRUIT

After the frosts of April 1989, growers reported that plum and cherry crops for that year would be light. As with the top fruit, subsequent warm weather helped to give good fruit. Cherries ripened very quickly in the hot weather, and the quality was good. Most plum varieties were one and a half to two weeks early. The relative scarcity and good quality of crops demanded good prices.

The mild winter of 1989/90 encouraged early bud formation, and by February 1990 plum and cherry buds were two and a half to three weeks earlier than in 1989. Most plum varieties were in full flower by the third week in March. This early development meant that orchards were vulnerable to the frosts of late March and early April. Crops in some orchards were decimated by this event. Because of the cold spell, fruit set was light, although the warm summer of 1990 again provided ripening conditions conducive to good quality.

SOFT FRUIT

Strawberry crops in 1989 were about one week early and in 1990, 7–10 days early. In spring there was prolific flowering in warm weather. There were reports of damage due to the high levels of insolation, which was scorching plants on black polythene. In many places, crops needed picking early and very quickly due to unusually rapid ripening. The season was also shortened because of the heat, and crops of different varieties ripening at the same time. This led to gluts on the market and low prices. Because the harvest was early, fruit pickers were not always available, and consequently, some crops were left to rot.

Some "everbearing" varieties in the south and autumn-fruiting varieties were temporarily without blossom due to high temperatures in midsummer. Yields from these plants were therefore late but of reasonable quality.

GRAPES AND WINE

English vines had ideal conditions during the 1989 summer. They grow best in dry soils, and high temperatures and high levels of insolation produce fruit with a large sugar content. There was good foliage and bud development during the spring and good weather in the flowering period of July, enabled the flowers to set; in previous years, flowers had been destroyed by rain resulting in poor fruit set. Grapes ripened well in the 1989 summer. The hot 1989 summer also resulted in good wood development for the following year.

Warm temperatures in March 1990 stimulated early growth. A severe frost on the night of 4 April 1990 killed a large proportion of this new growth with some producers reporting 80% of the potential crop lost. However the continuing warm weather enabled some second growth in late April and May. Those that were not affected by the frost reported that the 1990 harvest was the biggest ever although mildew was a problem due to ideal micro climate conditions.

English wine producers predicted that the quality of 1989 fruit would yield a very good product, with 2.25 million litres of wine being produced. In the northern extremities of the wine producing area, where the sugar level of the fruit is not high enough, chaptalisation is often necessary. This involves adding sugar to increase the potential alcohol content to 10–11%. This was not necessary for wine produced from 1989 fruit.

BULBS AND FLOWERS

Hot summer weather in 1989 and 1990 induced rapid deterioration, and consequent reduction in shelf life, of cut flowers. The flowering of *Alstrameria* depends on light conditions. The above-average amount of insolation early in the summer induced crops to flower early and in synchronization. This caused a glut at a time when few flowers were purchased. (People spend less time in their homes in warm, bright weather and demand for cut flowers is less). Early, glasshouse-grown daffodils were not in great demand because so many were flowering in the open, in gardens.

B4.6 GRASS GROWTH AND ASSOCIATED ANIMAL PRODUCTION

4.6.1 Grass growth and silage production

Grass growth through the summers of 1989 and 1990 varied tremendously with region. Generally, northern and western counties experienced good growth and high yields, whilst southern and eastern counties had poor growth. This was a feature of differing soil moisture deficits, soil type and regional rainfall.

Warm weather in early summer in 1989 produced silage of high dry matter. However, although quality was good, quantities were about 10% less than in 1990 in Scotland and Northern Ireland and 25% less in the south and south west. In 1990, silage cutting began early, by about 10 days in Devon and Dyfed, and 2 weeks in north Wales, in ideal conditions. Yields compared favourably with 1989 at around 21t/ha. In the drier counties *e.g.* Somerset and Dorset, yields were estimated to be 10–15% below 1989 yields, but quality was good nation-wide, as it was also in 1976.

In 1989, some potential silage was baled as hay, surplus hay providing a useful cash crop as hay prices increased with grass shortage. Hay quality was reported to be very high. In 1990, hay and second cut silage was more variable in quantity and quality, as regrowth in many areas was restricted by the prolonged drought (Figure 2) compared to 1989 and an average year (1985). In areas of the south and east, few farmers managed any second or third cuts, and many were looking to bulk feeds to supplement restricted quantities of grass and silage through the summer and 1990/91 winter.

As in 1976, supplementary feeding of hay, straw and concentrates began early in 1989 and 1990 but the situation was much more severe in 1990. The demand for feed varied regionally, and was reflected in prices (Table 13). As prices increased, farmers struggled to find feed for summer calvers.

In 1990, in areas of grass shortage, the problem was compounded by forage crop yields being 30–50% below target. In Hampshire, some commercial wheat crops were

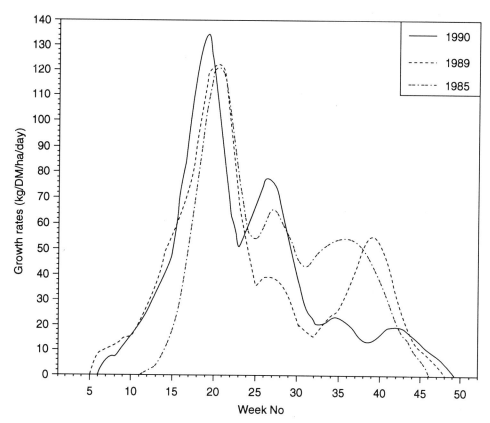

2   Growth rate of non-irrigated Cropper Perennial Ryegrass at North Wyke, Devon, where 1985 represents an average year. Based on four-weekly cuts throughout the growing season. (Courtesy of R Sheldrick, IGER).

Table 13: Hay and straw prices 1990, 1989 and 1985 (average year) (from Farmers Weekly 21–9–90, 22–9–89, 20–9–85).

| | PRICE £/t | | | | | |
| | Hay | | | Straw | | |
Region	1990	1989	1985	1990	1989	1985
South and east	90	45–60	60–62	60	16–22	16–18
South west	70–80	60	75	50	35	28
West	<70	55–65	50–55	30	30	20–22
North	<70	50–60	65–90	26	15–30	20–30

cut for arable silage because of the drastic shortfall in forage maize (15–20%). Extensive use was made of big bale silage, and hay was transported to regions of shortage. Much straw from cereal harvests was moved to stock farms.

4.6.2 Dairy cattle and milk production

Grazing practices very much reflected the pattern of grass growth, although many herds were on supplementary feed earlier in 1989 and 1990 than in 1988 (Figure 3). In some areas (mainly the north and west) increased grass growth necessitated increased stocking rates to maintain body condition, prevent over-fatness (which could lead to problems at calving and metabolic disorders) and to maintain sward height at the optimum height of 7–9cm. In other areas however low growth rates meant increasing the grazing area; this impinged upon land set aside for

silage production. For example, in 1990 at Bridgets EHF, near Winchester, 50% of the grass area was being grazed, compared to a normal 30%.

In July and August 1989 milk yields were 8% below those forecast. This, combined with an increased consumption of fresh milk during the hot weather, meant that some manufacturers of dairy produce, (but not hard cheese manufacturers), had a 13% cut in supplies (Milk Producer, September 1989).

Due to a shortfall in milk production, in some parts of the country there were also logistical problems in transporting milk. Reallocation of supplies to consumers was as severe a problem as it had been in 1976. There was also concern about maintaining low enough temperatures in bulk milk vats over the hot summer (Milk Producer, November 1989).

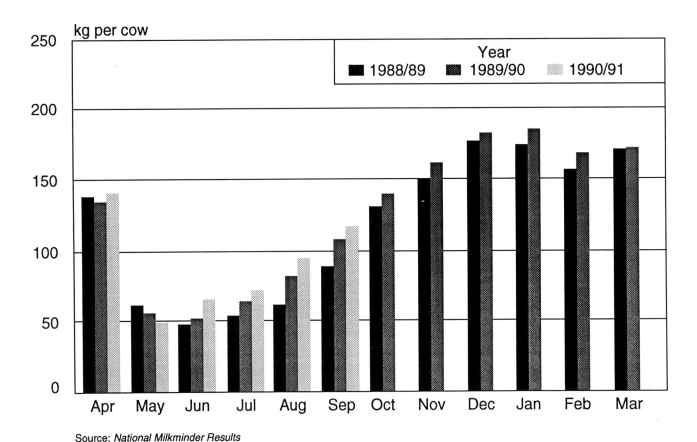

kg per cow

Year
■ 1988/89 ▦ 1989/90 ▨ 1990/91

Source: *National Milkminder Results*

3 Monthly concentrate used in the UK (kg/cow), 1988–1990. Data courtesy of Milk Marketing Board, National Milkminder Results.

Similar problems occurred in 1990. Cows were milking well in the north and west, but in the south there was a rapid decline in production and many farmhouse cheese producers again had to decrease production as milk supplies were diverted to the liquid market. Some herds in the south were already on full winter rations, increasing concern that winter fodder supplies were being depleted long before winter began.

By mid-October most stock was fully housed either due to drought conditions (south) or deteriorating soil conditions following heavy rains (north).

Despite these management practices, milk production remained below quota (Figure 4), which assumes "normal" weather conditions and anticipates the trend towards summer calving. Spring milk production in 1990 peaked two weeks ahead of 1989 due to earlier turn out, but was often below quota due to the weather effects upon grazing conditions. Nationally, over the period April-October 1990, production was 2% below quota, which is equivalent to a loss of 114 million litres.

4.6.3 Beef cattle and sheep

As with dairy cattle, grazing shortages for beef cattle occurred in both years. Not only did these follow the NW/SE pattern, but hill farms generally fared better than lowland ones, maintaining adequate grazing for longer. In 1989, in order to reduce stocking rates and reduce costs in areas short of grass, cattle were sold off when prices were low over the summer. Some beef producers delayed calf weaning as there was no grass for them to feed on. In 1990, the problem of tight grazing was heightened by low market prices, which meant that livestock remained on farms longer than normal. For beef cattle this was mainly due to the BSE scare creating low demand.

Sheep also suffered from grass shortages in 1989 and 1990. Conditions were most severe in England, eliminating overfat sheep and lambs which had gorged themselves on the abundant grass earlier in the year, whereas in the north, ideal finishing conditions meant that lambs remained fat. Sheep were sheared earlier due to high temperatures, and lambs weaned earlier due to the shortage of forage. By August, stock was deteriorating in condition as well as in growth rate and supplementary feeding was widespread. The lack of adequate grazing meant that many lambs were under condition for market and ewes were in poor condition for breeding. It also proved expensive to maintain sheep in good condition ready for tupping later in the year. Hot weather around tupping time can reduce ewe fertility, and rams are less active and reticent to mate.

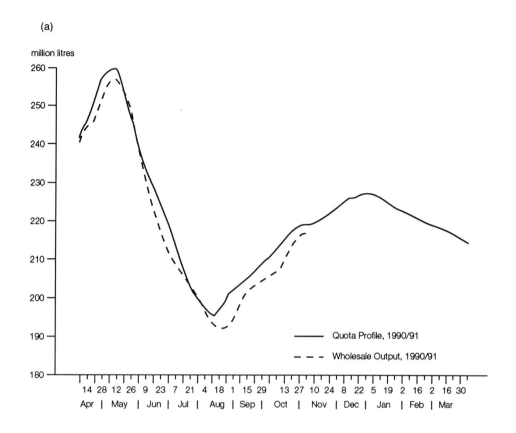

(a)

million litres

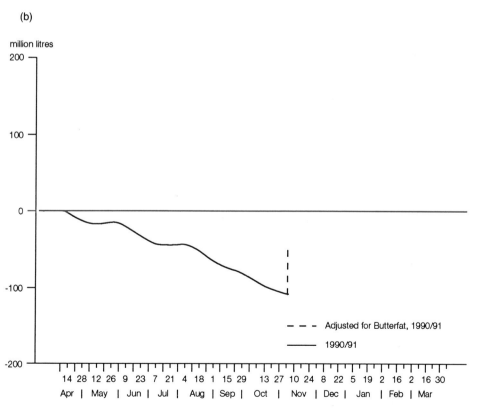

(b)

million litres

4 UK national milk production for the year 1990/91. (a) Weekly wholesale output and quota; (b) cumulative difference from quota (courtesy of the Milk Marketing Board).

B4.7 CONCLUSIONS

1. The dominant physical factor affecting agriculture and horticulture in the summers of 1989 and 1990 was soil moisture. Crops in the south were affected by drought more than those in the north. Restrictions on water for irrigation were widespread, starting as early as May, and affecting more than 1000 farms in East Anglia in 1990.

2. The dry weather reduced the incidence of many fungal diseases and blight was infrequent. Take-all disease of cereals was a problem, being favoured by the mild winters and dry hot summers. Powdery mildew was the main foliar disease, occurring earlier and spreading further north than normal.

3. Aphids occurred in considerable number and spread several virus diseases to severe levels. However, increases in predator numbers and use of aphicides prevented populations from reaching critical levels.

4. Winter cereals withstood the drought better than spring-sown cereals. Generally yields were lower than average especially on lighter soils of the midlands and East Anglia. Cereal protein content was high in 1989 but surprisingly variable in 1990, for reasons that are not understood.

5. Sugar beet was sown and harvested early. Although drought kept yields below the potential record (typically by 35%), national sugar yields were still above average.

6. Yields of spring-sown oilseed rape were below average in both years although crop quality was generally good. Late-sown oilseed crops such as sunflower and linseed did well on water-retentive soils.

7. When potato crops could be irrigated, yields and quality were good. Early potatoes were well ahead of schedule. Unirrigated maincrop potatoes suffered from drought and in 1990 were damaged in quality by rain in September.

8. Vegetable crops were highly variable, depending on soil properties, management and availability of irrigation. Some crops (lettuce, cabbage, sprouts) bolted in high temperatures. Yields were below average by 10–80% depending on crop and region, and quality was often below average. Tomatoes were badly affected by the hot summer, with low humidity reducing quality, and prices remained low.

9. Grapes and top fruit developed early because of the mild winters but in 1990 were decimated by frosts of late March – early April. These events affected yield much more than the following summer conditions. Areas unaffected by frosts had excellent yields. Grape quality was good, though mildew was a problem, and UK wine from the 1989 and 1990 harvests was of high quality.

10. Grass growth began early and was initially very good, but productivity later in the season was severely restricted by drought in the south and east. There were consequent problems in maintaining milk production from cattle in pastures of droughted regions. Nationally, milk output fell increasingly below planned quota from April to October.

11. Heat stress affected animal production in some areas outdoors and indoors. Animal health was generally good, although restricted grazing for ewes (and consequent poor condition) may have affected twin lamb production in 1990/91.

APPENDIX

Diseases of Sugar Beet in 1989 and 1990

Disease		Incidence of disease in 1989 and 1990	Control procedures	Consequences
Virus yellows	The virus is transmitted from the host plant to beet by aphids. The main aphid vector is the peach-potato aphid. Brassica crops act as hosts for the pathogen and vector,	In 1989 large numbers of aphids survived the winter building up into swarms. Early flights of infected aphids caused heavy infestations particularly in northern regions.	In high risk areas growers sowed seed with a granular insecticide. Spraying against aphids was above average with some growers using three times more aphicide than usual.	Reported average yield loss in 1989 was 4%.
		Fewer aphids survived the 1989/90 winter due to a combination of sharp November frosts, wet windy weather in December and high predation. Main aphid migration was delayed by frosts in April and did not occur until crops were growing well.	Aphid numbers were not as high in 1989 possibly due to the increased use of granular insecticides in sowing and the increase in numbers of aphid predators such as ladybirds and the mite *Anystis*.	At Brooms Barn, loss of yield was 2 t/ha.
Powdery mildew	Overwinters on wild beet, seed beet – and fodder clamps.	Optimum temperatures for the disease were frequently attained in 1989 and 70% of the crop area was infected. Because of the mild winter and lack of frosts, the disease was greater in 1990 appearing as early as July.	Despite 70% infection, only 17% of crop was sprayed because good yields were likely despite mildew.	
Rhizomania	Soil-born disease	Three cases occurred in 1989 and five in 1990. The soil born fungus required high soil temperatures but also moisture. Hence only irrigated crops were at risk.		

Section C

Conclusions

Section C
Conclusions

In this section the most important points from each of the chapters are listed under the chapter headings, followed by general conclusions on the impacts of the mild winters and hot summers. More detailed summaries can be found at the end of each chapter or section.

(A) MILD WINTERS, 1988/89, 1989/90

A1 CLIMATE

Temperature and windiness

- In central England, December-March 1988/89 was the mildest since 1659, and 2.5°C warmer than the 1961–80 mean; December-February 1989/90 was 2.2°C above the 1961–80 mean. January-March 1990 was the warmest three month start to a year in central England since 1659. The two winters together were the two mildest successive winters in the central England record.

- In 1988/89, the greatest temperature anomalies were centred over north eastern England and eastern Scotland, whereas in 1989/90, the greatest anomalous warmth occurred over south eastern England.

- The 1989/90 winter was exceptionally windy. The November to April 1989/90 period had the second greatest number of gale days, and damaging gales occurred in 25 January and 25 February 1990.

Hydrology

- The winter of 1988/89 was not only mild but also very dry. This was unusual, as mild winters in the UK tend to be wet. The distribution of rainfall was also unusual being wetter than normal in the north west and drier than normal in the east and south.

- River flows and ground water levels were very low from November to February 1989, and in many parts of eastern England soil moisture contents failed to return to field capacity. Spring 1989 was wet, and by the end of April river flows and ground water levels in many regions were almost up to average values.

- In contrast, winter 1989/90 was warm and wet. However, the rainfall was concentrated in a short period from mid December to February, and fell mainly in the west. Parts of eastern Scotland and England received below average winter rainfall for the second year in succession.

- The rise in groundwater levels and river flows in western Britain was very rapid following the short, intense period of winter rainfall in 1989/90, and there was widespread flooding in February in the west. Not all the surplus water could be stored in reservoirs, and, in the absence of normal rain in the spring 1990, some reservoirs were low at the start of the 1990 summer.

A2 IMPACTS ON THE TERRESTRIAL ENVIRONMENT

Impacts on plants

- The two mild winters had a major impact on plant phenology. Observations of up to 17 native plant species at 6 ITE stations, and of over 200 garden plants in East Lothian, showed that most plants that normally flower before April, flowered several days or weeks earlier than normal in 1989 and 1990. Late flowering species were less affected. Not all species responded to early warming (*e.g.* Cox's apple, honesty, yellow alyssum), probably because their phenology is controlled by daylength and/or winter chilling.

- The unusually vigorous spring growth of species (with low nuclear DNA content) such as goosegrass in 1988/89 suggested that a succession of mild winters could lead to competitive suppression of vernal species (with high nuclear DNA amounts) such as bluebell in many hedgerows and woodlands.

- Many species suffered frost damage in late spring 1989 and 1990, although the damage was not as severe as expected. In the event of regular mild winters, the timing of spring frosts will affect the performance and survival of individual species.

- A lack of hardening of Sitka spruce seedlings in forest nurseries in 1988/89 led to the death of 2–3 million transplants in cold storage and a similar number after planting out.

- In the event of continued mild winters, changes in species composition may be caused directly, *e.g.* by the absence of prolonged chilling, or indirectly by the competitive suppression of vernal herbaceous species, and an increased capacity for insect pests to overwinter (see below).

- The impacts of these gradual progressive changes in vegetation must not be over-emphasised. A storm on 25 January 1990 blew down 1.3 million m³ of timber over an area of 4,800 ha representing not only a loss of stock but also a loss of much woodland habitat.

Impacts on animals

- During the winters of 1988/89 and 1989/90 insects and other animals moved about and fed more actively than normal. The phenology of many species was altered and temperature dependant developmental/growth events and reproductive behaviour occurred earlier than normal.

- Rothamsted suction traps caught aphids very early in 1989 and 1990 (April) and in record numbers by July. However, numbers caught in 1990 were not quite as large as in 1989, because ladybird and hoverfly predator numbers had increased in 1989/90. In 1989, aphids did major damage in gardens and on crops (see below), and a major outbreak occurred of the great green spruce aphid.

- Both moths and butterflies were unusually active in the winters 1988/89 and 1989/90. Some normally migratory species such as the red admiral and painted lady butterflies and hummingbird hawkmoth over-wintered successfully in southern England.

- In spring 1989, slug populations were higher than for about 10 years, owing to a wet summer and autumn in 1988, and continued growth of vegetation and crops in the mild 1988/89 winter.

- The common frog spawned several weeks or months earlier in 1989 and 1990 than in previous years in England and southern Scotland. Common toads spawned about 20 days earlier than normal in Dorset in 1989, but the natterjack toad was unaffected.

- Lizards and snakes (cold-blooded reptiles) were active in both winters.

- Notable observations on birds included (i) full breeding behaviour during the winter, (ii) early return of oystercatchers to agricultural fields from overwintering estuaries, (iii) the presence of large flocks of some species feeding on bumper berry/seed crops in 1989/90, and (iv) possibly enhanced survival of small insectivorous passerines.

- There was no consistent evidence for change in populations of voles, mice and shrews as a result of the mild winters, possibly due to buffering effects of corresponding changes in predator populations.

- Rat populations were high in 1988/89 and 1989/90 but the mild winter temperatures were only one contributory factor.

- In 1988/89, red deer mortality was high in western Scotland because of wet windy weather from autumn

1988 to spring 1989. Muntjac deer in eastern England and the Midlands, on the other hand, benefitted from the long mild breeding season and absence of severe winters and reached pest proportions in some woodlands.

A3 IMPACTS ON FRESHWATER SYSTEMS

- During the winters of 1988/89 and 1989/90, water temperatures were about 2°C higher than average, and many lakes and rivers that normally freeze remained ice-free.

- Freshwaters received less sodium and chloride than normal from road salt.

- Populations of winter phytoplankton were less affected by the increase in temperature than by periods of heavy rain in shallow lakes or the timing and intensity of wind mixing in deep lakes. A population model of *Daphnia* suggested that the warm winter temperature in 1988/89 and 1989/90 probably had little effect on numbers of many freshwater invertebrates.

- The mild winters led to earlier hatching and emergence of fish such as brown trout, but appeared to have little effect on fish numbers.

- The survival of some river birds was favoured by mild winter temperatures.

A4 IMPACTS ON AGRICULTURE AND HORTICULTURE

- The mild winters affected agriculture and horticulture by (i) speeding crop growth and development, (ii) increasing the number and activity of pests and pathogens, and (iii) decreasing the degree of freeze-thaw weathering of soil and hence its workability.

- A number of pest species were a problem because of the absence of severe winters. Pigeon numbers were high in 1989/90, although damage was generally less than normal on crops like oil seed rape because alternative food supplies were plentiful. In contrast, rooks damaged many autumn-sown crops as they foraged for unusually active soil living organisms. Rat and mouse populations were larger than normal and mice damaged emerging sugarbeet and legumes. Slugs were very active in 1988/89; repeated doses of molluscicides and sometimes resowing were necessary. Many black and green aphids survived both the winters, and despite the use of aphicides new waves of aphids quickly reinvaded crops in 1989.

- Weeds germinated throughout the winters, and together with "volunteer" crop plants, provided "green bridges" on which pests and pathogens overwintered.

- Some cereal crops were affected early and severely with mildew, yellow rust and barley yellow dwarf virus. Unusually large quantities of fungicides (and aphicides) were used.

- Winter cereal crops were generally advanced in both seasons, and good yields were obtained on water retentive soils. Spring-sown cereals suffered from poor seedbeds, and early and severe attacks from pests and pathogens.

- Potatoes were readily infected by virus diseases and potato blight, owing to aphid activity, and potatoes were prone to rot in warm conditions in winter stores.

- Horticultural crops were generally advanced over the winters and springs of 1989 and 1990. Yields were usually good, often leading to an over-supply on a depressed market. Quality of produce was frequently poor due to disease or other damage during storage.

- In many regions of Britain, grass growth continued throughout both winters. Stocks of silage were plentiful in 1988/89. Hay and silage was of good quality, owing to warm, sunny weather.

- In 1989/90 the winter grown grass reduced costs of overwintering animals. However some farmers over-estimated the nutritional value of the lush grass and failed to feed adequate supplements which led to nutritional disorders.

GENERAL CONCLUSIONS – MILD WINTERS 1988/89, 1989/90

Many of the most conspicuous effects of the mild winters occurred because the cumulative day-degree or temperature thresholds for growth and development of plants and animals were reached earlier than usual. Thus:

- leafing and flowering of many native and alien plant species was remarkably earlier than usual;
- many insects emerged early, and animals such as snakes and hedgehogs emerged early from hibernation;
- early development and reproduction of invertebrates meant that several generations were produced in one year, *e.g.* butterflies, moths, grasshoppers;
- some bird species were active and exhibited full breeding behaviour during the winters; and
- frogs and toads spawned much earlier than usual.

However, as expected, not all organisms were affected equally. Species that are normally active very early in spring such as vernal plants in woodlands, were less advanced than some other spring-flowering plants. Species that normally flower or leaf very late were least affected. Cox's apple flowered in early May in both 1989 and 1990 as normal. The natterjack toad, which spawns late, was little affected. Plant species requiring prolonged winter chilling did not flower or leaf early, and some species seemed to flower at a prescribed daylength irrespective of temperature. Clearly, such differences in phenology could, in time, lead to changes in the relative abundance of species, where temperature responsive and unresponsive species occur together. However, the outcome of such interactions may be complicated by the occurrence of late spring frosts.

The absence of prolonged cold temperatures, very low freezing temperatures, and of snow and ice had notable impacts of many organisms. Thus:

- many invertebrates, such as aphids, butterflies and moths, survived, and some migrants overwintered;
- weeds germinated and provided 'green bridges' for pathogens and food for slugs;
- nursery plants failed to become fully frost hardy;
- some bird and mammal species seemed to have survived the winters in larger numbers than normal; and
- animals that emerged from hibernation were active, sometimes to their detriment, sand lizards were killed by frosts, and hedgehogs were killed on the road.

One general effect seemed to be an increase in some of the species that are regarded as pests, pathogens or weeds. Consequently, it is possible that more insecticides, fungicides, and perhaps herbicides, were used than normal.

However, it cannot be assumed that a succession of mild winters will increase these problems, because natural feedbacks occur such as the build-up of insect predators, and farmers and nurserymen modify their management practices. It is also noteworthy that a 2°C increase in freshwater temperatures, and an absence of ice, seems to have had relatively little effect on freshwater organisms.

The impacts on agriculture and horticulture mainly concerned crop phenology, pests and pathogens, and the timing of operations. In general, winter crops were favoured relative to spring-sown cereals. Many horticultural crops gave good yields, but produced a glut on the spring market. The long growing season increased grass growth, with knock on effects on animal grazing and nutrition. Overall, one suspects that farming practices, and the choice of crops would change rapidly to adjust for any continued occurrence of mild winters.

Finally, the gales of 25 January and 25 February 1990 reminded us that extreme events may have more impact in the short term than a slow progressive change in climate.

(B) HOT SUMMERS 1989, 1990

B1 CLIMATE

Temperature and sunshine

- The May to October period in 1989 was the equal fourth warmest such period in central England since

1659; the average temperature in England was 1.3°C above the 1961–80 average. The June to August period in 1989 was less exceptional. During most months the greatest temperature anomalies in 1989 were located over southern England.

- May to October 1989 was exceptionally sunny, recording more sunshine hours (*ca.* 1250) than any other such period since 1909. For the July to August season, the 1989 total was the second highest (*ca.* 740), exceeded only slightly in 1976.

- In 1990, the May to October period was the equal 17th warmest in central England since 1659. The average temperature in England was 0.9°C above the 1961–80 average. Spatially, the summer was very similar to 1989, with the warmest temperatures over south eastern England.

- The most unusual feature of the 1990 summer was a heat wave 1–4 August. The maximum temperature recorded was 37.1°C on 3 August at Cheltenham.

- The 1990 summer was not as sunny as 1989 because of a cloudy June in 1990. It was, however, still the seventh sunniest May to October period since 1909.

Hydrology

- Overall, the period May–September 1989 was the second driest in England and Wales since records began in 1766.

- Potential evapotranspiration rates during the summer of 1989 were among the highest on record, and actual evapotranspiration over the entire country was higher than during the summer of 1976 (because of the greater availability of water in 1989). Large soil moisture deficits occurred in many parts of eastern Britain during the summer of 1989, and in many places deficits were maintained throughout the winter of 1989/90.

- Both groundwater levels and river flows were higher during the summer of 1989 than in 1976, but the lack of widespread autumn rainfall meant that levels and flows in many areas continued to decline until December.

- Average rainfall in the summer of 1990 (June, July, August) was not exceptionally low, because June rainfall was above average. The unusual feature of the rainfall in England in 1990 was the contrast between winter and spring; 1989/90 was the third wettest winter since 1766, and the 1990 spring was the driest in 100 years – more like a Mediterranean climate.

- Despite the rainfall in June, there was an exceptionally long period with high soil moisture deficits in the summer 1990 in most of England, owing to low rainfall in spring and the highest potential evaporation rates on record (since 1961) in summer (June–August).

- The high rainfall in January and February 1990 led to rapid rises in groundwater levels (and considerable flooding) with the notable exception of wells in the chalk in eastern England. However, the dry spring meant that both groundwater levels and river flows fell rapidly, and by early summer were below 1989 values. Levels and flows continued to decline during the summer, but remained above those recorded during the 1976 drought until August 1990. As in 1989, the autumn was dry, and the seasonal recovery in river flows and groundwater levels was delayed. Levels and flows in November 1990 were lower than the values recorded at the end of the 1976 drought across large parts of southern and eastern England. Groundwater-fed catchments were particularly affected, especially in the east. River flows in some groundwater-fed catchments fell below average in summer 1988 and had not risen above average by January 1991. In contrast, river flows remained close to average (and in some months well above average) in catchments in the north west.

B2 IMPACTS ON THE TERRESTRIAL ENVIRONMENT

Impacts on plants

- In general, the high soil moisture deficits had more direct and conspicuous effects on vegetation during the two hot summers than the high temperatures *per se*. However, despite exhibiting severe drought symptoms during the summer, most vegetation seemed to recover in the autumn or spring.

- Notable observations related to the droughts in southern and eastern England were as follows:

  – grasslands and lawns went brown, but species with deep tap-roots, like ribwort plantain and greater knapweed, remained green;
  – broadleaved trees wilted and exhibited leaf discoloration and premature defoliation; beech in southern England was badly affected in 1990 and branch dieback occurred on oak in Berkshire;
  – species of moist habitats, especially ferns, such as the hart's tongue fern growing in rocky cliffs, suffered shoot death;
  – on some heathlands, *Calluna* died back.

- Hot, dry summers are associated with high incidences of fires, and 1989 and 1990 were no exception. However, fires in natural vegetation were less numerous and/or extensive than in 1976.

- Some species, particularly those occurring in warmer southern regions of the country appeared to respond directly to increased temperatures and sunshine duration.

- The American duckweed (*Lemna minuscula*), first recorded in the UK in 1977, flourished in water bodies in Cambridge in 1990, replacing native duckweeds. A similar population explosion was recorded in Surrey in 1989.
- Populations of bearded fescue (*Vulpia ciliata* spp. *ambigua*), which was on the verge of extinction in its UK distribution in the Breckland in 1988, increased substantially following the two hot, dry summers of 1989 and 1990.
- Sooty bark disease of sycamore killed many trees in the London area, Berkshire and Bedfordshire in 1990, and was a problem in previous hot, dry summers (1947, 1959, 1976). The fungus (*Cryptostroma corticale*) has a high temperature optimum (25°C) and develops rapidly in water-stressed trees.

- The combination of high temperatures and drought conditions affected the flowering of many species.

  - Many tree species flowered and seeded heavily in 1990. It was a second consecutive "mast" year for beech. Hornbeam bore conspicuous clusters of fruits. Many berry-bearing trees were spectacular (hawthorn, apple, *Sorbus*). However, acorn production was low, possibly owing to frosts in April. The demands of the developing fruit crops may have exacerbated the drought stresses on trees.
  - March gentian (*Gentiana pneumonanthe*) which occurs on wet, acid heaths in lowland England flowered profusely in 1990, apparently in response to high temperatures or drought during 1989.
  - Long-term observations on orchid species showed that populations of musk orchid (*Herminium monorchis*) declined in 1976 and took four years to recover; in 1990 only 4 out of 331 plants in a sample plot in Cambridgeshire flowered, and none produced viable seed, causing concern that this species could die out.
  - Summer-flowering woody perennials, including roses, flowered unexpectedly early in 1990 in an East Lothian garden, suggesting some carry-over effect of the prolonged warm temperatures.

- It is stressed that several years of observation may be necessary before the impacts of the hot, dry summers of 1989 and 1990 on plant communities can be evaluated.

Impacts on animals

- The hot, dry summers favoured the multiplication and spread of many insects.

  - As mentioned, aphid numbers were high in 1989, but not so large in 1990 when ladybirds and other predators were abundant.
  - Many moths and butterflies produced second and third broods, and were seen in large numbers, especially in 1989; in 1990, drought damage to plants adversely affected the larvae and adult numbers.
  - Some butterfly species extended their ranges northwards, *e.g.* hedge brown and speckled wood.
  - Grasshoppers and crickets became more numerous and bush crickets produced more long-winged dispersive forms and spread further north.
  - Yields of honey per bee colony in 1989 and 1990 were the highest for 32 years, owing to the warm sunny weather and the absence of a drought as severe as that in 1976.
  - There was a marked increase in social wasp populations in 1989, and 1990 was regarded as a "wasp year".
  - Pests such as cockroaches, fleas and mites in buildings continued to increase and disperse owing to high temperatures and mild winters.

- The drought conditions adversely affected the habitats of some species.

  - Aquatic communities were damaged by drying out of their habitats. Midges, crane flies, and molluscs were probably adversely affected.
  - Fires damaged some habitats; coastal dune reserves had more fires than heathland or woodland reserves in 1989 and 1990.

- In the summer of 1989, there was some evidence that the hot dry weather improved the breeding success of some bird species, probably by enhancing their foraging success (sparrowhawk and red kite) or the abundance of their invertebrate prey (sedge warbler, reed warbler and capercaillie).

B3 IMPACTS ON FRESHWATER SYSTEMS

- During the summers of 1989 and 1990, river and lake surface water temperatures were above average, but not exceptionally so, mostly falling within the range recorded in recent decades, and below the high temperatures recorded in 1976.

- A detailed study of water flowing from a wetland in mid-Wales found high concentrations of dissolved organic matter, reduced-N and iron in the outflow water when it rained after dry spells. These peaks were most pronounced in 1989.

- Blooms of blue-green algae occurred on 25% of lakes and reservoirs surveyed by the National Rivers Authority in 1989 and many blooms were toxic. The calm, warm early summer of 1989 following a mild winter, was observed to favour a build-up in populations of the blue-green algae *Oscillatoria* in Windermere and *Aphanizomenon* in Esthwaite Water.

- The hot summers, like the mild winters, had no major effects on freshwater fish numbers, although drought restricted salmon migration in some streams, and warm temperatures may have increased trout weight in otherwise cool forest streams.

B4 IMPACTS ON AGRICULTURE AND HORTICULTURE

- As with natural vegetation, the high soil moisture deficits had more direct impact on agriculture and horticulture than the high temperatures *per se*. Restrictions on water for irrigation were widespread, starting as early as May, and affecting more than 1000 farms in East Anglia in 1990.

- The dry weather reduced the incidence of many fungal diseases, including potato blight. However, take-all disease of cereals was a problem, being favoured by the mild winters and hot, dry summers. Powdery mildew was the main foliar disease, occurring earlier and spreading further north than normal.

- The large aphid numbers spread virus diseases, especially in 1989.

- Winter cereals withstood the drought better than spring sown cereals. Yields were generally lower than average, especially on the lighter soils of the Midlands and East Anglia.

- Sugar beet yields were also reduced by the drought, although national sugar yields were still above average.

- Yields of spring sown oilseed rape were below average in both years, but late sown oilseed crops such as sunflower and linseed did well on water retentive soils.

- When irrigated, potato crops yielded well and quality was good. Unirrigated maincrop potatoes were damaged by drought.

- Vegetable crop responses were variable, depending on soil properties, management and the availability of irrigation. Some crops (lettuce, cabbage, sprouts) bolted in high temperatures. Tomatoes were badly affected by the hot summer, with low humidity reducing quality, and prices remained low.

- Grapes and top fruit developed early because of the mild winters, but in 1990 were adversely affected by late frosts. Areas unaffected by frosts had good yields. Grape sugar contents were high.

- Grass growth began early and was initially very good, but productivity later in the season was severely restricted by drought in the south and east. Nationally, milk output fell increasingly below the quota from April to October.

- Animal health was generally good although heat stress affected animal production in some areas outdoors and indoors.

GENERAL CONCLUSIONS – HOT SUMMERS 1989, 1990

In 1976, the main impacts of concern were those related to the drought conditions, including water supplies, fires and agricultural production. The same concerns were raised in 1989 and 1990, and, at the time of writing, water supplies and water deficits are still causing concern in the south and east.

The impacts on natural vegetation were generally related to the large soil water deficits in the south and east. Lasting damage may have been done to some mature broadleaved trees, as in 1976, and the vegetation in some wet habitats and in some areas that were burned, may take several years to recover. By contrast, much of the grassland and heathland, which partially or completely died aboveground in 1989 and 1990, has already recovered. However, it is likely that some individual species may have been lost from some areas, while some deep-rooting species, which avoided severe drought stress, may have become relatively more abundant.

Although individual farms and some crops were adversely affected by the droughts, overall, agricultural and horticultural production faired better than might be expected. Even in 1976, it was estimated that crop production was only 20–25% less than normal (Roy *et al.* 1978). In 1989 and 1990, winter sown cereals weathered the drought well, national sugar beet yields were above average, some horticultural crops produced gluts on the market, grape yields and quality were high, and many irrigated crops gave high yields. The main adverse effect was on grass growth (and milk yields), the yield of spring-sown cereals and of unirrigated crops on light soils.

The main effect of the high temperatures *per se* in 1989 and 1990 was an increase in the abundance, activity and geographic spread of many insects. Some of these insects were pests, such as aphids in 1989, wasps in 1990, and some indoor pests. Other insects, such as butterflies, moths and crickets may be said to have enriched the natural environment. Increased honey production by bees was certainly welcomed by producers. The populations of some insects were regulated in 1990 by a build-up in predators and by adverse drought conditions on food plants. Even so, it is to be expected that one of the most immediate and noticeable impacts of sustained climatic warming would be on the abundance and distribution of invertebrates. The knock on effects may include desirable improvements in the breeding success of birds, and an undesirable increase in the use of insecticides.

The combination of mild winters followed by hot summers had a marked effect on freshwater biota. Nuisance blooms of blue-green algae occurred on many lakes and reservoirs. American duckweed flourished in some water bodies in the south and east, and, of course, some streams and ponds dried out completely.

Finally, it is noteworthy that the combination of two hot, dry summers promoted the flowering of some warmth-loving herbaceous species, and produced heavy fruit and seed crops on many trees. If sustained, this response may have consequential effects on bird and other vertebrate populations, and on the composition of some plant communities.

REFERENCE

Roy, M.G., Hough, M.N. and Starr, J.R. 1978. Some agricultural effects of the drought of 1975–76 in the United Kingdom. Weather 33, 64–73.

M.G.R. Cannell and C.E.R. Pitcairn,
February 1992.

References

Aldhous, J.R. 1981. Beech in Wessex – a perspective on present health and silviculture. *Forestry*, **54**, 197–210.

Alford, D.V. 1975. *Bumblebees*. London: Davis-Poynter.

Al-Mufti, M.M., Sydes, C.L., Furness, S.B., Grime, J.P. & Band, S.T. 1977. A quantitative analysis of shoot phenology and dominance in herbaceous vegetation. *Journal of Ecology*, **65**, 759–791.

Anderson, P. 1986. Accidental moorland fires in the Peak District. Peak District Moorland Restoration Project. Sheffield, 164 pp.

Anon 1990. *1989 Yearbook, Hydrological data UK series*. Institute of Hydrology, Wallingford, Oxon, UK.

Anon. 1991. *1990 Year Book, Hydrological data, UK series*. Institute of Hydrology, Wallingford, Oxon, UK.

Anonymous, 1949. The weather of 1948 in Great Britain, *Weather*, **4**, 2–5.

Archer, M.E. 1985. Population dynamics of the social wasps *Vespula vulgaris* and *Vespula germanica* in England. *Journal of Animal Ecology*, **54**, 473–485.

Archer, M.E. 1990. The solitary aculeate wasps and bees (Hymenoptera: Aculeata) of an English suburban garden. *Entomologist's Gazette*, **41**, 129–142.

Archer-Lock, A. 1989. Butterflies in winter. *Entomologist's Record*, **101**, 117–120.

Armitage, P. 1987. Compensation flow and river biology. In: *A study of compensation flows in the UK*, edited by A. Gustard, G. Cole, D.C.W. Marshal and A.C. Bayliss. Institute of Hydrology Report 99.

Avery, M.I. 1985. Winter activity of pipistrelle bats. *Journal of Animal Ecology*, **54**, 721–738.

Baille, S.R., Clark, N.A. & Ogilvie, M.A. 1986. *Cold weather movements of waterfowl and waders: an anlaysis of ringing recoveries*. A report from the British Trust for Ornithology to the Nature Conservancy Council.

Baines, D. 1990. Black grouse densities and habitat requirements. *The Game Conservancy Reviews of 1989*, **21**, 136–138.

Baker, B.R. 1990. 1989 – a year for the holly blue, *Celastrina argiolus* L. *Entomologist's Record*, **102**, 40–41.

Bale, J.S. 1989. Cold hardiness and overwintering of insects. In: *Biology and population dynamics of invertebrate crop pests*, edited by G.E. Russell, 305–341. Andover: Intercept.

Barkham, J. & Macguire, F. 1990. The heat is on. *Natural World*, **30**, 24–28.

Beirne, B.P. 1955. Natural fluctuations in abundance of British Lepidoptera. *Entomologist's Gazette*, **6**, 21–51.

Benn, S. 1990. Raptor round up 1989. *Scottish Bird News*, **18**, 8–10.

Benn, S. 1991. Raptor round up 1990. *Scottish Bird News*, **22**, 8–10.

Bourn, N.A.D. 1989. *The ecology and conservation of Aricia agestis in southern England*. M.Sc. thesis, University College, London.

Bourn, N.A.D. & Thomas, J.A. 1992. The ecology and conservation of the brown argus butterfly *Aricia agestis* in Britain. Biological Conservation, **63**, 67–74.

Bourne, W.R.P. 1990. Bird mortality on North Eastern Scottish beaches in the spring of 1990. *Scottish Bird News*, **19**, 3.

Brian, M.V. & Brian, A.D. 1952. The wasp, *Vespula sylvestris* Scopoli: feeding, foraging and colony development. *Transactions of the Royal Entomological Society of London*, **103**, 1–26.

Briffa, K.R., Jones, P.D. & Kelly, P.M. 1990. Principal component analysis of the Lamb Catalogue of daily weather types: Part 2, Seasonal frequencies and update to 1987. *International Journal of Climatology*, **10**, 549–563.

Brugge, R. 1991. The record-breaking heatwave of 1–4 August 1990 over England and Wales. *Weather*, **46**, 2–10.

Canter, H.M., Heaney, S.I. & Lund, J.W.G. 1990. The ecological significance of grazing on planktonic populations of cyanobacteria (blue-green algae) by the ciliate *Nassula*. *New Phytologist*, **114**, 247–263.

Carter, C.I. 1972. Winter temperatures and survival of the green spruce aphid. *Forestry Commission Forest Record*, **84**, HMSO, London.

Carter, C.I. 1989. The 1989 outbreak of the green spruce aphid, *Elatobium abietinum*. *Research Information Note*, **161**, Forestry Commission.

Carter, N. 1989. Britain's unchecked plague of aphids. *New Scientist*, **1068**, 29–30.

Casey, H. & Clarke, R.T. 1979. Statistical analysis of nitrate concentrations from the river Frome (Dorset) for the period 1965–76. *Freshwater Ecology*, **9**, 91–97.

Cavalloro, R. & Sunderland, K.D. (Eds.) 1988. *Integrated Crop Protection in Cereals*. Proceedings of EC Experts Meeting, Littlehampton 1986.

Chapman, S.B., Rose, R.J. & Clarke, R.T. 1989. The behaviour of populations of the marsh gentian (*Gentiana pneumonanthe*): a modelling approach. *Journal of Applied Ecology*, **26**, 1059–1072.

Cherril, A.J. & Brown, V.K. 1991. Effects of the summer of 1989 on the phenology of the wartbiter, *Decticus verrucivorus* (L.) (*Orthoptera: Tettigoniidae*) in Britain. *British Journal of Entomology and Natural History*, **5**, 163–168.

Clutton-Brock, T.T. & Albon, S.D. 1989. *Red deer in the highlands*. BSP Professional Books.

Crick, H.Q.P. & Glue, D.E. 1990. Nesting seasons old and new. *BTO News*, **168**, 12.

Crick, H., Glue, D., Pearman, D. & Stockley, C. 1989. Breeding birds in 1988. *BTO News*, **164**, 9–12.

Crisp, D.T. 1981. A desk study of the relationship between temperature and hatching time for the eggs of five species of salmonid fish. *Freshwater Biology*, **11**, 361–368.

Crisp, D.T. 1988a. Water temperature data from streams and rivers in northeastern England. *Occasional Publication No 26, Freshwater Biological Associations*.

Crisp, D.T. 1988b. Prediction from temperature, of eying, hatching and "swim-up" times for salmonid embryos. *Freshwater Biology*, **19**, 41–48.

Crisp, D.T. & Howson, G. 1982. Effect of air temperature upon mean water temperature in streams in the north Pennines and English Lake District. *Freshwater Biology*, **12**, 359–367.

Davis, N.E. 1968. An optimum summer weather index. *Weather*, **23**, 305–317.

Dennis, R.L.H. & Shreeve, T.G. 1989. Butterfly wing morphology variation in the British Isles: the influence of climate, behavioural posture and the hostplant-habitat. *Biological Journal of the Linnean Society*, **38**, 323–348.

Dickenson, S. & Wheeler, B.E.J. 1981. Effects of temperature and water stress in sycamore on growth of *Cryptostroma corticale*. *Transactions of the British Mycological Society*, **76**, 181–185.

Dixon, A.F.G. 1985. *Aphid Ecology*. Blackie, Glasgow.

Doornkamp, J.C., Gregory, K.J. & Burn, A.S. 1980. *Atlas of Drought in Britain, 1975–76*. Institute of British Geographers. 86pp.

Dorset Naturalist's Trust & Royal Society for the Protection of Birds 1977. *Heath Fires in Dorset*. Report. Poole.

Dunn T.C. 1989. Early appearance of some spring moths. *Vasculum*, **74**, 5–6.

Dunn, T.C. (ed) 1990a. The weather during 1990. *Vasculum*, **75**, 45–46.

Dunn, T.C. (ed) 1990b. The long hot summer. *Vasculum*, **75**, 34–5.

Eden, G.P. 1991. A statistical review of 1990. *Weather*, **46**, 76–85.

Edmondson, W.T. 1960. Reproductive rate of rotifers in natural populations. *Memorie dell Instituto Italiano di Idrobiologia*, **12**, 21–77.

Edmondson, W.T. & Winberg, G.G. (eds) 1971. *A Manual on Methods for the Assessment of Secondary Productivity in Fresh Waters*. IBP Handbook No. 17. Oxford, Blackwell.

Elliott, J.M. 1975. The growth of brown trout (*Salmo trutta* L.) fed on maximum rations. *Journal of Animal Ecology*, **44**, 805–821.

Elliott, J.M. 1981. Some aspects of thermal stress on freshwater teleosts. In: *Stress and Fish*, edited by A.D. Pickerling, 209–245, London, Academic.

Elliott, J.M. 1984. Numerical changes and population regulation in young migratory trout *Salmo trutta* in a Lake District stream, 1966–83. *Journal of Animal Ecology*, **53**, 327–350.

Elliott, J.M. 1985. Population dynamics of migratory trout, *Salmo trutta*, in a Lake District stream, 1966–83, and their implications for fisheries management. *Journal of Fish Biology*, **27**, (Supplement A). 35–43.

Elliott, J.M. 1989. The critical-period concept for juvenile survival and its relevance for population regulation in young sea-trout, *Salmo trutta*, *Journal of Fish Biology*, **35**, (Supplement A), 91–98.

Elliot, J.M. 1992. A 25–year study of production of juvenile sea-trout, *Salmo trutta*, in an English Lake District stream. *Canadian Bulletin of Fisheries and Aquatic Science* (in press).

Elmes, G.W. 1990. Queen number as an adaptable trait: evident from wild populations of two red ant species (genus *Myrmica*). *Journal of Animal Ecology*, **59**, 675–688.

Emmett, B.A. & Reynolds, B. 1991. Preliminary conclusions on the effects of an upland wetland on streamwater quality (Llanbrynmair). Contract report to the Wesl Office, pp. 8.

Eversham, B.C. 1990. Changes in the mollusc fauna of a Huntingdom garden. *Annual Report Huntingdonshire Fauna and Flora Society* (in press).

Frazer, D. 1983. *Reptiles and amphibians in Britain* (New Naturalist Series). London: Collins.

Flowerdew, J. 1989. Mammal society national small mammal survey – comments on results up to May/June 1989. Unpublished report.

Flowerdew, J. 1990. Mammal society national small mammal survey – comments on results up to Nov/Dec 1989. Unpublished report.

Fox-Wilson, G. 1946. Factors affecting populations of social wasps. Vespula species, in England (Hymenopters). *Proceedings of the Royal Entomological Society of London(A)*, **21**, 17–27.

George, D.G. 1989. The thermal characteristics of lakes as a measure of climate change. Conference on Climate and Water, Helsinki, Finland. *The Publications of the Adacemy of Finland*, 402–412.

George, D.G., Hewitt, D.P., Lund, J.W.G. & Smyly, W.J.P. 1990. The relative effects of enrichment and climate change on the long-term dynamics of *Daphnia* in Esthwaite Water, Cumbria. *Freshwater Biology*, **23**, 55–70.

Gibbs, J.N. & Greig, B.J.W. 1977. Some consequences of the 1975–1976 drought for Dutch elm disease in southern England. *Forestry*, **50**, 145–154.

Glue, D. 1989a. Winter raven, grebe, robin nests 1988–89 – the never ending season. *BTO News*, **161**, 14.

Glue, D. 1989b. Unseasonal nesting by birds during mild midwinter 1988–89. *Journal of Meteorology*, **14**, 90–91.

Glue, D. 1989c. Nest record scheme: 1989 breeding season. Quail abound as shrikes dwindle. *BTO News*, **165**, 18–19.

Glue, D.E. 1989d. Impact of high temperatures and low rainfall on Britain's breeding birds during 1989. *Journal of Meteorology*, **143**, 373–5.

Glue, D.E. 1990. Nightjars flourish as rooks struggle – the 1990 breeding season. *BTO News*, **170**, 6–7.

Gordon, P. 1990. The 1990 Breeding Season. *Scottish Bird News*, **19**, 1–2.

Gregory, P.T. 1982. Reptilian hibernation. In: *Biology of the Reptilia*, edited by C. Gans and F.H. Pough, **13**, 53–154. London: Academic Press.

Gregory, S.C., MacAskill, G.A., Redfern, D.B. & Pratt, J.E. 1991. *Disease Diagnostic and Advisory Service*: Scotland and Northern England. Report on Forest Research 1990, 47–48.

Grime, J.P. & Mowforth, M.A. 1982. Variation in genome size – an ecological interpretation. *Nature*, **299**, 151–153.

Grime, J.P., Shacklock, J.M.C. & Band, S.R. 1985. Nuclear DNA contents, shoot phenology and species coexistence in a limestone grassland community. *New Phytologist*, **100**, 435–445.

Haes, C.M. 1990. Orthoptera recording scheme Newsletter, **17**, 1–7.

Hamer, M. 1990. Hot summer comes up to scratch. *New Scientist*, **1731**, 17.

Hammond, J.M. 1990. The strong winds experienced during the late winter 1989/90 over the United Kingdom: Hostorical perspectives. *Meteorology Magazine*, **119**, 211–219.

Harrington, R. 1989. Greenhouse greenfly? *Antenna*, **13**, 169–172.

Harrington, R., Tatchell, G.M. & Bale, J.S. (in press). Weather, life cycle strategy and spring populations of aphids. *Acta Phytopathologica and Entomologica Hungarica*.

Harris, M.P. & Wanless, S. 1990. Breeding success on British kittiwakes in 1986–88: evidence for changing conditions in the northern North Sea. *Journal of Applied Ecology*, **26**, 172–187.

Heaney, S.I. 1985. Long-term algal changes in the south basin of Windermere. In: "A general assessment of environmental and biological features of Windermere and their susceptibility to change." Report compiled by J.F. Talling for North West Water.

Heathwaite, A.L. 1990. The effect of drainage on nutrient release from fen peat and its implications for water quality – a laboratory simulation. *Water Air Soil Pollution*, **49**, 159–173.

Herron, A.C. 1989. Butterflies in midwinter. *Journal of Meteorology*, **14**, 285.

Howard, M.T. & Dixon, A.F.G. 1990. Forecasting of peak population density of the rose grain aphid *Metopolophium dirhodium* on wheat. *Annals of applied Biology*, **117**, 9–19.

Hulme, M. & Jones, P.D. 1991: Temperatures and windiness over the United Kingdom during the winters of 1988/89 and 1989/90 compared with previous years. *Weather*, **46**, 126–136.

Hunter, P.J. 1966. The distribution and abundance of slugs on an arable plot in Northumberland. *Journal of Animal Ecology*, **35**, 543–557.

Hurst, G.W. 1970. Temperatures in high summer, and honey production. *Meteorological magazine*, **99**, 75–82.

Hynes, H.B.N. 1983. Groundwater and stream ecology. *Hydrobiologia*, **100**, 93–99.

Innes, J.L. 1991. Observations on the effects of the 1989 and 1990 summer droughts on the condition of beech (*Fagus sylvatica* L.) in Britain in 1990. *Forestry*, **65**, 35–60.

Innes, J.L., Moffat, A.J. & Londale, D. 1989. Weather conditions during the summer of 1989 and their effects on trees. *Research Information Note*, **162**, Forestry Commission.

Jeffree, E.P. 1960. Some long-term means from The Phenological Reports (1891–1940) of the Royal Meteorological Society. *Quaternary Journal of the Royal Meteorological Society*, **86**, 95–103.

Jenkinson, A.F. & Collison, F.P. 1977. An initial climatology of gales over the North Sea. *Synoptic Climatology Branch Memorandum No 62*, Meteorological Office, Bracknell.

Jones, D. 1979. Steatoda nobilis (Thorell) 1875, its occasional appearance in Britain. *Newsletter of the British Arachnological Society*, **24**, 3–5.

Jones, D.E. 1987. Daily Central England temperature: recently constructed series. *Weather*, **42**, 130–133.

Jones, P.D. & Hulme, M. 1990. Temperatures and sunshine duration over the United Kingdom during the period May to October 1989 compared with previous years. *Weather*, **45**, 430–437.

Jones, P.D. & Kelly, P.M. 1981. Principal component analysis of the Lamb Catalogue of daily weather types: Part 1: Annual Frequencies. *Journal of Climatology*, **2**, 147–157.

Kennard, A. 1990. Another spring hummingbird hawkmoth. *Entomologist's Record*, **102**, 238.

Kenward, R.E. 1990. The red squirrel population of Furzey Island in 1989. Report to British Petroleum Developments Ltd., 1–9.

Kenward, R.E. & Holm, J.L. 1989. What future for British red squirrels? *British Journal of the Linnaean Society*, **38**, 83–89.

Knill-Jones, S.A. 1991. A comparison of the early spring emergence of the macro-moths 1989–1991 taken at Freshwater, Isle of Wight at mercury vapour light. *British Journal of Entomology and Natural History*, **4**, 129–131.

Kuusisto, E. 1989. Snow and ice – nonrenewable natural resources in the future? *Conference on Climate and water. The Publications of the Academy of Finland, Helsinki*, **1**, 300–318.

Lamb, H.H. 1972. British Isles weather types and a register of the daily sequence of circulation patterns, 1861–1972. *Geophysical Memoir*, **116**, London: HMSO, 85 pp.

Lavigne, D.M., Brooks, R.J., Rosen, D.A. & Galbraith, A.D. 1989. Cold, energetics, and populations. In: *Animal adaptation to cold*, edited by L.C.H. Wang. *Advances in Comparative and Environmental Physiology*, **3**, 403–432. Berlin: Springer-Verlag.

Leach, C.K. & Mason, G. 1990. Cynipid update 1990. The "Uncommon" spangle Gall. *British Plant Gall Society occasional paper*, **1**, 1–8.

Le Cren, E.D. 1958. Observations on the growth of perch (*Perca fluviatilis*) over twenty-two years with special reference to the effects of temperature change and population density. *Journal of Animal Ecology*, **27**, 287–334.

Lees, M.L., Bryant, S.J. & Marsh, T.J. 1990. The 1988/89 drought – a hydrological review. In: *1989 Yearbook Hydrological data UK series*. 25–44. Institute of Hydrology.

Legg, T.P. 1989. Removal of urbanization effects from the Central England temperature data sets. *Long-range Forecasting and Climate Memorandum No 33*, U.K. Meteorological Office, Bracknell.

Lonsdale, D. 1980. *Nectria coccinea* infection of beech bark: variation in disease in relation to predisposing factors. *Annales des Sciences Forestieres*, **37**, 307–317.

Lonsdale, D. 1983. Some aspects of the pathology of environmentally stressed trees. *International Dendrology Society Year Book 1982*, 90–97.

Lonsdale, D., Hickman, I.T., Mobbs, I.D. & Matthews, R.W. 1989. A quantitative analysis of beech health and pollution across southern Britain. *Naturwissenschaften*, **76**, 571–573.

Lowrance, R.R., Leonard, R. & Sheridon, J. 1985. Managing riparian ecosystems to control nonpoint pollution. *Journal of Soil and Water Conservation*, **40**, 87–91.

Lund, J.W.G. 1959. Buoyancy in relation to the ecology of the freshwater phytoplankton. *British Physiological Bulletin*, **1**, 1–17.

Majerus, M. 1990. The Cambridge ladybirds survey newsletter, **12**, 1–2.

Manley, G. 1974. Central England Temperatures: monthly means 1659 to 1973. *Quarterly Journal of the Royal meteorological Society*, **100**, 389–405.

Marquiss, M. & Newton, I. 1990. Effects on Birds. In: *The greenhouse effect and terrestrial ecosystems of the UK*, edited by M.G.R. Cannell and M.D. Hooper, 38–42. Institute of Terrestrial Ecology research publication 4. HMSO, London.

Marchant, J.H., Hudson, R., Carter, S.P. & Whittington, P.A. 1990. *Population trends in British breeding birds*. BTO/NCC, Tring.

Marchant, J.H. & Whittington, P.A. 1990. Common Birds Census 1988–1989 index report. *BTO News*, **171**, 9–12.

Marchant, J.H., Musty, L. & Carter, S.P. 1991. Common Birds Census: 1989–90 index report. *BTO News*, **177**, 11–14.

Marsh, T.J. & Bryant, S.J. 1991. *1988–90: A ride on a hydrological rollercoaster*. In press, Geography Review, May 1991.

Marsh, T.J. & Monkhouse, R.A. 1990. Hydrological aspects of the development and rapid decay of the 1990 drought. *Weather*, **45**, 290–299.

Matthews, P.S. & Heaney, S.I. 1987. Solar heating and its influence on mixing in ice covered lakes. *Freshwater Biology*, **18**, 135–149.

McCulloch, N.H. 1989. Natural mortality in red deer stocks in Scotland, winter 1988/89. *Scottish Forestry*, **43**, 322–324.

Mearns, R. & Newton, I. 1988. Factors affecting breeding success of peregrines in south Scotland. *Journal of Animal Ecology*, **57**, 903–16.

Morrison, G. 1989. *Frogwatch 89*. Lincoln: Royal Society for Nature Conservation.

Morrison, J.I.L. & Spence, R.A. 1989. Warm spring conditions and aphid infestations. *Weather*, **44**, 374–381.

Moss, R. 1986. Rain, breeding success and distribution of Capercaillies and Black Grouse in Scotland. *Ibis*, **128**, 65–72.

National Rivers Authority 1990. Toxic Blue-green Algae. *Water Quality Series*, No. 2, September 1990, pp 127.

Newton, I. 1986. *The Sparrowhawk*. Calton, Poyser.

Newton, I., David, P.E. & David J.E. 1989. Age of first breeding, dispersal and survival of Red Kites *Milvus milvus* in Wales. *Ibis*, **131**, 16–21.

Ormerod S.J. & Tyler, S.J. 1987a. Dippers *Cinclus cinclus* and Grey Wagtails *Motacilla cinerea* as indicators of stream acidity in upland Wales. In: *The value of birds* edited by A.W. Diamond and F. Filion, 191–208. *I.C.B.P. Technical Publication No 6*, Cambridge.

Ormerod, S.J. & Tyler, S.J. 1987b. Aspects of the breeding ecology of Welsh Grey Wagtails *Motacill cinerea*. *Bird Study*, **34**, 43–51.

Ormerod, S.J., Tyler, S.J., Pester, S.J. & Cross, A.V. 1988. Censusing distribution and population of birds along upland rivers using measured ringing effort: a preliminary study. *Ringing and Migration*, **9**, 71–82.

Parker, D.E., Legg, T.P. & Folland, C.K. 1991. A new Daily Central England Temperature Series 1772–1991. CRTN No. 11, Hadley Centre, Bracknell.

Pawsey, R.G. 1962. Resurgence of sooty bark disease of sycamore. *Plant Pathology*, **11**, 138.

Peach, W. & Baillie, S. 1990. Population changes on constant effort sites 1988–1989. *BTO News*, **167**, 6–7.

Peach, W.J. & Baillie, S.R. 1991. Population changes on constant effort sites 1989–1990. *BTO News*, **173**, 12–14.

Peterson, R.C., Madsen, B.L., Wilzbach, M.A., Magadza, C.H.D., Pearlberg, A., Kullberg, A. & Cummins, W.K. 1987. Stream management: emerging global similarities. *Ambio*, **16**, 166–179.

Philp, R.G. 1990. An early hummingbird hawkmoth in Kent. *Entomologist's Record*, **102**, 102.

Pollard, E. 1988. Temperature, rainfall and butterfly numbers. *Journal of applied Ecology*, **25**, 819–828.

Pollard, E. 1991a. Synchrony of population fluctuations: the dominant influence of widespread factors on local butterfly populations. *Oikos*, **60**, 7–10.

Pollard, E. 1991b. Changes in the flight period of the hedge brown butterfly *Pyronia tithonus* during range expansion. *Journal of Animal Ecology*, **60**, 737–748.

Pollard, E. & Yates, T.J. 1989. Butterfly monitoring scheme 1988. *Report to recorders*. Huntingdon: Institute of Terrestrial Ecology.

Pollard, E. & Yates, T.J. 1990. Butterfly Monitoring Scheme 1989. *Report to recorders*. ITE, Monks Wood.

Pollard, E. & Yates, T.J. 1991. Butterfly Monitoring Scheme 1990. *Report to recorders*. ITE Monks Wood.

Potts, D. 1990. Woodcock increase? *The Game Conservancy Review of 1989*, 21–100.

Da Prato, S. 1989. The 1989 breeding season in Scotland. *Scottish Bird News*, **15**, 4.

Da Prato, S. 1990. The 1990 breeding season. *Scottish Bird News*, **19**, 1–2.

Quine, C.P. 1991. Recent storm damage to trees and woodlands in southern Britain. In: *Research for Practical Aboriculture*, edited by S.J. Hodge, Forestry Commission Bulletin **97**, 83–89.

Radley, J. 1965. Significance of major moorland fires. *Nature*, **205**, 1254–1259.

Reynolds, C.S. 1989. Physical determinants of phytoplankton succession. In: *Plankton Ecology: The determinants of succession*, edited by V. Sommer, 9–56, Science Publishers, Madison.

Ricker, W.E. 1954. Stock and recruitment. *Journal of the Fisheries Research Board of Canada*, **11**, 559–623.

Riley, A.M. 1990. Twenty years of moth monitoring at Broom's Barn. Transactions of the *Suffolk Naturalist's Society*, **26**, 19–29.

Royal Meteorological Society. Phenological Report for various years between 1891–1948 in *Quarterly Journal of the Royal Meteorology Society*.

Savage, R.M. 1961. *The ecology and life history of the common frog*. London: Pitman and Sons.

Skidmore, P. 1991. Report on the Diptera Cyclorrhapha taken in the 1990 Entomological Survey of Thorne and Hatfield Moors. Thorn & Hatfield Conservation Forum (unpublished).

Smith, E.M. & Smith, R. 1991. Odonata recording Scheme Newsletter, **13**, 1–6.

Smith, K. 1981. The prediction of river water temperatures. *Hydrological Sciences Bulletin*, **26**, 19–32.

Smith, S.G. 1982. An index of windiness for the United Kingdom. *Meteorology Magazine*, **111**, 232–247.

South, A. 1989a. A comparison of the life cycles of the slugs *Deroceras reticulatum* (Müller) and *Arion intermedius* Normand on permanent pasture. *Journal of Molluscan Studies*, **55**, 9–22.

South, A. 1989b. The effect of weather and other factors on numbers of slugs on permenent pasture. *BCPC Monographs*, **41**. Slugs and snails in world agriculture, 355–360.

Spradbery, J.P. 1973. *Wasps, an account of the biology and natural history of solitary and social wasps*. London: Sidgwick & Jackson.

Stebbings, R.E. & Griffith, F. 1986. *Distribution and status of bats in Europe*. Huntingdon: NERC, Institute of Terrestrial Ecology.

Steinberg, C.W. & Hartmann, H.M. 1988. Planktonic bloom-forming Cyanobacteria and the eutrophication of lakes and rivers. *Freshwater Biology*, **20**, 279–287.

Storey, A., Folland, C.K. & Parker, D.E. 1986. A homogeneous archive of daily Central England temperature 1772 to 1985. *Synoptic Climatology Branch Memorandum No 107*, U.K. Meteorological Office, Bracknell.

Strong, D.R., Lawton, J.H. & Southwood, R. 1984. *Insects on plants*, Oxford: Blackwell Scientific Publications.

Strouts, R.G., Rose, D.R. & Reffold, T.C. 1991. Disease Diagnostic and Advisory Service: Southern England and Wales. Report on Forest Research 1990, 48–50.

Sutcliffe, D.W. & Carrick, T.R. 1983a. Relationships between chloride and major cations in precipitation and streamwaters in the Windermere catchment (English Lake District). *Freshwater Biology*, **13**, 415–441.

Sutcliffe, D.W. & Carrick, T.R. 1983b. Chemical composition of waterbodies in the English Lake District: relationships between chloride and other major ions related to solid geology, and a tentative budget for Windermere. *Freshwater Biology*, **13**, 323–352.

Talling, J.F. 1971. The underwater light climate as a controlling factor in the production ecology of freshwater phytoplankton. *Mitt. Internat. Verein. Limnol.*, **19**, 214–243.

Tapper, S. & Cook, S. 1990. The 1989/90 shooting season: a perspective from the game bag records. The Game Conservancy Review of 1989, **21**, 28–33.

Thomas, J.A. & Merrett, P. 1980. Observations of butterflies in the Purbeck hills in 1976 and 1977. *Proceedings of the Dorset Natural History and Archaeological Society*, **99**, 112–119.

Thompson, N., Barrie, I.A. & Ayles, M. 1981. *The Meteorological Office rainfall and evaporation calculation system: MORECS*. Met. 0 8, Hydrological Memorandum 45, Met. Office, Bracknell.

Townsend, M.C. & Riley, A.M. 1990. Rothamsted farmland light trap network: interesting Lepidoptera records for May 1990. *Entomologist's Record*, **102**, 214.

Tremewan, M.A. 1989. An early *Vanessa atalanta* (L.) (Lepidoptera: Nymphalidae) in Cornwall. *Entomologist's Gazette*, **40**, 92.

Turner, P.C., Gammie, A.J., Hollinrake, K. & Codd, G.A. 1990. Pneumonia associated with contact with cyanobacteria. *British Medical Journal*, **300**, 1440–1441.

Varley, G.C., Gradwell, G.R. & Hassel, M.P. 1973. *Insect Population Ecology: an Analytical Approach*. Blackwell, Oxford.

Walsh, P.M. 1990. Seabird monitoring: some 1989 results. *BTO News*, **168**, 7.

Walters, K.F.A. & Dewar, A.M. 1986. Overwintering strategy and the timing of the spring migration of the cereal aphids *Sitobion avenae* and *Sitobion fragariae*. *Journal of Applied Ecology*, **23**, 9050915.

Weatherley, N.S. & Ormerod, S.J. 1990. Forests and the temperature of upland streams in Wales: a modelling exploration of the biological effects. *Freshwater Biology*, **24**, 109–122.

Wells, T.C.E. 1971. A comparison of the effects of sheep grazing and mechanical cutting on the structure and botanical composition of chalk grassland. In: *The Scientific Management of Animal and Plant Communities*, edited by E. Duffey and A.S. Watt. *BES Symposium*, **11**, 497–515. Blackwell Scientific Publications, Oxford.

Wells, T.C.E. & Cox, R. 1989. Predicting the probability of the bee orchid (*Ophrys apifera*) flowering or remaining vegetative from the size and number of leaves. In: *Modern methods of orchid conservation: the role of physiology, ecology and management*, edited by H.W. Pritchard, C.U.P.

Welton, J.S., Beaumont, W.R.C. & Clarke, R.T. 1989. Factors affecting the upstream migration of salmon in the River Frome, Dorset. *Atlantic Salmon Trust Workshop*, Bristol, April 1989.

Woiwood, I.P., Riley, A.M. & Townsend, M.C. 1990. The Rothamsted farmland light trap network. *Entomologist's Record*, **102**, 200–210.

Young, C.W.T. 1978. Sooty bark disease. *Arboricultural Leaflet*, 3, 8pp.

Young, A.G. & Port, G.R. 1989. The effect of microclimate on slug activity in the field. British Crop protection monograph No 41. *Slugs and snails in world agriculture*, 263–269.

Printed in the UK for HMSO
Dd 0295809 9/93 C28 531/3 12521